MEETING ASIA'S
INFRASTRUCTURE NEEDS

50 YEARS

ADB

ASIAN DEVELOPMENT BANK

ISBN 978-92-9257-753-7 (Print), 978-92-9257-754-4 (e-ISBN)
Publication Stock No. FLS168388-2
http://dx.doi.org/10.22617/FLS168388-2

Cataloging-In-Publication Data

Asian Development Bank.
        Meeting Asia's infrastructure needs.
Mandaluyong City, Philippines: Asian Development Bank, 2017.

1. Infrastructure. 2. Climate change. 3. Infrastructure gap. 4. Infrastructure needs.
I. Asian Development Bank.

Notes:
In this publication, "$" refers to US dollars.
Corrigenda to ADB publications may be found at http://www.adb.org/publications/corrigenda
ADB recognizes "China" as the People's Republic of China; "Hong Kong" as Hong Kong, China; and "Korea" as the Republic of Korea.

Contents

Tables

Figures

Boxes

Appendixes

Foreword

In 2009, the Asian Development Bank (ADB) and the ADB Institute projected infrastructure needs for developing Asia from 2010 to 2020 in *Infrastructure for a Seamless Asia (Seamless Asia)*. The study covered 32 of ADB's 45 developing member countries (DMCs) and four sectors: transport, power, telecommunications, and water supply and sanitation. It projected that total investment needs for the four infrastructure sectors would be slightly above $8 trillion (in 2008 prices) over the 11-year period, or almost $750 billion a year.

This report updates these estimates by presenting infrastructure investment needs for all 45 DMCs from 2016 to 2030, the final year of the United Nations Sustainable Development Goals. Two sets of estimates are presented. The first includes the costs of climate mitigation and adaptation (climate-adjusted estimate). Using this set of estimates, developing Asia will need to invest $26 trillion over the 15-years from 2016 to 2030, or $1.7 trillion per year. The second set of estimates does not include climate-adjusted costs (baseline estimate), and amounts to $22.6 trillion, or $1.5 trillion per year.

The baseline estimates are generated closely following the methods of *Seamless Asia*, but using more refined data and deriving key parameters from ADB project experience and the latest literature. The climate-adjusted estimates add the costs of climate mitigation and adaptation to the baseline estimates based on recent ADB studies. Incorporating the effects of climate change on infrastructure investment needs is one important contribution of this report.

The second contribution of the report is that it provides a detailed analysis of infrastructure investment gaps. The estimates of infrastructure needs are compared with current investment levels to get a concrete sense of the gaps countries need to bridge. Based on an assessment of how much the public sector can invest in infrastructure with public finance reforms, the report provides a sense of how much private finance will be required for developing Asia to meet its infrastructure needs and what policies will allow this to happen.

The third contribution of the report relates to measurement of infrastructure investment. Given the lack of comprehensive data on actual infrastructure investment data across countries, this report seeks to better understand how much countries have been investing in infrastructure by considering several ways of measuring infrastructure investments. It adopts a benchmark measure that relies on country infrastructure expenditures from government budget documents plus information on private investment in infrastructure from a World Bank database. There is certainly room for improvement on measurement of infrastructure investments, and the report suggests a way forward through collaboration between national accounts statisticians in the region and international agencies.

The preparation of this report was helped by the active cooperation of colleagues from many different parts of ADB. Staff from ADB's regional departments and resident missions provided insights on country budget data to better capture public sector investments in infrastructure. Experts from ADB's sector and thematic groups shared data and provided assistance in estimating the costs of different types of infrastructure. Many colleagues also contributed to the report's policy discussion and boxes highlighting special issues. This collaborative approach should provide a good basis for future ADB dialogue and engagement with relevant authorities.

As ADB celebrates its first 50 years of operations, I am confident this report will be useful for both experts and policy makers as they search for efficient and effective ways of providing the infrastructure that is prerequisite to sustainable and inclusive growth in Asia and the Pacific.

Takehiko Nakao
President
Asian Development Bank

Acknowledgments

This report was prepared by the Development Economics and Indicators Division (ERDI) of the Economic Research and Regional Cooperation Department (ERCD) as a special supplement to ADB's Key Indicators for Asia and the Pacific. Valuable contributions were made by ADB sector and thematic groups—energy, transport, water, climate change and disaster risk management, finance, and regional cooperation and integration; the five regional departments; the Office of Public-Private Partnership and Private Sector Operations Department; and ADB Country Offices.

Rana Hasan, Director of ERDI, headed a core team of staff in preparing the report: Yi Jiang and Zhigang Li led much of the analysis; Abdul Abiad served as advisor and contributed the analysis on fiscal space; and Orlee Velarde and Priscille Villanueva provided essential research and administrative support. Important contributions were made by Kaushal Joshi, Kijin Kim, Trevor Lewis, Mahinthan Mariasingham, Thiam Hee Ng, and Vivek Rao. Additional inputs were provided by Eileen Capilit, Melissa Pascua, Iva Sebastian, and Eric Suan.

A team of consultants, namely, Christine Ablaza, Erik Jan Eleazar, Paul Feliciano, John Paul Flaminiano, Janine Lazatin, and Rhea Molato provided research support, with additional inputs from Mel Lorenzo Accad, Renz Adrian Calub, and Angelica Maddawin.

Technical advice and inputs on estimating infrastructure needs were provided by Tyrrell Duncan, Vijay Padmanabhan, David Raitzer, and Yongping Zhai. Additional contributions were provided by Sharad Saxena and Naren Singru.

Material for the boxes on special issues were contributed by Noritaka Akamatsu, Charlotte Benson, Johanna Boestel, Alexandra Pamela Chiang, Saugata Dasgupta, Maria Vicedo Ferrer, Kanupriya Gupta, Aziz Haydarov, John Cheong Holdaway, Xinglan Hu, Yoshiaki Kobayashi, Trevor Lewis, David Ling, Rommel Rabanal, Abhijit Sen Gupta, Manoj Sharma, Gurjyot Singh, Akiko Terada-Hagiwara, Frederic Thomas, James Michael Trainor, Norio Usui, Hanna K. Uusimaa, and Qingfeng Zhang. Outside contributors Marco Gonzalez-Navarro, Eui-Young Shon, and Zhirong Zhao conducted independent studies which were condensed into boxes in the report. Grateful acknowledgment is also given to Koki Hirota (Chief Economist of the Japan International Cooperation Agency) and his team, Takeshi Saheki and Ishizuka Fumiaki for contributing boxes for this report.

Other written contributions and/or advice on private finance were provided by Arup Chatterjee, Georg Inderst, Alexander Jett, Lars Johannes, Sung Su Kim, and Lotte Schou-Zibell.

Preety Bhandari, Sekhar Bonu, Bruno Carasco, Chen Chen, Xiaoxin Chen, Joao Pedro Farinha, Jesus Felipe, Robert Guild, Abid Hussain, Andrew Jeffries, Utsav Kumar, Dan Millson, Kee-Yung Nam, Jiangbo Ning, Olly Norojono, Rajesh Poddar, Charles Rodgers, and Jiro Tominaga provided advice on various topics related to the report.

The external advisors to this report were Douglas Brooks (who also contributed to the writeup) and Stephane Straub. Anupam Rastogi provided analytical inputs and contributed to the discussion on private sector finance.

Thanks are due to participants at the workshop on infrastructure finance held on 18–19 August 2016, Du Huynh, Edgare Kerwijk, Richard Michael, Alma Porciuncula, and Raman Uberoi, who gave presentations and provided background materials used in the report.

Guy Sacerdoti edited the manuscript extensively and ensured coherence and consistency. Rhommell Rico designed the cover and typeset the publication. Ma. Roselia Babalo, Oth Marulou Gagni, and Aileen Gatson provided administrative assistance in the workshop.

We also thank the national statistics offices of developing member countries, especially Fiji, India, and Pakistan, for providing detailed data on gross fixed capital formation compiled for the national accounts statistics.

Finally, the team also acknowledges Artur Andrysiak, Aniceto Orbeta, and Guntur Sugiyarto who helped initiate this study on Asia's infrastructure needs, and colleagues from ADB's Department of External Relations for their strong support on the report's dissemination.

Juzhong Zhuang
Officer-in-Charge and Deputy Chief Economist
Economic Research and Regional Cooperation Department

HIGHLIGHTS

- Developing Asia will need to invest $26 trillion from 2016 to 2030, or $1.7 trillion per year, if the region is to maintain its growth momentum, eradicate poverty, and respond to climate change (climate-adjusted estimate). Without climate change mitigation and adaptation costs, $22.6 trillion will be needed, or $1.5 trillion per year (baseline estimate).

- Of the total climate-adjusted investment needs over 2016–2030, $14.7 trillion will be for power and $8.4 trillion for transport. Investments in telecommunications will reach $2.3 trillion, with water and sanitation costs at $800 billion over the period.

- East Asia will account for 61% of climate-adjusted investment needs through 2030. As a percentage of gross domestic product (GDP), however, the Pacific leads all other subregions, requiring investments valued at 9.1% of GDP. This is followed by South Asia at 8.8%, Central Asia at 7.8%, Southeast Asia at 5.7%, and East Asia at 5.2% of GDP.

- The $1.7 trillion annual estimate is more than double the $750 billion Asian Development Bank (ADB) estimated in 2009. The inclusion of climate-related investments is a major contributing factor. A more important factor is the continued rapid growth forecasted for the region, which generates new infrastructure demand. The inclusion of all 45 ADB member countries in developing Asia, compared to 32 in the 2009 report, and the use of 2015 prices versus 2008 prices also explain the increase.

- Currently, the region annually invests an estimated $881 billion in infrastructure (for 25 economies with adequate data, comprising 96% of the region's population). The infrastructure investment gap—the difference between investment needs and current investment levels—equals 2.4% of projected GDP for the 5-year period from 2016 to 2020 when incorporating climate mitigation and adaptation costs.

- Without the People's Republic of China (PRC), the gap for the remaining economies rises to a much higher 5% of their projected GDP. Fiscal reforms could generate additional revenues equivalent to 2% of GDP to bridge around 40% of the gap for these economies. For the private sector to fill the remaining 60% of the gap, or 3% of GDP, it would have to increase investments from about $63 billion today to as high as $250 billion a year over 2016–2020.

- Regulatory and institutional reforms are needed to make infrastructure more attractive to private investors and generate a pipeline of bankable projects for public-private partnerships (PPPs). Countries should implement PPP-related reforms such as enacting PPP laws, streamlining PPP procurement and bidding processes, introducing dispute resolution mechanisms, and establishing independent PPP government units. Deepening of capital markets is also needed to help channel the region's substantial savings into productive infrastructure investment.

- Multilateral development banks (MDB) have financed an estimated 2.5% of infrastructure investments in developing Asia. Excluding the PRC and India, MDB contributions rise above 10%. A growing proportion of ADB finance is now going to private sector infrastructure projects. Beyond finance, ADB is playing an important role in Asia by sharing expertise and knowledge to identify, design, and implement good projects. ADB is scaling up operations, integrating more advanced and cleaner technology into projects, and streamlining procedures. ADB will also promote investment friendly policies and regulatory and institutional reforms.

Infrastructure's pivotal role in developing Asia's economic growth and poverty reduction

- **This report estimates infrastructure investment needs in Asia and the Pacific between 2016 and 2030.** The analysis covers transport, power, telecommunications, and water supply and sanitation.[1] The report describes how much the region will need to invest in infrastructure to continue its economic growth momentum, eradicate poverty, and respond to climate change. It examines how much countries have been investing in infrastructure, using data from a variety of sources—including government budget data, components of gross fixed capital formation, and information on private sector investment. It also presents a snapshot of infrastructure stocks currently available. It concludes with a discussion of the financial and institutional challenges the region must overcome to meet future infrastructure needs.

- **The region's infrastructure has improved rapidly but remains far from adequate.** Developing Asia has seen dramatic improvements in its transportation network, electricity generation capacity, and telecommunications and water infrastructure, among others. Better access to infrastructure has driven growth, reduced poverty and improved people's lives. Yet over 400 million Asians still lack electricity; roughly 300 million have no access to safe drinking water and 1.5 billion lack basic sanitation. Poor quality remains a problem. In many countries, power outages constrain economic growth. And city traffic congestion alone costs economies huge amounts daily in lost productivity, wasted fuel, and human stress.

- **This report updates ADB's earlier assessment of the region's future infrastructure investment.** In 2009, ADB and the Asian Development Bank Institute (ADBI) projected infrastructure needs for developing Asia from 2010 to 2020 in *Infrastructure for a Seamless Asia (Seamless Asia)*.[2] The study was based on 32 of ADB's 45 developing member countries (DMCs). It projected that total investment needs for the four infrastructure sectors would reach a little more than $8 trillion (in 2008 prices) over the 11-year period—or almost $750 billion a year. These projections must be updated as the region continues to grow robustly, better data are available, and the role of infrastructure in tackling the impact of climate change has become clearer.

- **The new estimates cover all 45 DMCs over the 15-year period from 2016 to 2030.** Following the "top-down" methodology adopted by *Seamless Asia*, estimates of infrastructure needs are based on (i) the estimated empirical relationship between an economy's infrastructure stocks and key economic and demographic factors (such as per capita GDP, population density, share of urban population, and share of industry in the economy, controlling for country-specific characteristics) over the last four decades; (ii) projections of these economic and demographic variables over 2016–2030; and (iii) estimates of the unit cost of building each type of infrastructure. The data indicate that the stocks needed for all types of infrastructure increase with income level, but at a declining rate; increased population density and urbanization require greater road and sanitation infrastructure; and a higher share of manufacturing in GDP requires greater stocks of seaports and power generation infrastructure.

---

1   For the most part, infrastructure in this report refers to physical infrastructure covering transport (roads, railways, airports, and seaports), power (generation, distribution, and transmission), telecommunications, and water supply and sanitation.

---

2   See ADB and ADBI (2009).

The two sets of estimates: (i) baseline; and (ii) climate-adjusted (baseline plus climate mitigation and adaptation costs)

- **Two sets of estimates are generated.** The first are baseline estimates. The second set of estimates incorporates the effects of climate change. It adjusts the baseline estimates by adding the costs of climate mitigation (in particular, for more efficient and cleaner power generation and electricity transmission) and adaptation (in particular, for "climate proofing," mainly in transport and water by making infrastructure more resilient to the impacts of climate change).

- **The baseline estimate is $22.6 trillion; the needs increase to $26.2 trillion including climate mitigation and adaptation costs.** The baseline scenario indicates that developing Asia will need to invest $22.6 trillion (in 2015 prices)—or $1.5 trillion annually—in infrastructure from 2016 to 2030. This is equivalent to 5.1% of projected GDP. Factoring in climate mitigation and adaptation costs raises the investment required to $26.2 trillion—$1.7 trillion annually—or 5.9% of projected GDP.

- **The $1.7 trillion annual climate-adjusted estimate is more than double the $750 billion ADB estimated in 2009.**[3] The inclusion of climate-related investments is a major contributing factor. An even more important factor that explains the difference between the two estimates is the continued rapid growth forecasted for the region, which generates new infrastructure demand. The inclusion of all 45 ADB member countries in developing Asia, compared to 32 in the 2009 report, and the use of 2015 prices versus 2008 prices also explain the increase.

- **There is wide variation across subregions.** Including climate change, East Asia—driven by the PRC—accounts for 61% of developing Asia's projected 2016–2030 infrastructure investment, followed by South Asia, Southeast Asia, Central Asia, and the Pacific (Table 1). South Asia accounts for about a quarter of the total needs. However, as a share of GDP, the Pacific's needs are highest at 9.1% of GDP, followed by South Asia's at 8.8%. Southeast Asia's economies will need to allocate 5.7% of GDP for infrastructure investment needs through 2030, and Central Asia at 7.8% of GDP.

- **Differences in existing infrastructure stocks, level of economic development and growth prospects are the main reasons for subregional variations.** As our analysis of the empirical relationship between an economy's infrastructure stocks and key economic and demographic factors reveals, an economy with lower infrastructure stocks, lower GDP per capita, and greater growth prospects will have higher investment needs as a percent of future GDP. As GDP per capita increases, the stock of infrastructure will rise, but annual infrastructure investment needs as a share of GDP will decline. For example, with South Asia's GDP per capita about 60% below that of Southeast Asia in 2015, and the projected average annual growth of South Asia 1.4 percentage points higher than Southeast Asia, infrastructure investment needs as a percent of GDP are significantly higher in South Asia.

- **Infrastructure investment needs vary considerably by sector** (Table 2). Power and transport are the two largest sectors, accounting for 52% and 35%, respectively, of total infrastructure investments for the baseline projections; and 56% and 32%, respectively, of total climate-adjusted investments. Telecommunications and water and sanitation are relatively small, accounting for 9% and

---

3   Annex Table 1 compares this report's estimates with those of *Seamless Asia* for the common 32 DMCs, expressed in 2008 prices.

Table 1: Estimated Infrastructure Investment Needs by Region, 45 DMCs, 2016–2030
($ billion in 2015 prices)

Region/Subregion	Projected Annual GDP Growth	2030 UN Population Projection (billion)	2030 Projected GDP Per Capita (2015 $)	Baseline Estimates			Climate-adjusted Estimates**		
				Investment Needs	Annual Average	Investment Needs as % of GDP	Investment Needs	Annual Average	Investment Needs as % of GDP
Central Asia	3.1	0.096	6,202	492	33	6.8	565	38	7.8
East Asia	5.1	1.503	18,602	13,781	919	4.5	16,062	1,071	5.2
South Asia*	6.5	2.059	3,446	5,477	365	7.6	6,347	423	8.8
Southeast Asia	5.1	0.723	7,040	2,759	184	5.0	3,147	210	5.7
The Pacific	3.1	0.014	2,889	42	2.8	8.2	46	3.1	9.1
Asia and the Pacific	**5.3**	**4.396**	**9,277**	**22,551**	**1,503**	**5.1**	**26,166**	**1,744**	**5.9**

Note: * Pakistan and Afghanistan are included in South Asia. ** Climate change adjusted figures include climate mitigation and climate proofing costs, but do not
            include other adaptation costs, especially those associated with sea level rise.
Source: 2015 Revision of World Population Prospects, United Nations; ADB estimates.

3%, respectively, of total climate-adjusted investments. However, the figures for these two sectors by no means suggest they are less important for the economy or individual welfare.

- **Climate mitigation costs are estimated at $200 billion annually.** These primarily come from the power sector, which is particularly important in controlling carbon emissions through investments in renewable energy, smart grids, and energy efficiency. The transport sector is also important for mitigating climate change through shifts from more carbon-intensive modes of travel (private cars) to less carbon-intensive modes (public transit and railways). However, over the longer term, these shifts in transport should be promoted by policy and regulations, and are unlikely to incur additional costs over baseline transport estimates. Countries may need to invest more in railways,

but less in highways; thus aggregate investment can be even lower. Hence, we do not introduce any mitigation-related adjustments to our transport sector investment needs estimates.

- **The costs of climate proofing, a subset of climate adaptation, are estimated at $41 billion annually.** Transportation accounts for the majority of climate proofing investments—estimated at $37 billion annually. Countries must ensure their infrastructure is resilient to the projected impacts of climate change, as phenomena such as sea level rise and intensified extreme weather can damage infrastructure, and affect its longevity and performance. This can be done by measures such as elevating road embankments, relocating upstream water intake and treatment works, and enhancing design and maintenance standards.

Table 2: Estimated Infrastructure Investment Needs by Sector, 45 DMCs, 2016–2030
($ billion in 2015 prices)

Sector	Baseline Estimates			Climate-adjusted Estimates			Climate-related Investments (Annual)	
	Investment Needs	Annual Average	Share of Total	Investment Needs	Annual Average	Share of Total	Adaptation	Mitigation
Power	11,689	779	51.8	14,731	982	56.3	3	200
Transport	7,796	520	34.6	8,353	557	31.9	37	–
Telecommunications	2,279	152	10.1	2,279	152	8.7	–	–
Water and Sanitation	787	52	3.5	802	53	3.1	1	–
Total	22,551	1,503	100.0	26,166	1,744	100.0	41	200

Note: – denotes not applicable.
Source: ADB estimates.

Data issues

- **An important and unique task in preparing this report was to better understand how much countries have been investing in infrastructure.** Given the lack of comprehensive data on actual infrastructure investments across countries, this report tries several ways of measuring actual infrastructure investment. It adopts a benchmark measure—infrastructure expenditures from government budget documents plus information on private investment in infrastructure from the World Bank's Private Participation in Infrastructure Project database.

- **National and international agencies should prioritize constructing more comprehensive, better quality data on infrastructure investments.** A promising approach is to partner with national accounts statisticians to estimate infrastructure investments using gross fixed capital formation data disaggregated by type of fixed asset, the institution undertaking the investment, and the industry in which investment is taking place. This approach would be comprehensive as it would capture investments by governments, state-owned enterprises (SOEs), and the private sector; allow disaggregation by sector and institution; and generate a time-series of infrastructure investments.

Boosting infrastructure investment to meet development and sustainability goals

- **Focusing on 25 DMCs and the 5-year period from 2016 to 2020, the gap between current and needed investment levels works out to $330 billion (baseline) or $460 billion (climate-adjusted) annually.** Information from government budgets and the World Bank's Private Participation in Infrastructure Project database for 25 DMCs with adequate data and covering 96% of the region's population suggest the region invested $881 billion in infrastructure in 2015 (Table 3). This is well below the estimated $1.2 trillion (baseline) or $1.3 trillion (climate-adjusted) annual investment needs over the 5-year period from 2016 to 2020 for the 25 DMCs. The baseline infrastructure investment gap is around $330 billion, equivalent to 1.7% of projected GDP of the 25 DMCs. If climate-related needs are included, the gap is around $459 billion, or 2.4% of the projected GDP.

- **These aggregate figures mask wide variations in infrastructure investment gaps across the region.** The PRC has a gap of 1.2% of GDP using climate-adjusted estimates. Without the PRC, the gap in the climate-adjusted scenario as a share of the remaining economies' GDP is much higher at 5%. In general, lower income economies tend to have larger gaps. Thus, the South Asia climate-adjusted gap is 5.7% of projected GDP—or 1.6 percentage points higher than that of more developed Southeast Asia. But, factors other than income levels are also at work, such as the prospects for economic growth.

- **The gap should be filled by both public and private sectors.** Public finance reforms could generate additional revenues estimated to bridge around 40% of the gap (or 2% of GDP) for the 24 economies (excluding the PRC) in the climate-adjusted scenario. For the private sector to fill in the remaining gap (or 3% of GDP), it would have to increase investments from about $63 billion today to as high as $250 billion a year over 2016–2020.

Table 3: Estimated Infrastructure Investments and Gaps, 25 DMCs, 2016–2020
($ billion in 2015 prices)

	Estimated Current Investment (2015)	Baseline Estimates			Climate-adjusted Estimates		
		Annual Needs	Gap	Gap (% of GDP)	Annual Needs	Gap	Gap (% of GDP)
Total (25)	881	1,211	330	1.7	1,340	459	2.4
Total without PRC (24)	195	457	262	4.3	503	308	5.0
Selected Central Asia Countries (3)	6	11	5	2.3	12	7	3.1
Selected South Asia Countries (8)	134	294	160	4.7	329	195	5.7
Selected Southeast Asia Countries (7)	55	147	92	3.8	157	102	4.1
Selected Pacific Countries (5)	1	2	1	6.2	2	2	6.9
India	118	230	112	4.1	261	144	5.3
Indonesia	23	70	47	4.7	74	51	5.1
PRC	686	753	68	0.5	837	151	1.2

PRC = People's Republic of China.
Numbers in parentheses refer to the number of selected countries.
Note: The gap as a % of GDP is based on the annual average of projected GDP from 2016 to 2020. The 25 DMCs covered here are listed in Annex Table 2.
Source: ADB (2016a); Country sources; Investment and Capital Stock Dataset, 1960–2015, IMF; Private Participation in Infrastructure Database, World Bank; World Bank (2015a and 2015b); World Development Indicators; World Bank; ADB estimates.

Financing infrastructure investment

- **The public sector currently dominates infrastructure financing.** The public sector currently finances around 92% of the region's infrastructure investment (as captured by the 25 DMCs with adequate available data).[4] There is a wide difference in the relative importance in public finance across subregions, however, with its share ranging from a high of over 90% in East Asia (driven by the PRC) to a low of 62% in South Asia. Public sector finance covers tax and nontax revenues, borrowing via bonds and loans, official development assistance from donor countries, and support from multilateral development banks (MDBs). The importance of each of these components varies across countries.

- **MDB operations in developing Asia, most of which provide support for public sector finance, are estimated to have contributed around 2.5% of the region's infrastructure investments in 2015.** However, the MDB contributions rise above 10% if both the PRC and India are excluded. MDB operations in Asia are led by ADB and the World Bank. In 2015, ADB approved $10 billion of financing in the four major infrastructure sectors covered in this report. In the same period, the World Bank Group also committed about $10 billion to the same group of countries, of which $3 billion went to the private sector through the International Finance Corporation. The Islamic Development Bank Group approved $3 billion in Asian infrastructure.

- **Governments in many DMCs can increase public investment in infrastructure by raising more revenues, reorienting spending, and through prudent borrowing.** Policy makers must evaluate how much fiscal space is available to increase infrastructure investment under various options for reforming public finance. Many countries in developing Asia can increase revenues through tax reform (including improving tax administration). There is also scope to reorient budget expenditures toward public investment by cutting energy subsidies, for example, and by borrowing prudently while keeping debt levels manageable.

- **Innovative approaches exist to expand government funds available for financing**

---

4   Public sector infrastructure investment covers SOEs in India, Indonesia and the PRC, but may underestimate SOE infrastructure investment in other DMCs.

infrastructure development. Given that increases in private sector infrastructure finance of the amounts needed will likely increase gradually, innovative ways to bolster government finance for infrastructure will be needed. These include, for example, using "land value capture" to finance infrastructure, or capital recycling (selling brownfield assets and auctioning concessions, and allocating proceeds to finance greenfield infrastructure). At the same time, other actions, like setting user charges for infrastructure services with greater regard to cost recovery will also help.

- **Private sector investments are particularly important in telecommunications and power generation.** In telecommunications, around 49% of investments have been made by the private sector in low to lower middle income countries, while it is much higher for upper middle income countries, at around 99%. For the power sector, the private share of investment averaged around 40% for both sets of DMCs. Especially in the subsector of power generation, independent power producers play an important role in some countries. Private sector finance in the transport and water supply and sanitation sectors tends to be far more limited. However, there are subsectors in transport and water where relatively high feasibility and desirability of cost recovery make private financing possible. Examples include airports, seaports, toll roads, and some types of water supply and treatment facilities.

- **Public finance reforms are estimated to cover a little less than half of the infrastructure gap, implying that private finance for infrastructure will have to increase dramatically**. This is best seen by examining data for selected DMCs. Public finance reforms can create extra fiscal space in many countries—increasing public infrastructure

financing from the current $133 billion to $254 billion annually for the selected DMCs as a whole, an increment equivalent to 2% of projected GDP (Figure 1, first and third bars from the left in both panels). With current private financing at around $63 billion (second bar from the left in both panels), an additional $141 billion–$187 billion annually will be needed from private sources, depending on whether climate related costs are included or not. This is equivalent to 3.0% of future GDP.

Attracting private participation and strengthening institutional capacity

- **An enabling environment that delivers well-prepared, viable proposals for private investment is critical for PPPs.** PPPs are an important modality for attracting private investment in infrastructure. However, to meet their potential, they need to be structured within a regulatory and institutional environment conducive to private investment and better project preparation capabilities that generate a robust pipeline of bankable PPP projects. Many countries are moving in this direction. For example, recent PPP reforms involve enacting PPP laws, streamlining procurement and bidding processes, using PPP tool kits, introducing dispute resolution mechanisms, building capacity for planning and managing projects, and establishing independent PPP government units.

- **Deepening bond markets is critical to attract long-term institutional investors.** While banks will remain important finance vehicles, increased capital requirements (like Basel III) and the inherent maturity mismatch related to long-term project lending implies bond financing must assume a greater role to complement banks. Credit enhancement

Figure 1: Meeting the Investment Gaps: Selected ADB Developing Member Countries,* 2016–2020
(annual averages, $ billion in 2015 prices)

A. Baseline Estimates

B. Climate-adjusted Estimates

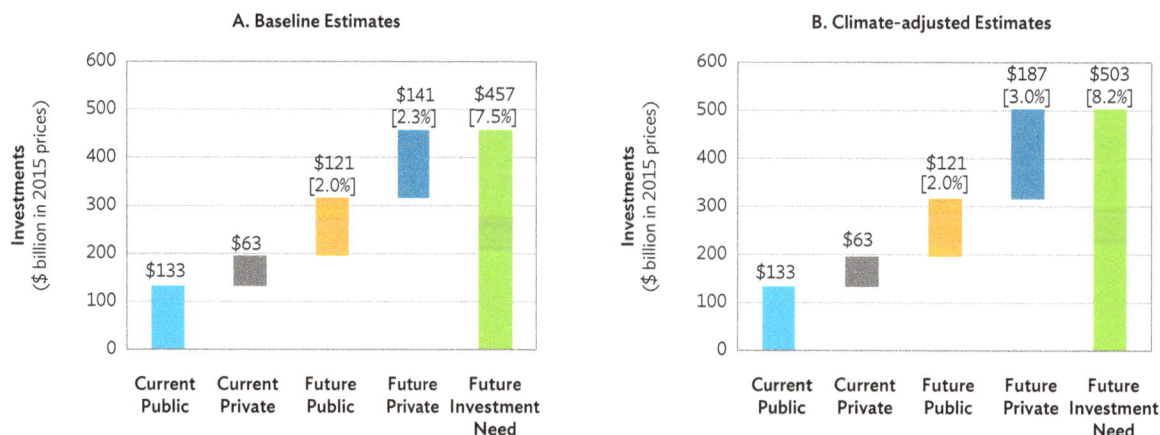

* Countries include the 25 DMCs in Table 3 minus the People's Republic of China; future public investments are based on the 50% fiscal space assumption. Numbers in brackets indicate investments as a percentage of GDP.
Note: Numbers may not add up due to rounding.
Source: ADB (2016a); Country sources; Investment and Capital Stock Dataset, 1960–2015, IMF; Private Participation in Infrastructure Database, World Bank; World Bank (2015a and 2015b); World Development Indicators, World Bank; ADB estimates.

through bond guarantees can allow long-term contractual investors like pension and insurance funds to invest in infrastructure bonds. More generally, to promote deeper and more liquid bond markets, countries need to introduce reforms such as strengthening bankruptcy laws and credit rating agencies.

- **A well-functioning, multi-stakeholder institutional "ecosystem" for infrastructure development is essential.** Close coordination across government levels—national, provincial, and local—is essential for infrastructure development. Also required is the capacity for high-quality planning and project design, feasibility studies and project implementation to get projects done on time and within budget. This "ecosystem" not only helps ensure that public investments in infrastructure are efficient; it also helps attract private investment by creating a pipeline of "bankable" projects.

The role of multilateral development banks

- **MDBs like ADB have an important role to play in public and private sector infrastructure financing.** ADB is scaling up its operations by 50% from $14 billion in 2014 to more than $20 billion in 2020, with 70% of this amount for sovereign and nonsovereign infrastructure investment. A growing proportion of ADB finance is expected to go to the private sector. Its nonsovereign operations—which mainly comprise private sector operations—are projected to grow from an average of 17% of nonconcessional approvals over 2012–2014 to 22% by 2019. ADB can also engage in cofinancing with bilateral development assistance and catalyze private foreign capital.

- **MDBs like ADB have been effective in building good infrastructure because they combine finance with expertise and knowledge, drawing on their experience across countries.** In addition to bringing advanced technologies to projects, ADB has helped strengthen government capacity in planning and implementing infrastructure projects. ADB can further help countries promote climate-proofing design; modernize procurement processes; enhance safeguard standards for social and environment impacts; support the development of a regulatory environment conducive to PPPs; and develop capital markets. It is urgent that ADB plays a pivotal role in helping identify bankable projects and provide transaction advisory services for PPPs. Finally, ADB—with experience in regional cooperation and integration, trust of DMCs and technical skills—can facilitate cross-border and regional infrastructure projects.

Annex

Annex Table 1: Baseline Scenario in Comparison with *Infrastructure for a Seamless Asia+*

Region/Subregion	Total for the Period ($ billion in 2008 prices)		Annual ($ billion in 2008 prices)	
	Seamless Asia+	This report	Seamless Asia+	This report
Time period	2010–2020	2016–2030	2010–2020	2016–2030
DMCs covered	32	32	32	32
Central Asia	374	396	34	26
East Asia	4,378	9,728	398	649
South Asia*	2,370	5,095	215	340
Southeast Asia	1,095	2,171	100	145
The Pacific	6	36	1	2
Asia and the Pacific	**8,223**	**17,426**	**748**	**1,162**

DMC= developing member country.
+*Seamless Asia* refers to the *Infrastructure for a Seamless Asia* (ADB and ADBI 2009).
*Pakistan and Afghanistan are included in South Asia.
Source: ADB and ADBI (2009); ADB estimates.

Annex Table 2: Country Coverage—Special Report versus *Seamless Asia*

Subregion/Economy	Seamless Asia 32 DMCs	This report 45 DMCs	25 DMCs	Subregion/Economy	Seamless Asia 32 DMCs	This report 45 DMCs	25 DMCs
Central Asia				**Southeast Asia**			
Armenia	✓	✓	✓	Brunei Darussalam		✓	
Azerbaijan	✓	✓		Cambodia	✓	✓	✓
Georgia	✓	✓		Indonesia	✓	✓	✓
Kazakhstan	✓	✓	✓	Lao PDR	✓	✓	
Kyrgyz Republic	✓	✓	✓	Malaysia	✓	✓	✓
Tajikistan	✓	✓		Myanmar	✓	✓	✓
Turkmenistan		✓		Philippines	✓	✓	✓
Uzbekistan	✓	✓		Singapore		✓	
				Thailand	✓	✓	✓
East Asia				Viet Nam	✓	✓	✓
People's Republic of China	✓	✓	✓	**The Pacific**			
Hong Kong, China		✓		Cook Islands		✓	
Republic of Korea		✓		Fiji	✓	✓	✓
Mongolia	✓	✓	✓	Kiribati	✓	✓	✓
Taipei,China		✓		Marshall Islands		✓	✓
				Micronesia, Fed. States of		✓	✓
South Asia				Nauru		✓	
Afghanistan	✓	✓	✓	Palau		✓	
Bangladesh	✓	✓	✓	Papua New Guinea	✓	✓	✓
Bhutan	✓	✓	✓	Samoa	✓	✓	
India	✓	✓	✓	Solomon Islands	✓	✓	
Maldives		✓	✓	Timor-Leste	✓	✓	
Nepal	✓	✓	✓	Tonga	✓	✓	
Pakistan	✓	✓	✓	Tuvalu		✓	
Sri Lanka	✓	✓	✓	Vanuatu	✓	✓	

DMC= developing member country; Lao PDR = Lao People's Democratic Republic.

Abbreviations

ACRAA	Association of Credit Rating Agencies in Asia
ADB	Asian Development Bank
ADBI	Asian Development Bank Institute
ADOU	Asian Development Outlook Update
BAPPENAS	Badan Perencanaan Pembangunan Nasional
BOT	build own operate transfer
CAREC	Central Asia Regional Economic Cooperation
CPC	United Nations Central Product Classification
CRA	credit rating agency
DAC	development assistance committee
DMC	developing member country
EIRR	economic internal rates of return
GDP	gross domestic product
GFCF	gross fixed capital formation
GFCF(CE)	gross fixed capital formation on construction excluding buildings
GFCF(GG)	gross fixed capital formation for general government
GHG	greenhouse gas
GMM-IV	generalized methods of moments-instrumental variables
GMS	Greater Mekong Subregion
GQ	golden quadrilateral
ICP	International Comparison Program
ICT	information and communication technology
IMF	International Monetary Fund
Lao PDR	Lao People's Democratic Republic
LCOE	levelized cost of electricity
MDB	multilateral development bank
MWh	megawatt-hour
NITI	National Institution for Transforming India
NSO	national statistics office
ODA	official development assistance
ODF	official development finance
OECD	Organisation for Economic Co-operation and Development
OLS	ordinary least square
PMGSY	Pradhan Mantri Gram Sadak Yojana
PPI	Private Participation in Infrastructure
PPP	public-private partnership
PPWSA	Phnom Penh Water Supply Authority
PRC	People's Republic of China
PV	solar photovoltaic
SASEC	South Asia Subregional Economic Cooperation
SOEs	state-owned enterprises
SPV	special purpose vehicle

STAR	Southern Tagalog Arterial Road
TEU	twenty-foot equivalent unit
TFP	total factor productivity
VAT	value-added tax
WDI	World Development Indicators Database
WEF	World Economic Forum

MEETING ASIA'S
INFRASTRUCTURE NEEDS

Section 1. Introduction

Infrastructure—defined here as transport, power, telecommunications, and water supply and sanitation—is essential for development. It is an essential input into the production of goods and services and raises productivity. It powers factories and businesses and enables firms to trade. It encourages innovation and generates new economic opportunities and jobs as firms interact and discover new products, processes, and markets. Efficient infrastructure lowers distribution costs and boosts living standards by making goods and services more affordable. One of infrastructure's most dramatic benefits is on the poor, allowing access to better health and educational services, improving living conditions, and fostering greater social and economic mobility. And decisions on infrastructure development—including the type of infrastructure and technology—have significant implications for economic sustainability, as climate change, pollution, and other environmental factors present new challenges.

Indeed, the many ways infrastructure affects economic activity and people's lives is engrained in the 17 United Nations Sustainable Development Goals—the 2030 global agenda to end poverty, protect the planet, and ensure prosperity for all. While Goal #9 is to "build resilient infrastructure, promote sustainable industrialization and foster innovation," goals #6 (water), #7 (energy), #8 (work and economic growth), and #11 (cities) have direct links to increased infrastructure investment and development.

This report presents a snapshot of the current condition of developing Asia's infrastructure. It examines how much the region has been investing in infrastructure and what will likely be needed through 2030. And it analyzes the financial and institutional challenges that will shape future infrastructure investment and development.

Section 2 begins with a brief look at how infrastructure is distributed across Asian Development Bank (ADB) developing member countries (DMCs). The region's dramatic infrastructure development over the past decades have spurred growth, reduced poverty, and improved people's lives. Yet over 400 million Asians still lack electricity; roughly 300 million have no access to safe drinking water and 1.5 billion people lack basic sanitation. More pervasively, quality remains a problem. In many countries, power outages restrain economic growth and underdeveloped transportation networks restrict the flow of people, goods, and services within cities and between urban and rural areas. City traffic congestion alone costs huge amounts in lost productivity and wasted fuel and adds to human stress. Moreover, the diversity in geography and development across the Asia and the Pacific region leaves vast differences in infrastructure provision across economies. Given the links between infrastructure and development, reducing deficiencies and closing infrastructure gaps makes sense.

Increasing infrastructure investment is key. But by how much and in which sectors is not nearly as obvious. How much is currently being invested by who is a good starting point. Yet this is surprisingly more difficult to determine than commonly thought. Section 3 deals with the types of data available and the problem of how to best measure infrastructure investment given the number of players involved—national and subnational governments, state-owned enterprises (SOEs), and increasingly, the private sector. Governments do not typically publish data on aggregate infrastructure investment, and there is no single way or international best practice to measure it.

To get around this problem, Section 3 considers several different data sources on infrastructure investment—including government budget documents, data on subcomponents of gross fixed capital formation (GFCF) recorded in national income accounts, and available data on private infrastructure investment. Three separate measures of infrastructure investment are derived. Each has its benefits and limitations. The report proposes a way to improve measuring infrastructure investment using GFCF data broken down by asset type, the institution investing in these assets, and the economic or industrial sector in which they operate. Applying this approach would require close collaboration among official national accounts statisticians and should be part of the medium-term knowledge agenda. In this report, however, the available measures—used judiciously—provide a reasonable comparison of the amounts individual countries invest in infrastructure.

Based on our preferred, more conservative measure—government budget data and information on private infrastructure investment (from the World Bank's Private Participation in Infrastructure or PPI Project Database)—over three quarters of current infrastructure investment in the Asia and the Pacific region is in the People's Republic of China (PRC), which invests around 6.8% of GDP in infrastructure. Among economies with relatively good data, Bhutan, India, Mongolia, the Maldives, and Viet Nam all invest more than 5% of GDP in infrastructure.

Section 4 presents our estimates of infrastructure investment needs for ADB's 45 DMCs for 2016–2030. The estimates are calculated in two major steps. First, analogous to earlier work—*Infrastructure for a Seamless Asia* (ADB and ADBI 2009), Fay and Yepes (2003), and Ruiz-Nunez and Wei (2015)—we rely on the historical, cross-country relationship between physical infrastructure stocks and key economic and demographic factors that influence demand and/or supply of infrastructure services. These are used to estimate the infrastructure investment required to sustain economic growth and demographic changes over the 15 years from 2016 to 2030. We call these our baseline estimates of investment needs; they in effect update the estimates in *Infrastructure for a Seamless Asia* (ADB and ADBI 2009) for the 11-year 2010 to 2020 period.

Second, we estimate infrastructure investment needs that factor in the effects of climate change on transport, power, telecommunications, and water and sanitation. We adjust our estimates of investment needs to account for the costs of climate change mitigation (in particular, costs for greener power generation and electricity transmission) and for climate change adaptation ("climate proofing" infrastructure). Based on key estimates and parameters from recent studies—especially ADB (2016b)—we adjust baseline estimates upward for infrastructure investment in power, transport, and water.

The infrastructure estimates here are not meant as forecasts of optimal future infrastructure investments for the region. There are certainly other ways of determining infrastructure needs. For example, they could be defined as investments required to ensure people have access to infrastructure services of the type and quality that average citizens in Organisation for Economic Co-operation and Development (OECD) countries have. (We consider estimates of infrastructure needs using this approach for the PRC and the Pacific economies—as expected, they are considerably larger.)

Rather, the estimates here represent a "birds-eye view" of infrastructure needs. They provide the big picture of the region's infrastructure needs under plausible scenarios—future economic growth and the need to deal with climate change, for example—and use the results to think more concretely about what it means for future infrastructure finance and the critical regulatory and institutional issues that help define how infrastructure projects should be planned, designed, and implemented.[1]

---

1   The report's projections cannot substitute for the detailed analysis of an individual economy's infrastructure needs—whether in aggregate or by subsector. This would require a granularity impossible at the cross-country level—for example, when thinking about transport infrastructure investment, details on precise topography, and current and projected traffic volumes at subnational levels are important factors, among others.

Keeping this in mind, our estimates show the region will need to invest around $22.6 trillion (in 2015 prices) from 2016–2030 ($1.5 trillion annually) in transport, power, telecommunications, and water and sanitation without taking climate change into account. This is based on a baseline assumption that economic growth will range from 3% to 7% across developing Asia's subregions. Power and transport are largest, accounting for 52% and 35% of future investments, respectively.

Incorporating climate change mitigation and adaptation, our projections rise substantially to $26.2 trillion for the region ($1.7 trillion per year) from 2016 to 2030. The majority of the increase covers greenhouse gas mitigation in the power sector, especially, and climate-proofing investments for roads. As a result, the share of investments in power rises to 56.3% of total future infrastructure investment.

How will these needs be met? Section 5 first considers the extent of infrastructure finance needed. The difference between estimated infrastructure investment needs and current infrastructure investment—a measure of the infrastructure financing gap—is calculated for 2016–2020. The gap reaches 2.4% of projected GDP, or 5% if the PRC is excluded. Section 5 then explores the fiscal resources available to the public sector—by far the dominant player in infrastructure finance—and how they can be increased. The remainder of the gap would need to be covered by the private sector. Several important ways the private sector could increase its investment in infrastructure development are discussed.

Section 5 also addresses institutional and capacity issues related to planning, designing, and implementing infrastructure projects. These include maintaining infrastructure assets to ensure infrastructure investment is well spent. Part and parcel to this is to view infrastructure investment as an integrated development priority—choosing appropriate technologies, especially with the challenge of climate change and the longevity of infrastructure projects. Section 6 concludes and summarizes the role of ADB in meeting Asia's infrastructure needs.

Section 2. Infrastructure's Role and Record: A Brief Review

2.1. Infrastructure and its role in development

Infrastructure is key to economic production, trade and improving everyday life. This report focuses on critical physical infrastructure—transport, power, telecommunications, and water supply and sanitation.[2,3] Roads and railroads ease the flow of people, commodities, and manufactures, allowing economic activities to be concentrated and specialized across regions. Electricity is needed for most modern production and essential for the quality of household life. Telecommunications, especially digital and cellular, enables real-time information transfer regardless of distance. Secure water supply and sewage safeguard human health and productivity. And increasingly, there is growing recognition of the role of infrastructure in helping societies deal with the challenges presented by climate change. In short, sound infrastructure promotes economic development, enhances welfare and helps provide the basis for more sustained, inclusive growth.

Infrastructure is characterized by a unique set of characteristics. Its services are typically delivered through complex and costly network systems; and although initial investments in infrastructure are large, the marginal cost of servicing additional customers is usually low and decreasing. Therefore, infrastructure has often been characterized as a natural monopoly, giving rise to the general dominance of government or public agencies in providing its services. Moreover, governments dominate these sectors as they are considered essential to human needs, influence social equity and stability, and/or generate externalities.

This natural monopolistic character is less accepted today, with the possible exception of water and sanitation. For example, in recent decades, technological and regulatory progress has made telecommunications highly competitive. This is also true for power generation and increasingly distribution (as it unbundles less competitive transmission processes). Transportation has become more competitive both across subsectors and between modalities. While this reduces some of the need for governments to intervene in what were natural monopolies, a strong regulatory environment is still needed to ensure infrastructure services can accommodate externalities and benefit the public good.

Policy makers, scholars, and practitioners increasingly recognize that the private sector can contribute in a variety ways in infrastructure investment, operations, and regulations. New technology allows the unbundling of infrastructure components, making the public and private agencies responsible for the costs and risks of these components more efficient. In practice, private companies build and operate power generating plants, water supply and wastewater treatment facilities, and compete in running telecommunication companies, airlines, many toll roads, and port facilities.

There are several ways of assessing infrastructure's contributions to an economy and society. It is widely accepted that infrastructure services directly contribute to the production of goods and services. Moreover, infrastructure may enhance the efficiency of other factors of production and thus improve productivity. Not surprisingly, there is a strong positive correlation between gross domestic product (GDP) per capita and indicators of infrastructure stock (Figure 2.1). Of course, correlation

---

2   The infrastructure covered varies in different sections based on data availability. For example, dams, irrigation, and flood control are important physical infrastructure—yet they are not covered in the analysis of infrastructure needs (Section 4 projections). Similarly, due to differences in data availability, gas and oil pipelines are included in estimates of existing "energy" infrastructure investments in Section 3, but are not included in the "power" infrastructure projected as future needs in Section 4. As explained, available information on investments does not always allow disaggregation of infrastructure categories into their various subcomponents.

3   Social infrastructure—education, health care, and public housing, for example—is not covered in this report. While just as critical, it raises very different issues in performance and delivery.

does not imply causation and the contribution of infrastructure capital to production and development more broadly need to be empirically verified and may vary over time, location, and context. Earlier studies using macrodata obtained estimates of elasticities of total output to infrastructure capital between 0.20 and 0.40 (Straub 2008), implying that a 1% increase in infrastructure stock was associated with a 0.20%–0.40% increase in output. However, these studies were generally plagued by measurement and endogeneity problems—for example, the possibility that infrastructure provision may be the result of growth or a response to some third factor (such as new technology) that also drives growth and other outcomes. More recent studies use microdata and pay more attention to endogeneity issues (Box 2.1). For example, Donaldson (2010) shows that, in India, railroads increased trade, reduced price differences across regions, and increased real incomes and welfare. Banerjee, Duflo, and Qian (2012) showed that in the PRC, proximity to transportation networks led to moderately higher GDP per capita. Alternatively, Allcott, Collard-Wexler, and O'Connell (2016) find that power shortages reduce Indian manufacturers' revenues and producer surpluses by 5% to 10%.[4]

Infrastructure benefits can also be evaluated by project. One way is to look at economic internal rates of return (EIRR) of infrastructure projects. The returns account for economic benefits and costs, thus reflecting a project's net impact on an economy. For instance, a road project will lead to shorter travel time, lower vehicle operation costs, and more trips. A water supply project will improve household health. Table 2.1 illustrates EIRR using data from completed ADB-financed projects. The average EIRR of infrastructure projects implemented by ADB in developing Asia in the last 50 years ranged from 14.3% for air transport to 33% for conventional power generation.

Table 2.1: Average Economic Internal Rate of Return of ADB-Financed Projects
(1966–present)

Sector	Number of Projects	EIRR (%)
Transport		
Air transport	11	14.3
Road transport	184	22.8
Rail transport	20	16.1
Water transport	38	20.1
Power		
Conventional power generation	33	33.1
Electricity transmission and distribution	71	20.0
Information and communication technology	17	24.1
Water and other urban infrastructure services	42	18.1

ADB = Asian Development Bank; EIRR = economic internal rates of return.
Source: InfrAsia Project Database, ADB.

Beyond the quantifiable benefits of infrastructure projects—such as EIRR—there are benefits that accrue to society at large. Aside from the direct benefits of transport projects, for example, indirect and qualitative benefits could include boosting local tourism or promoting more small and medium enterprise entrepreneurs to establish businesses.[5]

It is clear that the essential services or public goods infrastructure provides significantly benefit the poor. There is a robust negative correlation between infrastructure availability and poverty (Figure 2.2)—measured as the percentage of population below

Figure 2.1: Gross Domestic Product (GDP) per Capita and Infrastructure Index, 2011

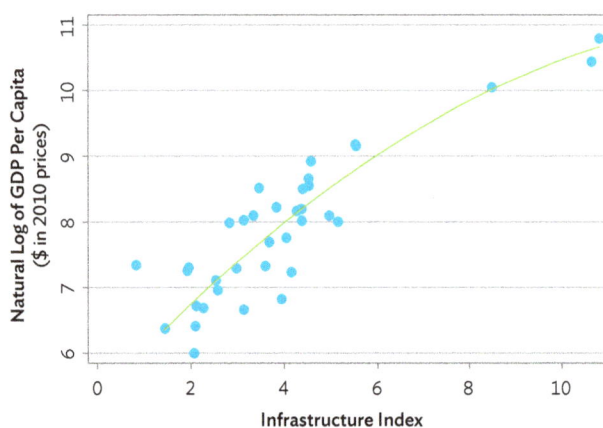

Note: Infrastructure index is computed based on first principal component of infrastructure stocks in roads, airport, electricity, telephone, mobile, broadband, water and sanitation. Higher values represent greater infrastructure availability.
Source: World Development Indicators, World Bank; ADB estimates.

---

4   Interested readers may see Sawada (2015) for a discussion of challenges in evaluating the impacts of infrastructure on economic development.

5   While economic returns generally outweigh the financial returns for infrastructure projects, the calculated economic benefits may still not capture the full benefits of an infrastructure project to society. For instance, new roads may help boost the local tourism industry, which is not quantified by the methodology used in this report.

Box 2.1: Microeconomic Studies of Impacts of Transport Infrastructure

Several studies use detailed microdata to examine how different types of transportation infrastructure impact economic development and individual welfare in developing Asia. Several examples stand out.

The Golden Quadrilateral (GQ) project is a large-scale highway construction and improvement project launched in India in 2001. Using firm-level data, Ghani, Goswami, and Kerr (2016) find that output levels, over the decade after construction began, in the districts located within 10 kilometers (km) from the GQ network grew by 50% while districts 10–50 km from the network did not. With inventory data and perception of firms in the World Bank's Enterprise Surveys Data, Datta (2012) finds that the GQ program led firms along the network to reduce input inventories, switch primary suppliers, and report decreased transportation obstacles to production.

The Li and Li (2013) study of the rapidly expanded road network in the People's Republic of China (PRC) echoes the effect that road infrastructure has on firm inventory. Specifically, they estimate that $1.00 of road spending saves about $0.02 of inventory costs, a non-trivial saving.

Faber (2014) finds that expanding the PRC expressway network reduced industrial output growth among peripheral counties. The lower trade costs between these counties and metropolitan areas from the expressway connection enhance the spatial concentration of production activities.

Yoshino and Pontines (2015) studied the Southern Tagalog Arterial Road (STAR) in Batangas, Philippines finding that the tollway increases tax and nontax revenues for the municipalities it passes through. This also extends to cities in neighboring provinces.

Several studies evaluating rural roads in different countries confirm the widely held belief that rural roads play an important role in reducing poverty. For example, Gibson and Rozelle (2003) show that rural roads are an important determinant of poverty status of rural households in Papua New Guinea.

Khandker, Bakht, and Koolwal (2009) find rural road investments in Bangladesh led to higher agricultural production, higher wages, lower input and transportation costs, higher output prices, and higher schooling of youth. In addition, they find rural roads benefited the poor more than the nonpoor.

Pradhan Mantri Gram Sadak Yojana (PMGSY) is a rural road program sponsored by the Government of India that aims to provide all-weather rural roads. Gupta et al. (2014) provide suggestive evidence that the program reduced poverty in the connected districts by enabling a transition of employment from low-paying agriculture to construction and, to a limited extent, manufacturing. Significantly, these effects are robust to control the national employment guarantee program. A more recent study (Asher and Novosad 2016) that uses more detailed spatial and individual level data adds further support to the effects of the rural road program. The authors find that the new roads resulted in the significant reallocation of rural labor from agriculture into wage jobs; and that this reallocation occurred most prominently in villages closer to major cities.

Railway infrastructure has also been the topic of several recent studies. Li and Chen (2013) studied a railway project that doubled the shipping capacity of a 1,200-mile-long railway in the PRC northwest, which was congested in one-direction before the expansion. They find that after the project the price gap of goods shipped in the congested direction dropped by 30% and shipping volumes increased by 40%, whereas goods moved in the non-congested direction were unaffected. The estimated social return of the investment reaches 10% annually in the most conservative case.

Yoshino and Abidhadjaev (2015) provide some evidence that a newly built railway in south Uzbekistan may have caused 0.4%~2.0% GDP growth in the regions affected. Finally, Chen and Whalley (2012) show that the opening of the new rail transit system in Taipei,China reduced air pollution from carbon monoxide, a key tailpipe pollutant, by 5%–15%. The results highlight the importance of urban public railway transit infrastructure.

the international poverty line $1.90 a day (2011 PPP). While many factors (income, for example) could underlie the negative relationship between infrastructure and poverty, today more studies examine how certain infrastructure investments impact the poor. For example, studying South Africa's mass roll-out of grid infrastructure to rural areas after the end of apartheid (Dinkelman 2011) finds household electrification raised employment by freeing women from home production and enabling microenterprises. Zhang and Xu (2016) show that the PRC government's substantial investment in

rural drinking water treatment since the 1980s generated significant long-term educational benefits among rural youth (in addition to improving health). On average, the program led to 1.1 additional years of education for rural beneficiaries—and girls gained more than boys. Jensen (2007) finds that, between 1997 and 2001, the widespread use of mobile phones by fisherfolk and wholesalers in south India substantially reduced price dispersion and eliminated waste. The technology (and associated infrastructure) improved both consumer and producer welfare.

Figure 2.2: Poverty Rate and Infrastructure Index, 2011

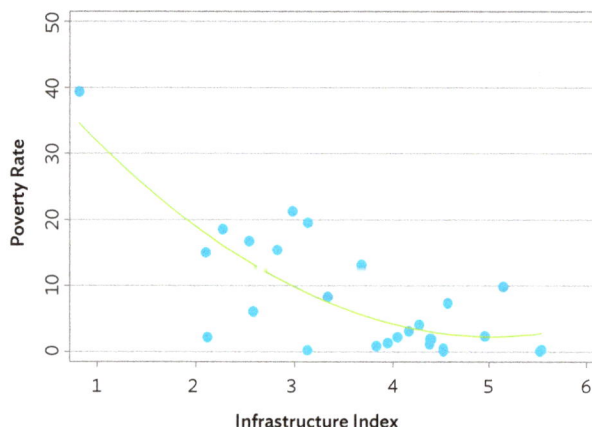

Note: Infrastructure index is computed based on first principal component of infrastructure stocks in roads, airport, electricity, telephone, mobile, broadband, water and sanitation. Higher values represent greater infrastructure availability.
Source: PovcalNet, World Bank; ADB estimates.

2.2. Infrastructure provision in the region

In the past decade, developing Asia has built more infrastructure across all sectors than any other developing region. Nonetheless, there remain significant gaps in infrastructure quantity and quality compared with more developed regions. And there is considerable variation across economies within developing Asia in the quantity and quality of infrastructure.

Between 2001 and 2010, developing Asia's road network expanded an average 5% annually—much faster than other developing economies and Organisation for Economic Co-operation and Development (OECD) economies as a whole (Figure 2.3). There are a few countries like Samoa, Azerbaijan, Thailand, and Afghanistan that have experienced double-digit annual growth in length of road networks (or road stock per land area). Malaysia, the PRC, and the Kyrgyz Republic have also seen rapid growth. However, road density in much of developing Asia remains low; and transport services provided mean less if road quality is poor.[6]

---

6   For instance, data suggest India has large road length. However, its high road density is accompanied by lower road quality, evident in perceptions of road quality.

Figure 2.3: Road Density and Annual Growth

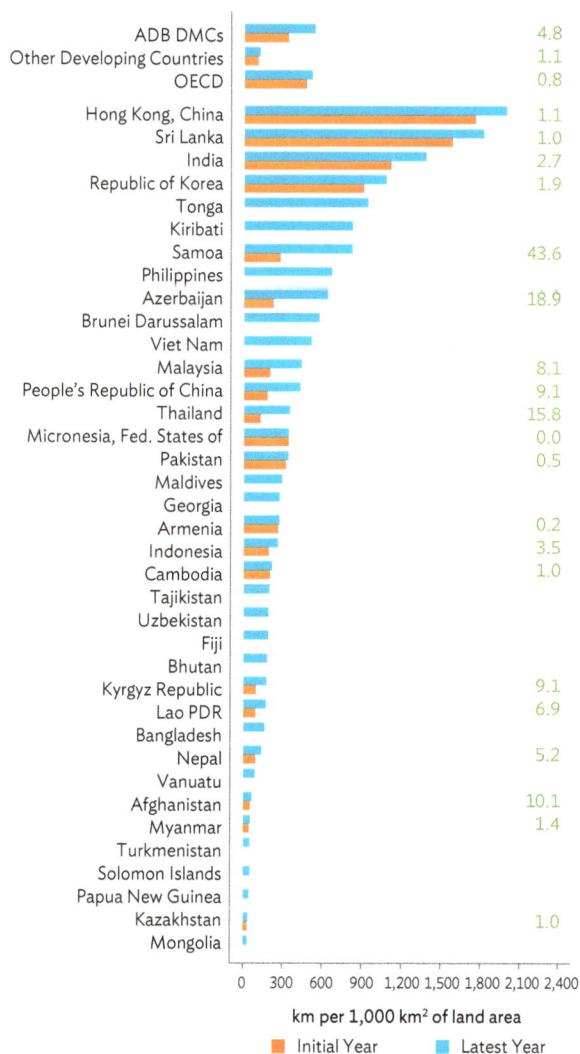

km per 1,000 km² of land area

■ Initial Year   ■ Latest Year

ADB = Asian Development Bank; DMC = developing member country; Lao PDR = Lao People's Democratic Republic; OECD = Organisation for Economic Co-operation and Development.
Note: Figures in green refer to annualized growth rate (2000–2010). Regional averages are calculated with land area as weights. Initial year is between 1996–2004 while latest Year is between 2006–2010.
Source: International Road Federation (2012); World Development Indicators, World Bank.

Indeed, road quality needs to substantially improve in economies across each developing Asian subregion—most urgently in lower income countries. Perceptions of road quality using a 7-point scale (higher scores mean better road quality) are compared across Asia's developing economies as well as between developing Asia, developing economies outside the region and OECD economies (Figure 2.4). Developing Asia' scores range from 2 to 6 with the regional average slightly above 4. This is higher than the average for other developing economies but one

Figure 2.4: Road Quality, 2015

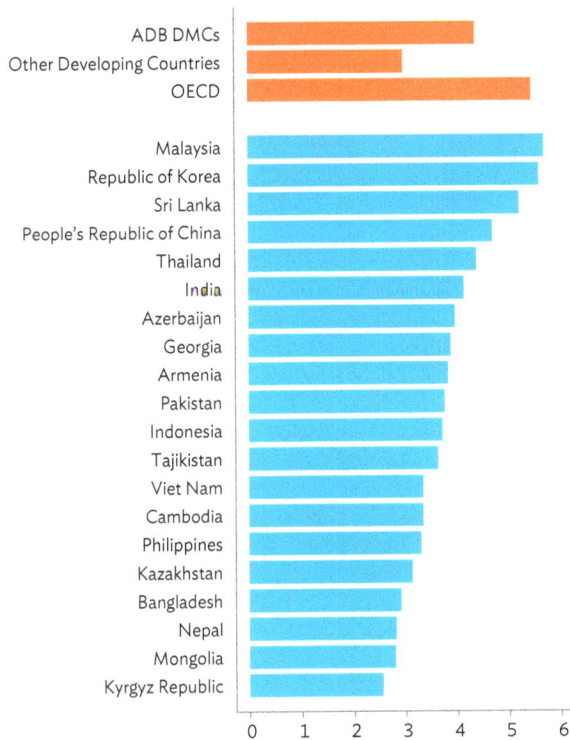

ADB = Asian Development Bank; DMC = developing member country;
OECD = Organisation for Economic Co-operation and Development.
Note: Regional averages of quality are calculated with length of road
as weights.
Source: World Economic Forum (2015).

Figure 2.5: Railroad Density and Annual Growth

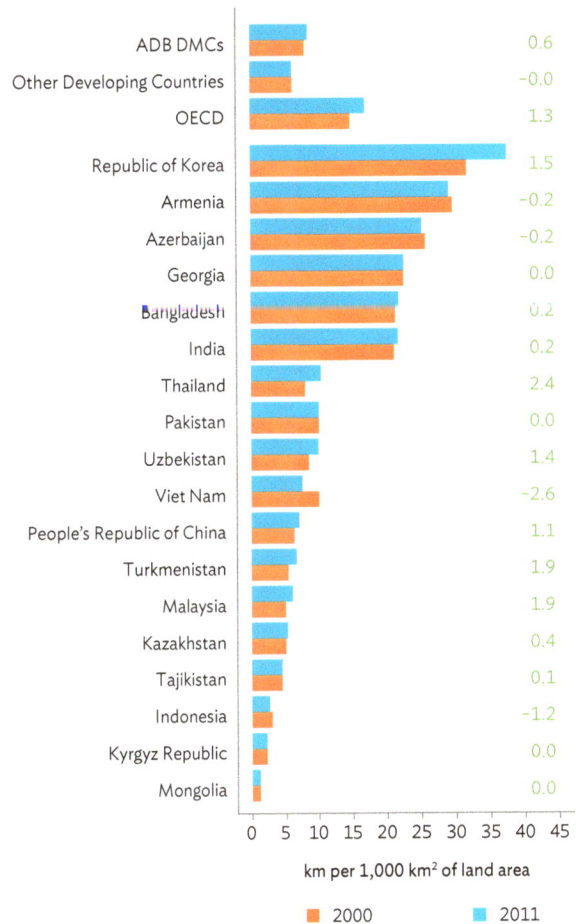

km per 1,000 km² of land area

■ 2000   ■ 2011

ADB = Asian Development Bank; DMC = developing member country;
OECD = Organisation for Economic Co-operation and Development.
Note: Figures in green refer to annualized growth rate (2000–2011).
Regional averages are calculated with land area as weights.
Source: World Development Indicators, World Bank.

point below the OECD average. The results suggest that quite a few regional countries need to increase investment in road rehabilitation and maintenance.

Railroads expanded moderately in developing Asia between 2000 and 2011, below OECD growth (Figure 2.5). While some economies such as the Republic of Korea, Thailand, Uzbekistan, Turkmenistan, and Malaysia intensified their railroad networks, others like Pakistan, the Kyrgyz Republic, and Mongolia did not expand despite their low railroad density in 2000. And some countries— Viet Nam, Indonesia, Armenia, and Azerbaijan— saw railroad density actually decline, probably due to obsolete railways going out of operation.[7] While geography and large initial investment costs may inhibit railroad development in some economies, their relatively benign environmental impact

compared with other modes of transportation suggest expanding rail networks may be highly desirable.

As with perceptions of road quality, developing Asia's railroad quality is considered better than other parts of the developing world, although they fall well below OECD quality. However, there is large variation within the region, with countries like the Republic of Korea, Malaysia, and the PRC registering railway quality scores exceeding the OECD average. At the same time, several economies, predominantly lower income ones, had scores below 3 on the 7-point scale (Figure 2.6). Again, rehabilitation as well as better management and maintenance are key for these countries to improve railroad system standards.

---

7   Though unverified, data error could also explain the decline in some cases.

Figure 2.6: Railroad Quality, 2015

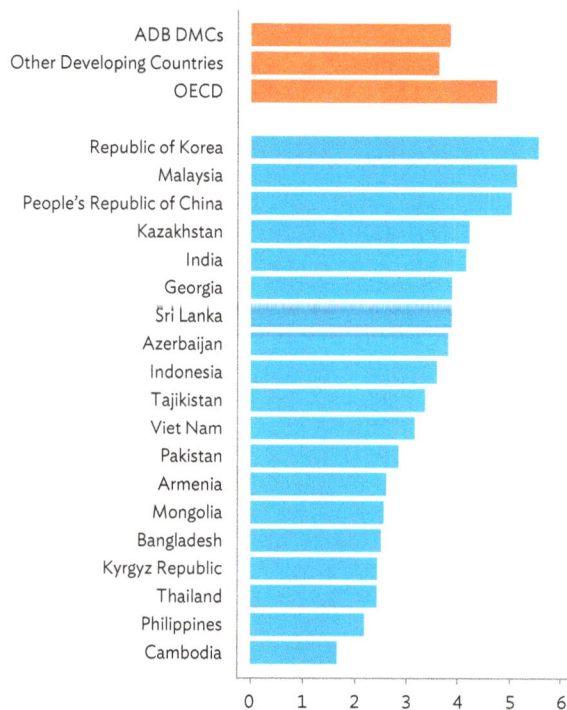

ADB = Asian Development Bank; DMC = developing member country;
OECD = Organisation for Economic Co-operation and Development.
Note: Railroad quality is measured based on perception scores in a
         7-point scale (higher scores mean better railroad quality).
         Regional averages of quality are calculated with length of
         railroad as weights.
Source: World Economic Forum (2015).

Figure 2.7: Electricity Generation Capacity and Annual Growth

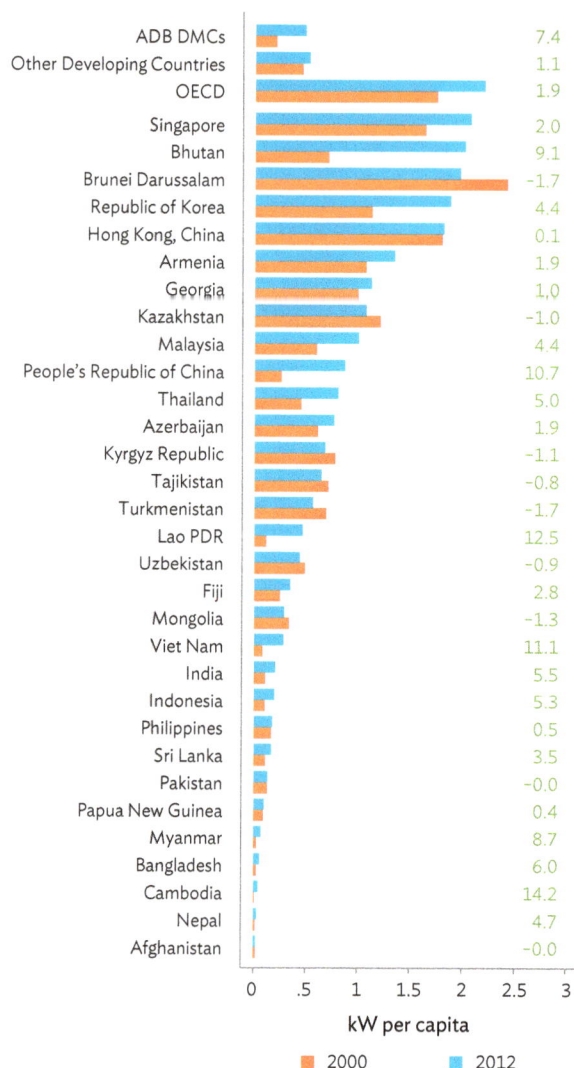

kW per capita
■ 2000   ■ 2012

ADB = Asian Development Bank; DMC = developing member country;
Lao PDR = Lao People's Democratic Republic; OECD = Organisation for
Economic Co-operation and Development.
Note: Figures in green refer to annualized growth rate (2000–2012).
         Regional averages are calculated with population as weights.
Source: International Energy Statistics, US Energy Information
         Administration.

Developing Asia's electricity generation capacity per capita, a key indicator to measure the power infrastructure of an economy, grew at a rapid average of 7.4% annually between 2000 and 2012; yet it remained slightly below the average for other developing economies and substantially below the OECD average (Figure 2.7). Several Southeast Asian, South Asian, and the Pacific economies have electricity generating capacity per capita well below the regional average, even if some have been expanding rapidly. Several Central Asian economies—along with Brunei Darussalam and Mongolia—saw capacity drop as population growth outpaced electricity capacity.[8] While an economy's structure strongly influences the optimal level of per capita electricity generation (including, in some cases, electricity exports to neighbors), transmission and distribution networks play a major role in the efficiency of electricity generated.

An important indicator for the efficiency of the power sector is thus the percentage of electricity lost in transmission and distribution. In 2013 developing Asia still lost about 8% of generated electricity. This was lower than the 12% of other developing economies but well above the 6% OECD average (Figure 2.8). Nepal and Cambodia lost as much as 30% of total electricity generated, while losses in Myanmar and the Kyrgyz Republic exceeded 20%. By contrast, developing Asian economies such as Bhutan, the PRC, the Republic of Korea, Papua New Guinea (PNG), and Singapore were more efficient than the OECD average, partly due to more up-

---

8   Though unverified, data error could also explain the decline in some
     cases.

Figure 2.8: Transmission and Distribution Loss, 2013

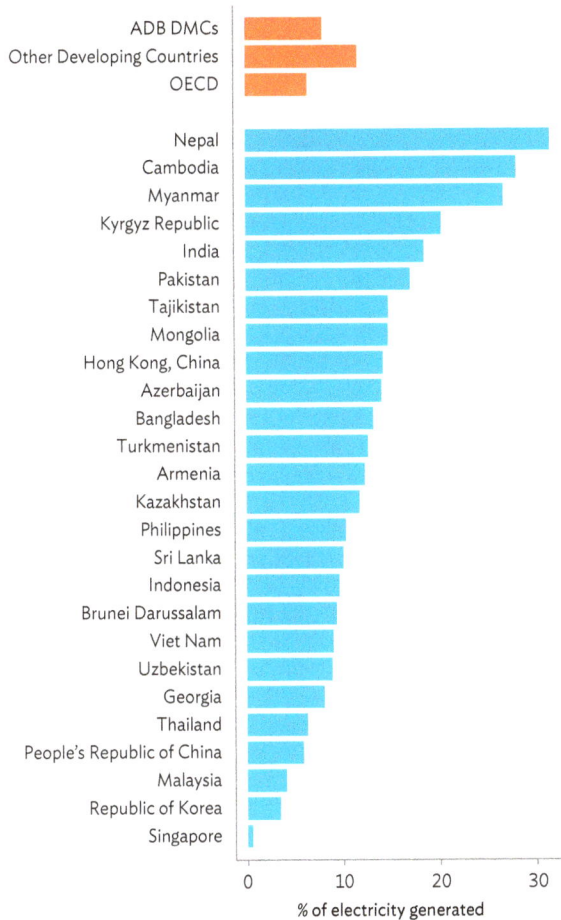

% of electricity generated

ADB = Asian Development Bank; DMC = developing member country;
OECD = Organisation for Economic Co-operation and Development.
Note: Regional averages are calculated with total electricity
         generated as weights.
Source: World Development Indicators, World Bank.

Figure 2.9: Frequency of Power Outages
(monthly)

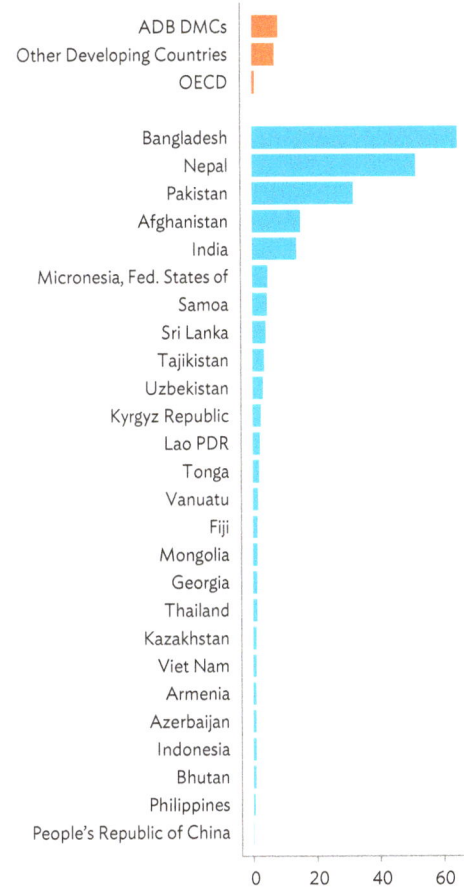

ADB = Asian Development Bank; DMC = developing member country;
Lao PDR = Lao People's Democratic Republic; OECD = Organisation for
Economic Co-operation and Development.
Note: Latest available data from 2006–2014.
Source: Enterprise Surveys Data, World Bank.

to-date transmission technology. This suggests the possibility for intraregion technological and knowledge sharing to improve the regional efficiency level.

Power outages reported by local firms can help measure the adequacy and stability of power supply. On average, firms in developing Asia experienced slightly more power outages than those in other developing countries (Figure 2.9). While most of developing Asia does not have severe power supply problems, several do—for example, Bangladesh (65 power outages in a typical month), Nepal (51), and Pakistan (31). Frequent power disruptions interrupt production and significantly reduce productivity. They also lower the efficacy of longer term planning and can disrupt entire supply chains.

Developing Asia heavily relies on coal for power generation. Statistics from World Bank's World Development Indicators database show that in 2013, 66% of electricity was generated from coal-fired power plants in the region, as compared to 14% in non-Asian developing countries and 32% in OECD countries. Large economies in the region explain most of the high percentage, such as the PRC (75%), India (73%), Indonesia (51%), the Republic of Korea (41%), and Malaysia (39%). This poses significant local and global environmental challenges. While actions have been undertaken by some countries, considerable investment will be needed in the short to medium terms to make the power sector greener through reducing emissions and switching to renewable energy.

Good cross-country data on telecommunications and water infrastructure are unavailable. However, telephone subscriptions and the percentage of those with access to water and sanitation can be used as proxies for infrastructure capacity in those sectors.

From 2000 to 2015, there was rapid growth across developing Asia in telecommunications services, especially in cellular phone use (Figure 2.10). Many low and middle income economies rapidly caught up despite very low subscriptions of either landline or mobile phone in 2001. Average annual growth in mobile phone subscriptions reached 22% in the region, increasing from 46 to 923 subscriptions per 1,000 population, slightly lower than the rest of the developing world (1,019) and OECD countries (1,142). There remains great potential to increase investment in related infrastructure and expand coverage in countries like India, Pakistan, and Bangladesh given the sheer size of their populations.

Developing Asia has better urban and rural water supply than other developing economies, as measured by the percentage of population with access to improved water sources (Figures 2.11a, 2.11b).[9] There are large gaps across economies, however, especially in rural water supply. There was progress, in some cases, quite impressive progress, in several economies that had clean rural water coverage below 80% in 2000. However, 10%–20% of city dwellers in Afghanistan, Bangladesh, Kiribati, the Lao PDR, and PNG and over 50% of rural residents in Afghanistan, Kiribati, and PNG lacked access to clean water in 2015. Given water's core necessity—and the substantial benefits of clean water—the region must improve water supply, targeting OECD levels (95% access in both urban and rural areas) over the medium term. Investment in maintenance and new water supply facilities, along with institutional upgrades in metering and monitoring should be prioritized.

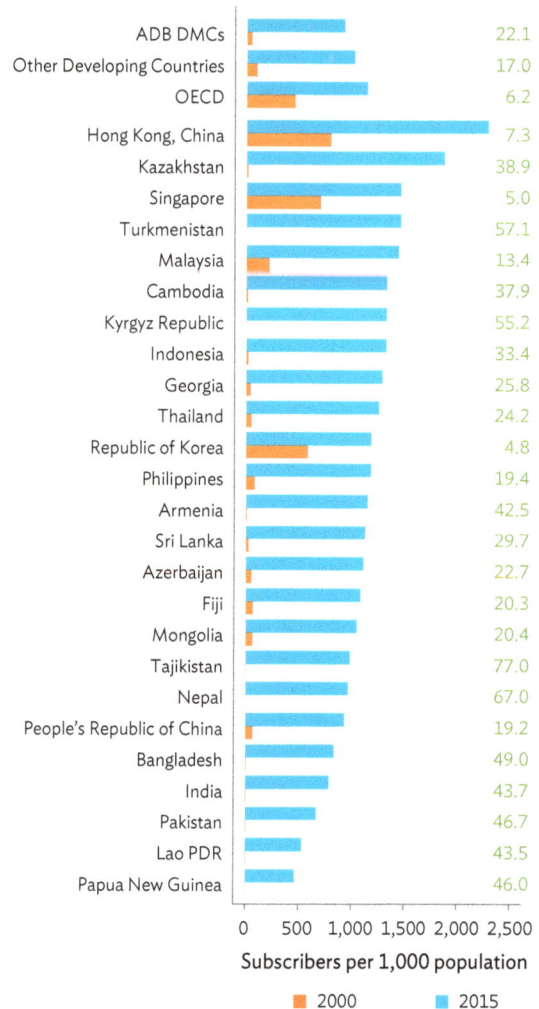

Figure 2.10: Mobile Cellular Phones and Annual Growth

Country	Growth
ADB DMCs	22.1
Other Developing Countries	17.0
OECD	6.2
Hong Kong, China	7.3
Kazakhstan	38.9
Singapore	5.0
Turkmenistan	57.1
Malaysia	13.4
Cambodia	37.9
Kyrgyz Republic	55.2
Indonesia	33.4
Georgia	25.8
Thailand	24.2
Republic of Korea	4.8
Philippines	19.4
Armenia	42.5
Sri Lanka	29.7
Azerbaijan	22.7
Fiji	20.3
Mongolia	20.4
Tajikistan	77.0
Nepal	67.0
People's Republic of China	19.2
Bangladesh	49.0
India	43.7
Pakistan	46.7
Lao PDR	43.5
Papua New Guinea	46.0

Subscribers per 1,000 population (0, 500, 1,000, 1,500, 2,000, 2,500)

■ 2000 ■ 2015

ADB = Asian Development Bank; DMC = developing member country; Lao PDR = Lao People's Democratic Republic; OECD = Organisation for Economic Co-operation and Development.
Note: Figures in green refer to annualized growth rate (2000–2015). Regional averages are calculated with population as weights.
Source: World Development Indicators, World Bank.

A relevant and important factor to consider here is the tremendous scope for urbanization in developing Asia in the next few decades. With significant numbers of people migrating from rural areas to cities, enormous investment in urban infrastructure including water supply and sanitation is required. On the other hand, when the rural population declines, the demand for infrastructure would be lower than what the statistics imply from a static point of view. Thus, rapid urbanization would affect the investment needs between urban and rural significantly, and from an economic perspective, it makes investment more efficient as urban infrastructure generally serves more people at the same cost.

---

9   Improved drinking water sources include piped water on premises (piped household water connections inside the user's dwelling, plot or yard), and other improved drinking water sources (public taps or standpipes, tube wells or boreholes, protected dug wells, protected springs, and rainwater collection).

Figure 2.11: Access to Improved Water Sources and Annual Growth

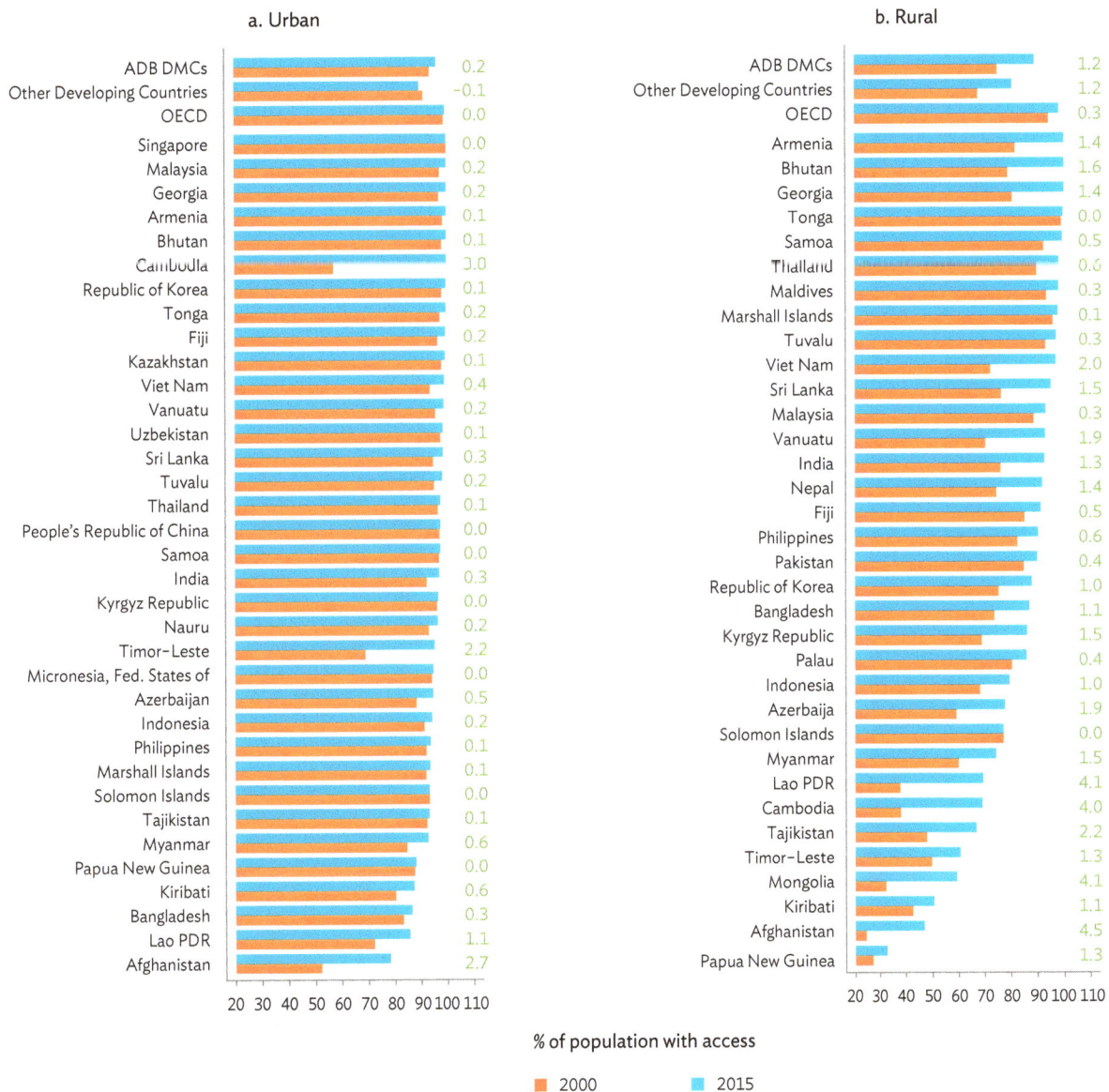

a. Urban

ADB DMCs	0.2
Other Developing Countries	-0.1
OECD	0.0
Singapore	0.0
Malaysia	0.2
Georgia	0.2
Armenia	0.1
Bhutan	0.1
Cambodia	3.0
Republic of Korea	0.1
Tonga	0.2
Fiji	0.2
Kazakhstan	0.1
Viet Nam	0.4
Vanuatu	0.2
Uzbekistan	0.1
Sri Lanka	0.3
Tuvalu	0.2
Thailand	0.1
People's Republic of China	0.0
Samoa	0.0
India	0.3
Kyrgyz Republic	0.0
Nauru	0.2
Timor-Leste	2.2
Micronesia, Fed. States of	0.0
Azerbaijan	0.5
Indonesia	0.2
Philippines	0.1
Marshall Islands	0.1
Solomon Islands	0.0
Tajikistan	0.1
Myanmar	0.6
Papua New Guinea	0.0
Kiribati	0.6
Bangladesh	0.3
Lao PDR	1.1
Afghanistan	2.7

b. Rural

ADB DMCs	1.2
Other Developing Countries	1.2
OECD	0.3
Armenia	1.4
Bhutan	1.6
Georgia	1.4
Tonga	0.0
Samoa	0.5
Thailand	0.6
Maldives	0.3
Marshall Islands	0.1
Tuvalu	0.3
Viet Nam	2.0
Sri Lanka	1.5
Malaysia	0.3
Vanuatu	1.9
India	1.3
Nepal	1.4
Fiji	0.5
Philippines	0.6
Pakistan	0.4
Republic of Korea	1.0
Bangladesh	1.1
Kyrgyz Republic	1.5
Palau	0.4
Indonesia	1.0
Azerbaija	1.9
Solomon Islands	0.0
Myanmar	1.5
Lao PDR	4.1
Cambodia	4.0
Tajikistan	2.2
Timor-Leste	1.3
Mongolia	4.1
Kiribati	1.1
Afghanistan	4.5
Papua New Guinea	1.3

20 30 40 50 60 70 80 90 100 110

% of population with access

■ 2000   ■ 2015

ADB = Asian Development Bank; DMC = developing member country; Lao PDR = Lao People's Democratic Republic;
OECD = Organisation for Economic Co-operation and Development.
Note: Figures in green refer to annualized growth rate (2000–2015). Regional averages are calculated with population as weights.
Source: World Development Indicators, World Bank.

The provision of sanitation facilities continues to differ significantly between developing Asia and OECD economies although the gaps have narrowed. In 2015, about 76% of those living in developing Asia's cities and 52% in rural areas had improved sanitation facilities (Figures 2.12a and 2.12b), compared to 98% and 96% in OECD countries, respectively.[10] A large number of the region's economies had urban coverage below 90%, while those with large populations—such as Indonesia and India—had coverage below 75%. More importantly, annualized growth rates in access in many countries were below 1% with the region averaging at 0.8%. A silver lining case, however, is Cambodia, which has increased its urban coverage from 43% to 88% with an average annual growth of 4.8% between 2001 and 2015.

_____

10   Improved sanitation facilities include flush/pour flush (to piped sewer system, septic tank, pit latrine), ventilated improved pit (VIP) latrine, pit latrine with slab, and composting toilet.

Figure 2.12: Access to Improved Sanitation Facilities and Annual Growth

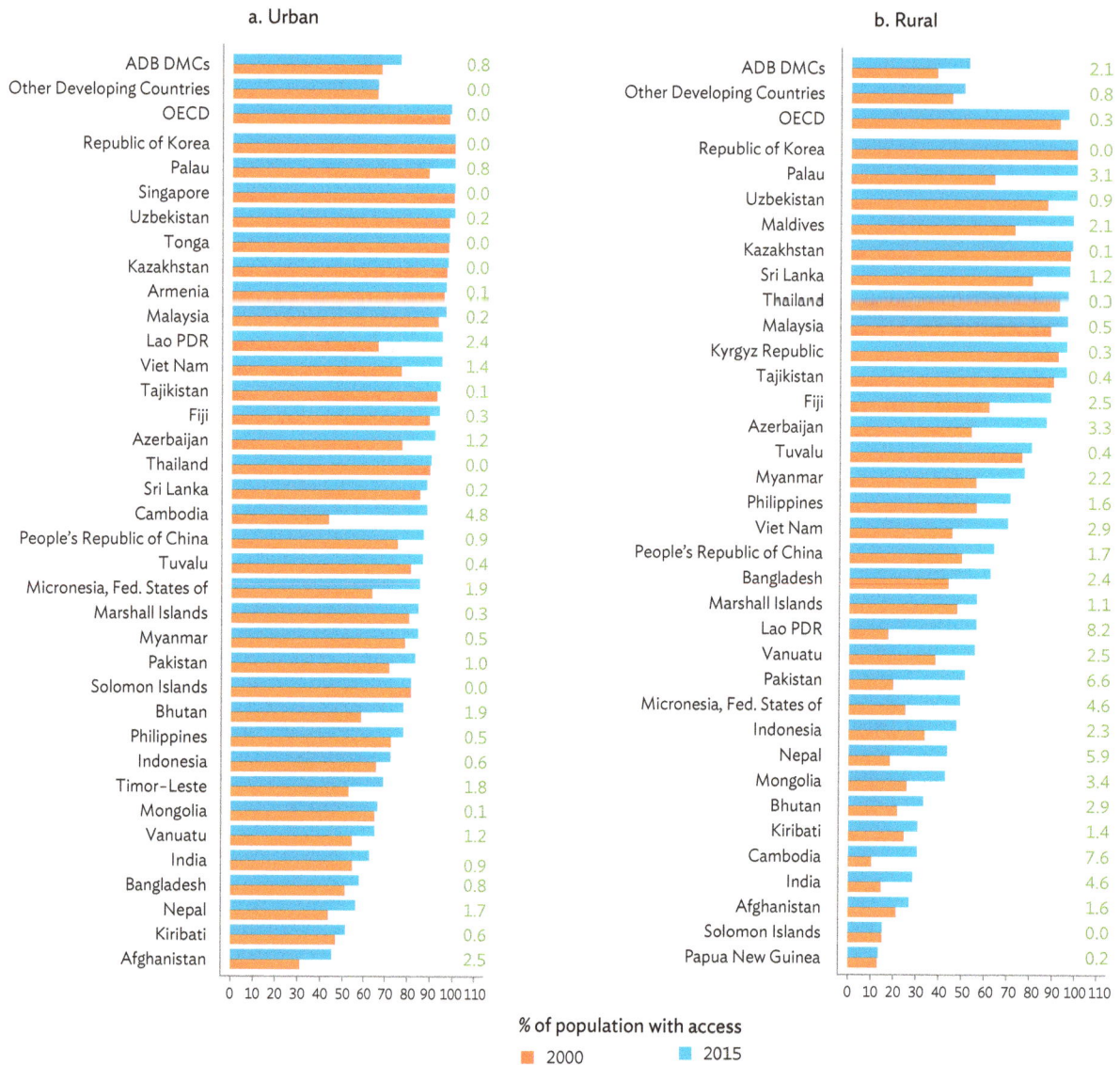

a. Urban

ADB DMCs	0.8
Other Developing Countries	0.0
OECD	0.0
Republic of Korea	0.0
Palau	0.8
Singapore	0.0
Uzbekistan	0.2
Tonga	0.0
Kazakhstan	0.0
Armenia	0.1
Malaysia	0.2
Lao PDR	2.4
Viet Nam	1.4
Tajikistan	0.1
Fiji	0.3
Azerbaijan	1.2
Thailand	0.0
Sri Lanka	0.2
Cambodia	4.8
People's Republic of China	0.9
Tuvalu	0.4
Micronesia, Fed. States of	1.9
Marshall Islands	0.3
Myanmar	0.5
Pakistan	1.0
Solomon Islands	0.0
Bhutan	1.9
Philippines	0.5
Indonesia	0.6
Timor-Leste	1.8
Mongolia	0.1
Vanuatu	1.2
India	0.9
Bangladesh	0.8
Nepal	1.7
Kiribati	0.6
Afghanistan	2.5

b. Rural

ADB DMCs	2.1
Other Developing Countries	0.8
OECD	0.3
Republic of Korea	0.0
Palau	3.1
Uzbekistan	0.9
Maldives	2.1
Kazakhstan	0.1
Sri Lanka	1.2
Thailand	0.3
Malaysia	0.5
Kyrgyz Republic	0.3
Tajikistan	0.4
Fiji	2.5
Azerbaijan	3.3
Tuvalu	0.4
Myanmar	2.2
Philippines	1.6
Viet Nam	2.9
People's Republic of China	1.7
Bangladesh	2.4
Marshall Islands	1.1
Lao PDR	8.2
Vanuatu	2.5
Pakistan	6.6
Micronesia, Fed. States of	4.6
Indonesia	2.3
Nepal	5.9
Mongolia	3.4
Bhutan	2.9
Kiribati	1.4
Cambodia	7.6
India	4.6
Afghanistan	1.6
Solomon Islands	0.0
Papua New Guinea	0.2

% of population with access

■ 2000   ■ 2015

ADB = Asian Development Bank; DMC = developing member country; Lao PDR = Lao People's Democratic Republic;
OECD = Organisation for Economic Co-operation and Development.
Note: Figures in green refer to annualized growth rate (2000–2015). Regional averages are calculated with population as weights.
Source: World Development Indicators, World Bank.

The progress in rural sanitation provision seems to be more encouraging in the region. Coverage has been growing on average by 2% annually, faster than developing countries outside the region. Over half the rural population obtained access to sanitation facilities by 2015. Countries like the Lao PDR, Pakistan, Nepal, Cambodia, and India have invested considerably and observed substantial growth in coverage although they started from a relatively low base. However, the region as a whole (52%) still lags far behind OECD level (96%). Among those with large rural populations, India, Indonesia, and Pakistan, for example, had rural access to sanitation below 50%, which means a significant amount of rural residents still suffer from the adverse impacts of lack of sanitation. Access to sanitation will remain an infrastructure priority for many in the future.

Section 3. Infrastructure Investment in Asia

How much has Asia invested in infrastructure? It is surprisingly difficult to answer. Governments invest—nationally and locally. Many countries create state-owned enterprises (SOEs) to build and operate major utilities, road and railway networks, seaports and airport facilities. And, increasingly, the private sector is involved—as participants in public-private partnerships and as direct private investors.[11] There is no single way—or international best practice—to measure infrastructure investment. Countries typically do not publish aggregate infrastructure investment figures, and how they report infrastructure-related data varies widely.

Government budgets would seem the obvious source for infrastructure investment by the public sector, encompassing not only national and subnational governments, but also public sector corporations (or SOEs). But not all economies publish budget data on investments by subnational governments; and investments by SOEs are typically excluded. Similarly, private sector[12] investments might not be published or even available. Thus comprehensive data on infrastructure investment by the government, SOEs, and the private sector are not readily available, making cross-country comparisons all the more difficult.

In principle, national accounts data on gross fixed capital formation (GFCF) is a potential source of information to determine how much the government, SOEs and the private sector invest in physical assets in an economy. But not all components of GFCF are related to infrastructure (Box 3.1). For example, investment in machinery and equipment such as a gas turbine by a power generating company supplying electricity would represent investment in infrastructure while investment in welding machines by an automobile assembler would not. As such, lack of details on GFCF subcomponents by type of asset (such as residential and nonresidential buildings, civil engineering works, and machinery and equipment) and the industry in which the asset is used to produce goods and services (such as manufacturing or electricity generation) makes it difficult to readily distinguish investments in infrastructure assets. In short, disaggregated data on GFCF that would help identify infrastructure investments are extremely scarce. Collating data this way would require national accounts statisticians to adjust some of their practices to enable data availability.

So how can one measure infrastructure investment? Government budget documents, national accounts data with sufficient breakdown on GFCF, and an international database on infrastructure investments undertaken by the private sector (the World Bank's Private Participation in Infrastructure or PPI Projects Database[13]) are viable options. Data from each of these sources have benefits and limitations. Constructing a reliable measure is a herculean task—and says much about what policy makers and governments need to consider in dealing with this major measurement issue. Nonetheless, within the limitations of available data it is possible to get a sense of how much each country actually invests in infrastructure.

This report covers as many of 45 developing member countries (DMCs) of the Asian Development Bank (ADB) as possible. But data limitations mean some DMCs are included in some analyses but not others. Details on country coverage of different data sources are outlined below—and summarized in Appendix 3.1.

---

11 Mixed ownership in SOEs (i.e., where both the private and public sectors hold shares in a special purpose vehicle) is also common.

12 Private sector includes private corporations and households (including unincorporated household enterprises).

---

13 This database reports project-level information in energy, transport, telecommunications, and water and sewerage sectors for 139 low and middle income countries. The database includes projects with at least 20% private participation. Details are also available on type of project—whether a project is a management and lease contract, a brownfield project, a greenfield project, or a divestiture.

It is important to note that our infrastructure investment estimates (in amounts and percentage of gross domestic product or GDP) may be different from other estimates due to differences in how infrastructure is defined and in methodologies used. For example, our budget-based measure excludes spending related to public housing and disaster management—which makes our estimate for Indonesia lower than existing estimates.

Box 3.1: Gross Fixed Capital Formation by Type of Asset and Institutional Sector Using National Accounts

National accounts are a coherent, consistent and integrated set of macroeconomic accounts, balance sheets and tables based on a set of internationally agreed concepts, definitions, classifications and accounting rules. National accounts provide a comprehensive accounting framework in which economic data can be compiled and presented in a format designed for economic analysis, decision-taking and policymaking (Glossary of Statistical Terms, OECD).

The key macroeconomic aggregate in national accounts relevant to assessing infrastructure investment is the expenditure category—gross fixed capital formation (GFCF). In simple terms, GFCF is the net value of assets acquired by producers of goods and services during the accounting period. In standard national accounts, an economy's GFCF can be further decomposed by type of institution making the investment—or institutional sector, as they are known in national accounts parlance. These include nonfinancial corporations (public and private), financial corporations (public and private), general government, households, and nonprofit institutions serving households. GFCF by the general government and public corporations can be further grouped together. GFCF can also be classified by type of asset—(i) construction (residential, nonresidential, and civil engineering structures), (ii) machinery and equipment (information and communication technology or ICT equipment, transport equipment, and other machinery and equipment), and (iii) others (cultivable biological assets, software, and research and development, among others) (Box table 3.1).

While GFCF records the value of fixed asset investments, not all fixed assets are infrastructure related. For example, most dwellings are not related to infrastructure. In contrast, the nonbuilding component of construction (cells shaded dark blue) mainly includes civil engineering works and is thus mostly infrastructure-related. As to buildings other than dwellings (cells shaded light blue), only those constructed for infrastructure such as transport, energy, telecommunication, and water and sanitation may be included as infrastructure investments.

Distinguishing between infrastructure- and noninfrastructure-related fixed assets is perhaps more difficult for machinery and equipment. For example, ICT assets are used in the production of a wide range of goods and services. Only a fraction of these are likely used by producers of infrastructure services. This is similar for both machinery and equipment assets as well as transportation assets. Thus, while gas turbines purchased by power plants for supplying electricity would be machinery and equipment classified as infrastructure investment, welding machines purchased by automobile assemblers would not. Similarly, the purchase of locomotives for rolling stock in railways would be classified as an infrastructure investment, while the purchase of trucks by the automobile assemblers for delivery of cars from the plant to auto dealers would not.

The challenge lies in the data availability on the economic activity or industrial sector of the entity investing in the fixed asset (for example, whether it is a producer belonging to the manufacturing or wholesale and retail trade services sectors, or an infrastructure related sector such as transport, storage, and communication; or electricity, gas, and water supply, for example). If available, then GFCF data can be used to generate fairly comprehensive estimates of infrastructure investments (see Box 3.2).

	Box table 3.1: GFCF by Asset Type and Institutional Sector							
	Total GFCF	Public			Private		**NPISH**	**HHs**
		General Government	Nonfinancial Corporations	Financial Corporations	Nonfinancial Corporations	Financial Corporations		
Total GFCF								
Construction								
Dwellings								
Buildings other than dwellings								
Other structures (civil engineering works) (code 532 of CPC 2.1)								
Machinery and equipment								
Transport equipment								
ICT equipment								
Other machinery and equipment								
Others								

Note: GFCF = gross fixed capital formation; ICT = Information and communication technology; NPISH = Nonprofit institutions serving households; HHs = households.

Section 3.1 discusses these data and measurement issues, while Section 3.2 attempts to provide the level of infrastructure investment and analyzes some investment patterns across DMCs. Section 3.3 briefly discusses how a proxy measure for infrastructure investment is associated with economic growth.

3.1. Measuring infrastructure investment

An ideal measure of infrastructure investment could be constructed based on gross fixed capital formation (GFCF) in national accounts data. It would require disaggregated information on infrastructure investment. In particular, it would distinguish investments in fixed assets by type of institution undertaking the investment (in particular, general government, SOEs, and private corporations) and type of asset (for example, civil engineering works or machinery and equipment). It would also provide information on the industry in which the investment takes place, which would allow, for example, investments in machinery and equipment to be distinguished between infrastructure investment (say, a gas turbine for generating electricity) against a noninfrastructure investment (say, welding machines used for assembling automobiles). This is illustrated in greater detail below, using the examples of India, Pakistan, and Fiji (Box 3.2).

For most DMCs, the detailed national accounts data needed to derive this ideal measure are not readily available. Thus, three alternative measures of infrastructure investment are examined in this report. The first measure uses government budget information taken from official websites of DMCs plus World Bank PPI Project database figures to capture private investment in infrastructure. The second measure mainly includes the civil engineering component of GFCF data from national accounts

statistics,[14] which covers all types of investors. And the third measure is derived from general government GFCF or GFCF(GG) available from the International Monetary Fund (IMF) plus the PPI Project database figures. Together, these three create a database covering 33 DMCs (with at least one measure each)—though years and number of economies covered vary by measurement method.

Defining infrastructure

Measuring infrastructure here includes fixed asset investments in four sectors—transport (road, rail, air, and ports); energy; telecommunications; and water and sanitation, which for the purposes of this section also includes dams, irrigation, and flood control waterworks.[15] These assets include civil engineering works, nonresidential buildings, and the machinery and equipment necessary to provide infrastructure output. Social infrastructure, defense, and other social services are excluded. To be more precise, each sector is defined below by product codes based on the United Nations Central Product Classification 2.1 (CPC 2.1) system.

- *Transport* includes civil engineering works on highways, bridges, streets, roads, railways, tunnels, airfield runways, ports/harbors, waterways, and related harbor and waterway facilities, among others. Residential buildings are excluded, but nonresidential buildings such as transport terminals are included. Except for railway and tramway locomotives and rolling stock, other transport equipment, such as vehicles, airplanes, and ships are excluded.

---

14 Total GFCF can be decomposed into construction; machinery/ equipment: and others. Construction can be further decomposed into dwellings (residential), buildings other than dwellings (non-residential), as well as other structures (mainly civil engineering works). This last component forms the basis of our second measure.

15 Including these items in this section is due to the nature of available data. In particular, it is difficult to separate broad categories of infrastructure (such as water and sanitation) into their separate subcomponents given the relatively aggregate nature of available data on investments.

Box 3.2: Improving Infrastructure Investment Estimates Using Disaggregated Data

When gross fixed capital formation (GFCF) is broken down by asset type and industrial sector of the investor, infrastructure investment can be estimated more accurately (Box table 3.2.1). Specifically, asset classes for each infrastructure sector are identified as follows:

- Transport—Civil Engineering Works, Buildings other than Dwellings, and Information and communication technology (ICT) and rail-related machinery and equipment;
- Energy—Civil Engineering Works, Buildings other than Dwellings, and machinery and equipment not transport related;
- Water supply and irrigation—Civil Engineering Works, Buildings other than Dwellings, and Machinery and equipment not transport related;
- Telecommunications—Civil Engineering Works, Buildings other than Dwellings, and Machinery and equipment not transport related.

Adding up asset-sector-specific infrastructure investment gives the total infrastructure investment. The example of Fiji has two implications:

i.   The majority of infrastructure investment—approximately 80%—went to civil engineering works. This lends support to

using GFCF on construction excluding buildings or GFCF(CE) to approximate infrastructure investment when there is no better alternative.

ii. A nontrivial amount of infrastructure investment is not captured by GFCF(CE). This is mainly on machinery and equipment (used mainly in telecommunications, energy, and water infrastructure)—accounting for about 20% of Fiji's infrastructure investment (with about a half in ICT equipment). Nonresidential buildings are also missing from GFCF(CE), but the amount is small.

One problem with this approach is that not all road investment is classified as transport. For example, Public Works (or Public Administration) may also contain information on road investment. The practice seems to vary by country. Nevertheless, the measure described above offers a conservative, or lower bound, estimate.

One way to address this issue is to include civil engineering works of all sectors, while keeping the investment in machinery/ equipment and nonresidential buildings in energy, water, and telecommunications unchanged. This creates an upper bound (higher estimate) as some noninfrastructure components in civil engineering would also be included (mines and industrial plants,

Box table 3.2.1: Using Disaggregated GFCF Data to Calculate Infrastructure Investment—Fiji					
Fiji's GFCF in Infrastructure per Sector, 2011 ($ million)	Road*	Energy	Water	Telecom	Total
2011 Fiji Gross Domestic Product (GDP) = $3,760.28 million					
Total (% of GDP)	2.24%	1.64%	0.95%	0.74%	5.57%
General Government					
a. Construction (Central Product Classification [CPC] 2.1)					
by Standard Industrial Classification (SIC) code:					
5311 Dwellings (Residential)	NI	NI	NI	NI	
5312 Buildings other than Dwellings (Nonresidential)	0.33	0.00	1.22	0.00	1.56
5320 Other Structures (Civil Engineering Works)	81.94	0.39	6.00	0	88.33
b. Machinery, equipment & others (CPC 2.1)					
49 Transport	NI	NI	NI	NI	
452 and 472 information and communication technology (ICT)	0.06	0.00	0.39	0.00	0.44
43 Others	NI	0.00	0.39	0.06	0.44
c. Other Products	NI	NI	NI	NI	
Total Public GFCF in Infrastructure	82.33	0.39	8.00	0.06	90.78
General Government	2.19%	0.01%	0.21%	0.00%	2.41%
Private Sector + SOEs					
a. Construction (CPC 2.1)					
5311 Dwellings (Residential)	NI	NI	NI	NI	
5312 Buildings other than Dwellings (Nonresidential)	...	...	...	...	...
5320 Other Structures (Civil Engineering Works)	1.83	53.67	23.50	0.06	79.06
b. Machinery, equipment & others (CPC 2.1)					
49 Transport	NI	NI	NI	NI	
452 and 472 ICT	0.06	0.00	0.50	19.94	20.50
43 Others	NI	7.50	3.89	8.00	19.39
c. Other Products	NI	NI	NI	NI	
Total Private GFCF in Infrastructure	1.89	61.17	27.89	28.00	118.94
Private + SOEs (% of GDP)	0.05%	1.63%	0.74%	0.74%	3.16%

... = missing values; GFCF = gross fixed capital formation; NI = noninfrastructure GFCF asset class.
*Data for Fiji shows no GFCF in other transport subsectors.
Market exchange rate from World Bank's World Development Indicators is F$1.80 to $1.00.
Source: ADB estimates; Country sources.

continued on next page

Box 3.2: Improving Infrastructure Investment Estimates Using Disaggregated Data *(continued)*

mining construction, other construction for manufacturing, outdoor sport and recreation facilities, and other civil engineering works such as satellite launching sites and defense).

Comparing alternative estimates for infrastructure investment in India, Pakistan, and Fiji show interesting results (Box table 3.2.2).

First, combining information from the alternative estimates may provide a more refined measure of infrastructure investment. For

example, in Pakistan the BUDGET+PPI, a conservative estimate, and the upper bound of the GFCF Breakdown approach are very close, suggesting that the actual infrastructure investment is near 2.1%.

Second, even using detailed GFCF data, the constructed lower and upper bounds may still show a fairly large gap, especially in India. For this to narrow, statistics on road investment in all relevant sectors, such as Public Works, need to be available.

Box table 3.2.2: Comparison of Alternative Estimates of Infrastructure Investment
(% of GDP)

	Fiji, 2011	India, 2013	Pakistan, 2011
Total Infrastructure Investment			
Ideal Measure: GFCF Breakdown	[5.58, 6.46]	[4.03, 8.39]	[1.23, 2.15]
Measure 1: Budget + PPI	3.78	5.50	2.14
Measure 2: GFCF(GG) + PPI	5.96	7.78	3.29
Measure 3: GFCF(CE)	5.48	5.79	2.21

GDP = gross domestic product; GFCF = gross fixed capital formation; GFCF(CE) = gross fixed capital formation in construction excluding buildings; GFCF(GG) = general government GFCF; PPI = Private Participation in Infrastructure Database.
Source: ADB estimates; Country sources.

Additionally, general and special purpose machinery and equipment in rail transport as well as information and communication technology (ICT) machinery and equipment for all transportation subsectors are also included.[16]

- *Energy* encompasses nonresidential buildings and civil engineering works for power plants, power stations, hydroelectric dams, electricity grids, long-transmission lines, power lines, transformer stations, and gas and oil pipelines, among others. It also includes ICT and general and special purpose machinery and equipment related to the generation, transmission, and distribution of energy, but excludes transport equipment.[17]

- *Water and sanitation* includes nonresidential buildings, civil engineering works and machinery and equipment for dams, irrigation and flood control waterworks, local water and sewer

mains, local hot-water and steam pipelines, sewage, and water treatment plants. Related ICT and general and special purpose machinery and equipment are included, but transport equipment is excluded.[18]

- *Telecommunications* comprises nonresidential buildings and civil engineering works for telephone and internet systems, land- and sea-based cables, communication towers, and telecommunication transmission lines, among others. It also includes general and special purpose machinery and equipment related to transmitting information along telecommunication networks along with ICT machinery and equipment in conducting everyday business, such as computers and telephone lines.[19]

Importantly, social infrastructure—such as health, education, and other social services—is excluded from infrastructure covered here.

16 Included are related items corresponding to CPC 2.1 codes 53122, 53129, 53211, 53212, 53213, 53221, 53222, and 53232; related items falling under CPC 2.1 division 43 and groups 452, 472, and 495.

17 Energy covers more than just the power sector. For example, gas and oil pipelines are included. Specifically included are related items corresponding to CPC 2.1 codes 53122, 53129, 53241, 53242, 53251, 53252, and 53262; related items falling under CPC 2.1 division 43 and groups 452 and 472.

18 Included are related items corresponding to CPC 2.1 codes 53122, 53129, 53231, 53232, 53233, 53234, 53241, 53251, and 53253; related items falling under CPC 2.1 division 43 and groups 452 and 472.

19 Included are related items corresponding to CPC 2.1 codes 53122, 53129, 53242 and 53252; related items falling under CPC 2.1 division 43 and groups 452 and 472.

Data sources

Data availability for measuring infrastructure as defined above is a big challenge. In this report, four major data sources are used to derive proxies for infrastructure investment. We discuss available data and their respective sources below (Table 3.1).

1. **Government spending on infrastructure.** Government budgets are the primary data source for assessing infrastructure investment by central, state, and local governments. These normally come from budgeting authorities such as ministries of finance or budgetary offices. We sifted through publicly available budget documents to compile data on budgetary government infrastructure spending by sector. A key advantage of this data is that they are typically broken down by economic sector and sometimes even activities within sectors. This makes it more useful when estimating infrastructure investment by sector. But there are several limitations to keep in mind when comparing budget-based estimates across DMCs.

   - Sufficiently disaggregated data may simply not be publicly available. Aggregation criteria—by sector, investor type, asset type—vary by economy. For example, while some DMCs report data by sector, others report by ministry.[20]

   - In ministries or sectors involved with infrastructure investment, fixed asset spending may include noninfrastructure assets (such as vehicles and ICT equipment unrelated to infrastructure). Only some economies—like the Philippines and the PRC—provide more detailed data that distinguishes between infrastructure and noninfrastructure fixed asset investments.

   - In most economies included in this report, budget spending may not cover SOE infrastructure spending, especially if funded by self-raised finance. Although government transfers to finance SOE infrastructure investment may be included in the budget, the amounts transferred are typically unclear. Nevertheless, where comprehensive data are available (India, Indonesia, and the PRC), SOEs are included in the estimates,[21] Box 3.3 describes the case for Indonesia.

   - Central government budgets are typically more accessible than subnational government budgets. This could underestimate infrastructure investment, for example in Armenia, Bangladesh, Fiji, Kiribati, Malaysia, Nepal and Thailand.

   - Executed values of budget spending are used when available. In several DMCs (Armenia, Bhutan, Georgia, the Maldives, Myanmar, and Thailand), only planned or estimated budget spending is available.

2. **General government GFCF or GFCF(GG).** This is a macroeconomic aggregate compiled following national accounting standards, covering total general government investment (thus, investment by central and subnational governments) on fixed assets—including buildings, civil engineering, machinery and equipment, weapon systems, cultivated biological resources, and intellectual property (United Nations 2009). The advantage is that data are readily available from the International Monetary Fund (IMF) and World Bank for most economies (and for long time periods). GFCF(GG) has also been frequently used as

---

20 For example, some economies (Fiji; Hong Kong, China; Kiribati; Nepal; Philippines; and Singapore) report budget spending by ministry. Others (Armenia, Bhutan, PRC, Georgia, India, Maldives, Myanmar, Thailand, and Viet Nam) report budget spending by sector (or product). Bangladesh reports data both by sector and ministry, with the ministry numbers using a more disaggregated breakdown (used here). Indonesia reports budget spending by implementing entity and sector.

21 For the PRC, data are sourced from the online *Statistical Year Book* published by the National Bureau of Statistics, which presents investments by the government and by SOEs. In India, data are derived from Annual Reports of the Government of India Planning Commission and NITI Aayog, which includes both public and private investments. Indonesian central and subnational government investments are from World Bank and BAPPENAS. Private investment is from the World Bank PPI Project database, and SOE investment is from World Bank *Indonesia Economic Quarterly* and the BAPPENAS Presentation "Alternatif Pembiayaan Infrastruktur".

Table 3.1: Data Source and Coverage[a]

	Measurement	Sources	Description	Items Covered	Items Not Covered
1.	Budget Spending on Infrastructure	Country Budget Offices	Capital expenditure in transportation, communication, energy, and water made by government Infrastructure investment by state-owned enterprises (SOEs) using budget transfers	Capital expenditures by general government in chosen infrastructure sectors	Capital spending by SOEs using self-raised funds are typically not covered in budget data.
2.	Gross fixed capital formation for general government GFCF(GG)	National Accounts[b]	Public investment by general government—national and subnational governments	Government investments in fixed assets (both infrastructure and noninfrastructure)	By definition, infrastructure investment by SOEs is not covered.
3.	GFCF on Construction excluding buildings or GFCF(CE)—mainly civil engineering works	National Accounts[c]	Investments in construction other than buildings	Infrastructure investment by government, SOEs, and the private sector in structures including highways, suburban roads, railways, airfield runways, bridges, tunnels, subways, waterways, harbors, dams, sewer systems, mines, pipelines, communication cables, transmission lines, power lines, and sports fields Some noninfrastructure investment, including mines and industrial plants, outdoor sports and recreation facilities, and other civil engineering works, such as military engineering works, satellite launching sites, waste dumps and waste incinerators, and plants for treating and processing of nuclear material	Buildings and machinery and equipment in infrastructure projects are purposely excluded to avoid overestimation.
4.	Private participation in infrastructure (PPI)	World Bank PPI Project database	Investment in Transportation, ICT, energy, and water projects that are owned or managed by private companies with at least 20% of private participation in the project contract	Some private investments with information from publicly available sources (for example, commercial news databases, publications, government reports, regulatory authorities, annual reports, multilateral development agencies) We limited our sample includes only those with private participation greater than 50% Projects reaching financial closure after 1983	Private infrastructure investments without publicly available information are not covered by the PPI project database. Projects with 50% or less private participation, divestitures and management and leasing projects, and cancelled projects may be covered by the PPI database but are excluded to avoid overestimating private infrastructure investment.

a ADB staff compilation.
b Investment and Capital Stock Dataset, 1960–2015, IMF.
c International Comparison Program of ADB and the World Bank.

a proxy for public infrastructure investments (Wagenvoort, de Nicola, and Kappeler 2010; Gonzalez Alegre et al. 2008). The major problem is that it includes noninfrastructure investment that could overstate general government infrastructure investment. Also, it may not cover SOE infrastructure investment, especially when self-financed. SOE investments are generally not included in GFCF(GG), except for transfers from government to SOEs for infrastructure-related expenditure. This could understate investment (Box 3.4).

3. **GFCF on construction excluding buildings or GFCF(CE)**[22] (CPC 2.1 division 53). This is a macroaggregate from GFCF classification of types of assets following national accounting standards and mainly includes civil engineering works (see United Nation's *System of National Accounts 2008* for the types of assets included under GFCF in typical national accounts). It

22 There is separate data on construction—buildings, which are excluded from this measure. This exclusion is considered because available GFCF data covers all economic sectors, such as industries and social infrastructure sectors. Including buildings could significantly overestimate infrastructure investment by including factory buildings, office space, schools, and hospitals.

Box 3.3: The Role of State-Owned Enterprises in Infrastructure Investment in Indonesia

Chapter XIV Article 33 of the 1945 *Constitution of the Republic of Indonesia* states that "Sectors of production which are important for the country and affect the life of the people shall be controlled by the state." Thus, the government of Indonesia is bound to rely on state-owned enterprises (SOEs) to provide infrastructure services. Indeed, staff calculations based on data from World Bank (2015a) and World Bank's Private Participation in Infrastructure Database show a significant portion of infrastructure investment is financed by SOEs. Nevertheless, the share of SOE investment in Indonesia's infrastructure sectors has gradually declined, while that of the general government steadily increased from 2007–2012. The private sector contributed an annual average of 10%, or 0.3% of GDP per annum (Box figure 3.3).

Indonesia's SOEs invested heavily in the energy sector in the mid-1990s up to 2000.[a] From 1995–2000, SOE investment in energy contributed about 56% a year of total SOE investment in infrastructure. The largest SOE supplying power is PT Perusahaan Listrik Negara (PLN), the country's major power utility which provides public electricity and electricity infrastructure. However, the huge rupiah devaluation during the 1997/98 Asian financial crisis seriously hampered energy infrastructure investment.[b] Energy investment consequently declined as a percentage of GDP by 2001, while SOE investments in telecommunications began to dominate SOE infrastructure investments. The two telecommunications SOEs—PT Telkom and PT Indostat—together

averaged 56% of SOE infrastructure investment (or 0.7% of GDP) per annum from 2001 to 2006. By 2007, SOE investments in energy regained the top spot in SOE infrastructure investment, overtaking telecommunications. SOE investments in transport have been increasing as a percentage of total SOE infrastructure investment. From 6% in 2009, SOE investment in transport increased to 30% of total SOE infrastructure investment in 2012.

Box figure 3.3: Breakdown of Infrastructure Investments in Indonesia by Investor Type, 2007–2012

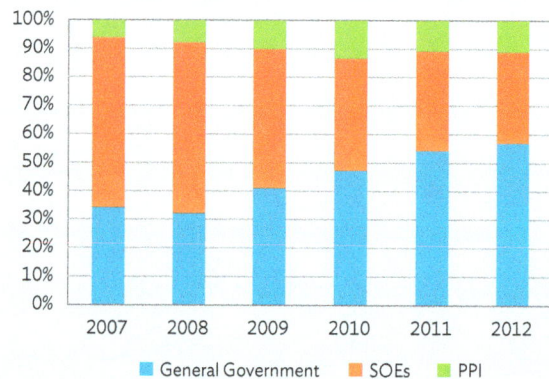

PPI = Private Participation in Infrastructure; SOE = state-owned enterprise.
Source: World Bank (2013).

---

a   Data limitations allow sectoral breakdown analysis to 2009.
b   According to PricewaterhouseCoopers (2015), the majority of PLN costs were denominated in US dollars, but its revenue base were in rupiah. Furthermore, the Independent Power Producer sector, established to supply energy to PLN, was set up as a US dollar-denominated chain. This added to the decline in energy investment (both for SOEs and the private sector).

---

has the advantage of being standardized and is recommended for reporting under the national accounting frameworks and are therefore comparable across countries. Moreover, it covers not only public investment (by national, subnational governments, and SOEs), but also private investment.[23] Its limitations are two-fold.

- As CPC 2.1 division 53 covers civil engineering structures (construction) only, investments in infrastructure-related buildings and machinery and equipment—such as turbines for power plants [CPC 2.1 division 43]—are not covered.[24]

- Some noninfrastructure investments in construction are included—mining related construction, other construction for certain manufacturing facilities, outdoor sport and recreation facilities, and other civil engineering works [CPC 2.1 subclasses 5326, 5327, and 5329].[25]

4. **Infrastructure investments with private participation.** For private sector infrastructure investment, we source data from the World Bank's Private Participation in Infrastructure (PPI) Project Database. This database covers infrastructure projects from as early as 1983. For low- to middle-income economies, it covers transportation, ICT, energy, and water projects

---

23   Private investment includes investments by private corporations and households including un-incorporated enterprises run by households.

24   National accounts include GFCF on machinery and equipment, some of which may be used in infrastructure investment—such as power stations. Including all machinery and equipment, however, may significantly overstate infrastructure investment because much machinery and equipment investment may be noninfrastructure capital.

25   Other civil engineering works include military engineering, satellite launching sites, waste dumps and waste incinerators, plants for treating and processing nuclear material, and other civil engineering works not elsewhere classified (n.e.c.). (United Nations 2015).

Box 3.4: Gross Fixed Capital Formation and Infrastructure Investment: How They Differ

The lack of complete data on infrastructure investment has made general government GFCF or GFCF(GG) a commonly used proxy (Gonzalez Alegre et al. 2008; Wagenvoort, de Nicola, and Kappeler 2010). This is reasonable for long-term investment trends, where cumulative GFCF(GG) is highly correlated with physical infrastructure stock across developing Asia (see Box 3.5). However, GFCF(GG) can be misleading. Box table 3.4.1 shows how GFCF(GG) could incorrectly measure infrastructure investment in Fiji, for example, while Box table 3.4.2 compares the structure of detailed GFCF data from India, Pakistan, and Fiji.

As expected, as GFCF(GG) includes noninfrastructure components, it could overestimate infrastructure investment. In Fiji, for example, noninfrastructure investments accounts for some 30% of GFCF(GG). In India and Pakistan, noninfrastructure shares of GFCF(GG) are 38% and 63%, respectively, even by conservative estimates. As Fiji provides the most detailed data, it also shows that

the noninfrastructure component in GFCF(GG) is evenly spread over machinery and equipment, as well as some civil engineering works and buildings.

But GFCF(GG) could also underestimate infrastructure investment, as some may be sourced from nongovernment investors, including SOEs and private enterprises. This can also be large. For example, in Fiji, private infrastructure investment including SOEs is slightly larger than GFCF(GG). This omitted infrastructure investment mainly comes from civil engineering works and machinery/equipment (mainly in energy production). The importance of private infrastructure investment is less in India and Pakistan, but still amounts to 67% and 30% of GFCF(GG), respectively. To partially address this issue, private infrastructure investment from the World Bank's Private Participation in Infrastructure (PPI) Project database can be used as a proxy for private investment.[a]

Box table 3.4.1: Decomposition of GFCF in Fiji, 2011
(% of GFCF)

	GFCF	General Government		Private + SOEs	
		Infrastructure	Noninfrastructure	Infrastructure	Noninfrastructure
Total	100	13.35	4.03	17.50	65.12
Construction	**53.1**	**13.22**	**2.15**	**11.63**	**26.10**
Dwellings	10.42	0.00	0.00	0.00	10.42
Buildings other than Dwellings	13.14	0.23	0.80	0.00	12.11
Civil Engineering Works	29.55	13.00	1.35	11.63	3.57
Machinery and equipment	**46.22**	**0.13**	**1.87**	**5.87**	**38.35**
Transport Equipment	15.46	0.00	0.64	0.00	14.82
ICT Equipment	4.85	0.07	0.15	3.02	1.61
Machinery and Equipment–others	25.93	0.07	1.09	2.85	21.92
Others	**0.67**	**0**	**0**	**0**	**0.67**

GFCF = gross fixed capital formation; ICT = information and communication technology.
Fiji national accounts do not report data on investment by SOEs.
Source: ADB estimates; Country sources.

Box table 3.4.2: Public vs. Private GFCF in Infrastructure and Noninfrastructure Sectors
(% of GFCF)

	General Government		Private	
	Infrastructure	Noninfrastructure	Infrastructure	Noninfrastructure
Fiji, 2011*	13.35	4.03	17.50	65.12
India, 2012	13.25	8.14	14.36	64.25
Pakistan, 2011	9.57	16.23	7.85	66.35

* Fiji's private GFCF includes SOEs
GFCF = gross fixed capital formation.
Fiji national accounts do not report data on investment by state-owned enterprises.
Source: ADB estimates; Country sources.

---

a   This could still underestimate nongovernmental infrastructure investment as not all private projects are included in the PPI database.

owned or managed by private companies with at least 20% private participation in the project contract. It only includes projects with publicly available information, so likely underestimates

total private infrastructure investment. Also, it only records investment at the time of commitment, not when actual disbursements are made.

Measuring infrastructure investment

Three alternative measures for infrastructure investment are computed by combining the four available data sources. Table 3.2 provides a snapshot of these measures, including their benefits and limitations.

Measure 1: Budget spending on infrastructure plus PPI or BUDGET + PPI

This is our benchmark measure. In principle, it offers a "conservative" estimate, as it likely omits SOE infrastructure investment from self-raised funds and private infrastructure investment not in the PPI Project database. The omission of SOEs is addressed for India, Indonesia, and the PRC by utilizing alternative data available. In the PRC, we replaced the BUDGET + PPI measure by official statistics that can be used to measure infrastructure investment, which covers SOEs. Similarly, the estimate for India is based on the Government of India Planning Commission and NITI Aayog Annual Reports, which cover all public and private investment in infrastructure. For Indonesia, SOE infrastructure investment provided by the World Bank is added to the BUDGET + PPI measure to arrive at the reported estimate.

Table 3.2: Alternative Measures of Infrastructure Investment[a]				
Measurement	Coverage	Sources	Benefits	Limitations
Measure 1: **[BUDGET + PPI]** **Budget spending on infrastructure + private participation in infrastructure (PPI)**	22 developing member countries (DMCs); time series available but vary by DMC.	Official government budget or statistical yearbook; World Bank PPI Project database Time series available; detailed sector breakdown	Measurement of government infrastructure spending conforms with definition;	Country and time coverage limited by availability of budget documents; Time series vary by DMC; State-owned enterprises (SOEs) only partially covered; Some economies include only central government, while others include both central and subnational data; Some economies report only planned expenditures; PPI only a partial sample of private infrastructure investment There is a possibility of double-counting if the projects with at least 50% private participation also has investment from the government or SOEs.
Measure 2: **[GFCF(GG) + PPI]** **General government gross fixed capital formation + private participation in infrastructure (PPI)**	27 DMCs; 1970–2013	National Accounts[b] and World Bank PPI Project database	Long time series and wide country coverage	No sector breakdown; Potentially significant measurement errors due to inclusion of noninfrastructure items; SOEs not covered; PPI only a partial sample of private infrastructure investment There is a possibility of double-counting if the projects with at least 50% private participation also has investment from the government or SOEs.
Measure 3: **[GFCF(CE)]** **GFCF on construction excluding buildings (mainly civil engineering works)**	27 DMCs; 2005 and 2011	National Accounts[c]	Easy to obtain as a standard national accounts item; Public-private breakdown possible; Sector breakdown possible	Limited time series; Some noninfrastructure items are included, such as mines and industrial plants, outdoor sports and recreation facilities, and other civil engineering works, such as military engineering works, satellite launching sites, waste dumps and waste incinerators, and plants for treating and processing nuclear material; Some infrastructure items are omitted, such as terminal buildings, communication buildings, rail-related machinery and equipment, and other machinery and equipment related to infrastructure. All types of investors are covered.

a ADB staff compilation.
b Investment and Capital Stock Dataset, 1960–2015, IMF.
c International Comparison Program of ADB and the World Bank.

Specifically, for public infrastructure investment, actual budget spending items associated with infrastructure (both new and for maintenance) are included. They are qualified by whether they are actual or planned, whether subnational governments or SOEs are included, and if the budget data are classified by ministry or by economic sector or product. Thus, caution is needed for comparing the measures across DMCs.[26]

Private infrastructure investment is the sum of investment in infrastructure projects included in the PPI Project database.[27] However, cancelled projects, those tagged as "divestitures" and "management and leasing" are excluded, as no new infrastructure comes from these types of projects. Also excluded are projects with 50% or less private ownership—to mitigate the double counting of public investments. Total investments are spread over 5 years to avoid "lumpy investment" because the PPI Project database records investment at the time of commitment, not when actual disbursements are made.[28] Moreover, as we do not have information to further break down these PPI numbers by private and public investment, we acknowledge that there is a possibility of double-counting if the projects with at least 50% private participation also has investment from the government or SOEs.

Measure 2: General government GFCF plus PPI or GFCF(GG) + PPI

Here, budget data (in Measure 1) is replaced by real general government GFCF or GFCF(GG) from

Investment and Capital Stock Dataset, 1960–2015, IMF. For private investment, the same PPI data is used as in Measure 1. Adding private investment as a share of GDP and the GFCF(GG) share of GDP gives the value of GFCF(GG) + PPI. The long time series for both databases allows this measure of infrastructure investment to start in 1990 for 27 DMCs.[29] As in Measure 1 above, there is also a possibility of double counting.

Measure 3: GFCF on construction excluding buildings or GFCF(CE)

Data from GFCF(CE)—or mainly civil engineering works—are collected from national statistics offices (NSOs) and compiled by the International Comparison Program (ICP). This measure consists mainly of infrastructure investment, but can either over- or underestimate actual investment (see Boxes 3.2 and 3.4). This measure is available for 27 DMCs in 2005 and 2011.

For three economies—Fiji, India, and Pakistan—NSOs provide detailed sector breakdowns, allowing for more accurate measurement (see Box 3.2).

3.2. Infrastructure investment in developing Asia

These alternative measures allow this report—for the first time—to draw a more comprehensive picture of infrastructure investment in developing Asia. Differences in data availability across DMCs make precise comparisons difficult. Yet it is possible—with clearly identified assumptions—to make some systematic analysis over those covered. Stylized facts about the DMC infrastructure investment landscape are given before summarizing lessons learned thus far from developing Asia's experience in infrastructure investment.

---

26 BUDGET+PPI would cover central government transfers to subnational governments or SOEs if the transfers are reported by infrastructure ministries or sectors. This could lead to double-counting of the transfers if data on central government, subnational governments, and SOEs are collected separately.

27 Investment figures in the PPI Project database are commitments rather than actual disbursements. This could overstate actual investment by private investors.

28 Actual disbursement of investment may vary systematically by sector, and empirical evidence is limited. According to McKinsey Global Institute (2014), projects can take 5 years or longer in development and construction stages before beginning to yield returns.

29 Hong Kong, China; the Republic of Korea; and Singapore PPI data are not included in the World Bank PPI database.

How much did Asian economies invest in infrastructure?

Of the measures described, the BUDGET + PPI measure offers a conservative estimate because it omits some SOE and private infrastructure investment. The other two measures can either over- or underestimate infrastructure investment, but it is typically unclear which. Thus, our discussion below is primarily based on the BUDGET + PPI measure.

Using this measure, total infrastructure investment of the 22 DMCs with available BUDGET + PPI data was $704 billion (in 2015 prices) in 2011. By subregion, both the infrastructure investment to GDP ratio and the share of total regional infrastructure investment varied widely (Figure 3.1). Infrastructure investment in East Asia accounted for almost 80% of the total. East Asia dominated not just

because of size, but also due to its high investment to GDP ratio—5.8% of GDP. South Asia followed at 4.8%, with Central Asia at 4.0% and the Pacific at 2.4%. Southeast Asia had the lowest infrastructure investment to GDP ratio at 2.1%, but accounted for 5.8% of total infrastructure investment due to its large economic size. These estimates may vary in different years, but their qualitative pattern generally remained the same.

The subregional estimates mask considerable variations by economy (Figure 3.2). Some results are not surprising, others more interesting. For example, large infrastructure investment in the PRC is well-known. The benchmark estimates show the PRC on average invested 6.8% of GDP in infrastructure from 2010 to 2014, modestly below estimates in existing studies (McKinsey Global Institute 2016) mainly due

Figure 3.1: Subregional BUDGET + PPI Infrastructure Investment, 2011

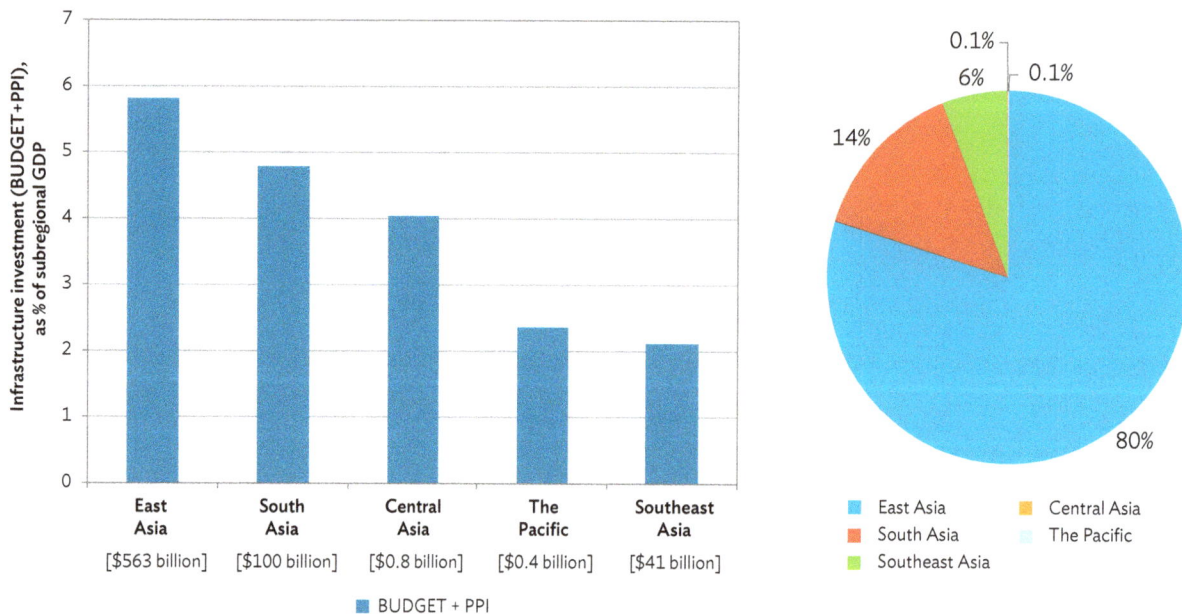

GDP = gross domestic product; PPI = private participation in infrastructure.
Figures in brackets indicate investment levels in 2015 prices.
Note: East Asia includes the People's Republic of China; the Republic of Korea; Hong Kong, China; and Mongolia. South Asia includes Bangladesh, Bhutan, India, Maldives, Nepal, Pakistan, and Sri Lanka. Southeast Asia includes Indonesia, Malaysia, Philippines, Singapore, Thailand, and Viet Nam. The Pacific includes Fiji, Kiribati, and Papua New Guinea. Central Asia includes Armenia and Georgia.
Source: Country sources; Private Participation in Infrastructure Database, World Bank; World Bank (2015a and 2015b); World Development Indicators, World Bank; ADB estimates.

Figure 3.2: BUDGET + PPI Infrastructure Investment Rate, various years
(% of GDP)

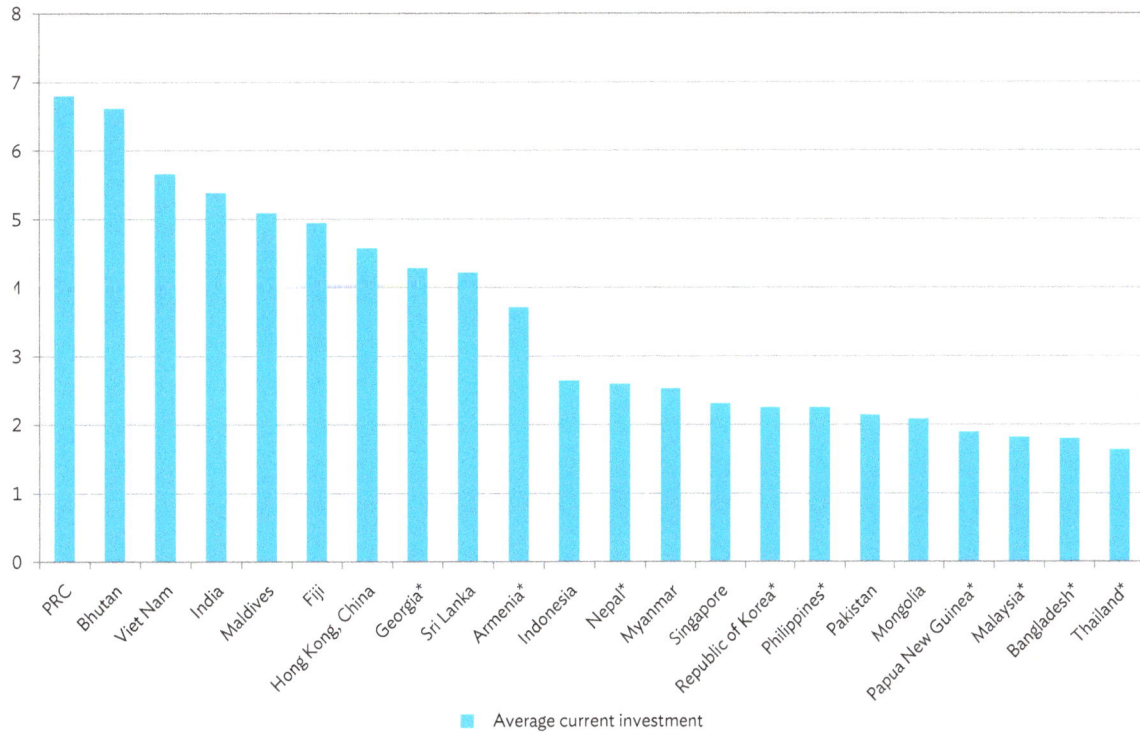

■ Average current investment

GDP = gross domestic product; PPI = private participation in infrastructure; PRC = People's Republic of China.
* Central government budget only.
Note: Actual budget investments except Armenia, Bhutan, Georgia, Maldives, Myanmar, and Thailand, which are planned or estimated budget investments.
         Periods covered are 2010–2013 average for Indonesia; 2010–2014 average for the PRC, Fiji, and Malaysia; 2010, 2011, and 2014 average for Hong Kong,
         China; 2011 for Armenia, Bangladesh and Georgia; 2011–2012 average for Nepal; 2012–2013 average for India; 2011–2013 average for Maldives; 2011,
         2012, and 2014 average for Singapore; 2011–2014 average for the Philippines, Sri Lanka, and Thailand and 2014 for Myanmar.
Source: Country sources; Private Participation in Infrastructure Database, World Bank; World Bank (2015a and 2015b); World Development Indicators, World Bank;
         ADB estimates.

to differences in sector coverage and methodology.[30] Less well known is that several DMCs—including India and Viet Nam—are investing more than 5% of GDP in infrastructure. Bhutan also shows high investment—partly because Bhutan exports power and its budget data are for planned rather than actual investment.[31] It is important to note that, for

relatively small economies, large fluctuations in infrastructure investment share can result from one-off "lumpy" infrastructure investments.[32]

By contrast, infrastructure investments in other developing Asian economies are relatively low. In particular, 12 economies in Figure 3.2 have infrastructure investment rates below 3%. Of these, two are high income economies—the Republic of Korea and Singapore; it is generally expected that high income countries need to invest less in infrastructure given the presumably high stock of quality infrastructure. Surprisingly,

30 The PRC infrastructure investment reported here is the average for 2010–2014. It excludes capital expenditures on civil engineering in sectors not classified as Transport, Energy, Water and Sanitation, and Telecommunications. Adding this excluded Civil Engineering component would raise the infrastructure investment to GDP ratio to 7.1%. The report estimate for the PRC also considers only 50% of the value of investment in Equipment and Instruments in most of the infrastructure sectors. Accounting for the total value of investment in Equipment and Instruments would raise the investment to GDP ratio to 8.3%.

31 Bhutan's Annual Financial Reports indicate that actual total investments are lower than planned investments, although data on actual infrastructure investment is unavailable. For instance, in FY 2014–2015, actual total investments were about 11.5% less than planned investments.

32 Kiribati invested over 12% of GDP in physical infrastructure each year from 2012 to 2014. The budget estimate for infrastructure investment in Timor-Leste was 44.7% of GDP in 2011, with 39% for energy, 3% transport, 2% water and sanitation, and 1% telecommunications. The high investment rates in these two DMCs are likely due to lumpy investment from a small number of projects, so they are not reported in Figure 3.2.

Hong Kong, China continues to invest heavily, but this is mainly due to the (likely one-off) mega-transport projects linking the territory to the PRC.[33]

Who tends to fund what infrastructure?

A breakdown by public and private sectors using BUDGET + PPI data shows wide variation across DMCs.[34] Countries such as the PRC, Bhutan, and Mongolia rely heavily on the public sector to finance infrastructure. In the PRC infrastructure investment was used heavily both to support economic development and as fiscal stimulus following the 2008/09 global financial crisis. And Bhutan's infrastructure investment in hydropower is primarily to boost electricity exports to India. At the other extreme, the Maldives relies heavily on private investment to finance infrastructure. Also, public spending as share of GDP declined in Indonesia, the Philippines, and Thailand since the 1997/98 Asian financial crisis, never recovering to precrisis levels. Their infrastructure spending maintains relatively low shares of GDP.[35]

Public and private investment in infrastructure also varies by sector. The feasibility to recover infrastructure investment costs through user charges may differ across sectors due to their different nature as public goods. For example, telecommunications and power consumption are primarily used by specific clients, making cost recovery through user charges feasible. In contrast, the significant social benefits of transport infrastructure—such as poverty reduction and agglomeration effects—may not directly benefit

transport users and thus are difficult to link to the private returns of investors. This is similar to water and sanitation projects.

Figure 3.3 shows the variation of public and private financing of infrastructure across subsectors (Figure 3.3). India and the PRC are excluded in the chart as they would dominate other economies in their income groups.[36] Telecommunications and energy—power plus oil and gas pipelines—both attract private investors. This is particularly evident in telecommunications, where almost all investment is from private investors. In energy, private participation is also significant although public investment still accounts for the majority. Key factors that support private investment in telecommunication and energy sectors include their normally favorable returns and predictable revenue streams. In addition, regulation and competition policy are also significant factors that influence private infrastructure financing. Large private investments in energy typically follow government procurement policies or energy sector privatization. For example, as of 2015, 29% of Viet Nam's power generation was private (ADB 2015a).

Water and sanitation and transport infrastructure are rarely financed privately. Except for the PRC, where water and sanitation infrastructure accounts for nearly 10% of private infrastructure investment, most DMCs rely on government investment for water infrastructure. This is generally true for transport infrastructure as well, with the notable exceptions of developing Asia's two largest economies—the PRC and India—where transport infrastructure accounts for over 30% of private infrastructure investment, primarily in roads, railways, airports, and seaports.

There is some indication that the degree of private participation is higher in more developed economies. This is particularly true in

---

33 The construction for the Hong Kong, China portion of the Guangzhou–Shenzhen–Hong Kong Express Rail Link alone accounts for approximately one quarter of the territory's total infrastructure investment.

34 Public infrastructure investment here is defined as infrastructure investment undertaken by the general government (i.e., consolidated national and subnational government) and SOEs. Due to data restrictions, in a number of DMCs only the component of SOE investment that is financed by transfers from the government can be covered, except in India, Indonesia, and the PRC, where data cover all SOEs investment in infrastructure.

35 Relative to the 1990–1997 precrisis period, public investment postcrisis 1998–2005 declined by 0.7% of GDP in Indonesia, 1.2% of GDP in the Philippines, and 2.2% of GDP in Thailand (Investment and Capital Stock Dataset, 1960–2015, IMF). Malaysia managed to raise public investment by 1.4% of GDP over the same period.

36 Adding India back to low-lower middle income group would not change the pattern much, although adding the PRC back to upper middle income group would significantly increase the share of public investment across all infrastructure sectors.

Figure 3.3: Public and Private Infrastructure Investment, by income group, 2011

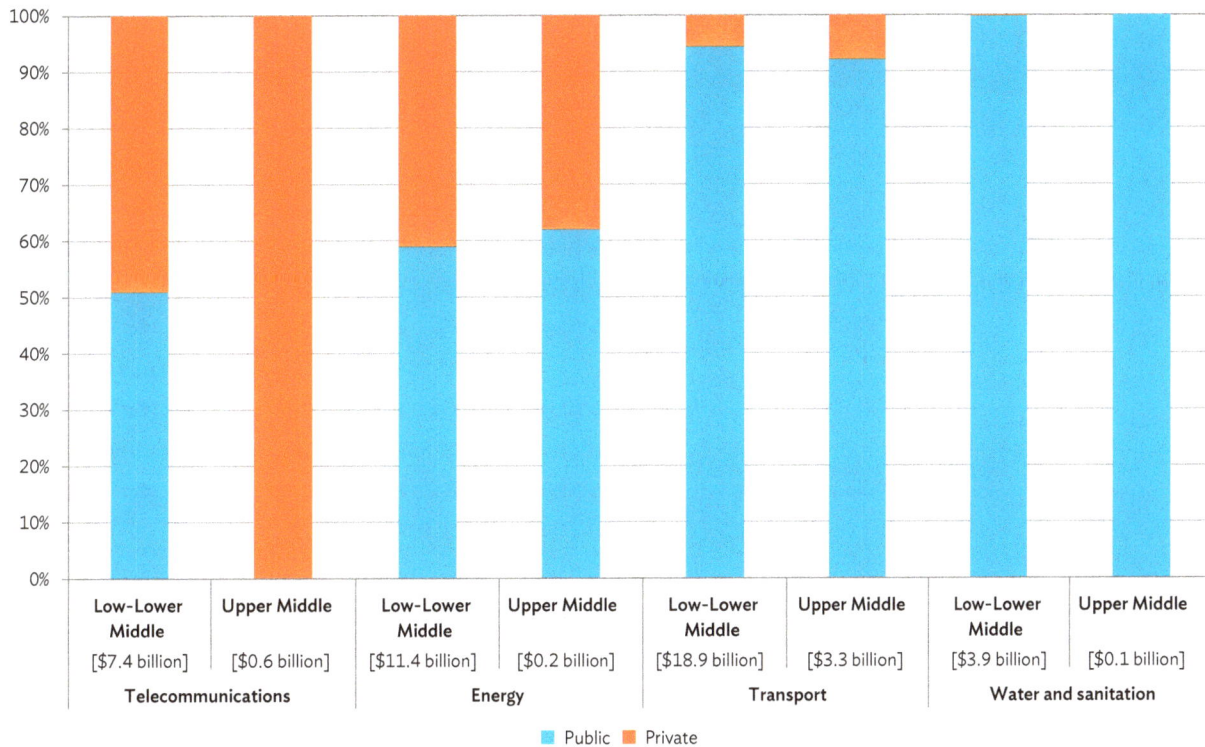

Low-Lower Middle [$7.4 billion]	Upper Middle [$0.6 billion]	
Telecommunications		
Low-Lower Middle [$11.4 billion]	Upper Middle [$0.2 billion]	
Energy		
Low-Lower Middle [$18.9 billion]	Upper Middle [$3.3 billion]	
Transport		
Low-Lower Middle [$3.9 billion]	Upper Middle [$0.1 billion]	
Water and sanitation		

■ Public ■ Private

Figures in brackets indicate investment levels in billion (in 2015 prices).

Note: Low to lower middle income countries include Armenia, Bhutan, Cambodia, Indonesia, Kiribati, Mongolia, Nepal, Pakistan, Philippines, Sri Lanka, and Viet Nam. Upper middle income countries include Fiji, Georgia, Malaysia, and Maldives. Government budget is for central government only in Armenia, Georgia, Nepal and Philippines.

Source: Country sources; Private Participation in Infrastructure Database, World Bank; World Bank (2015a and 2015b); World Development Indicators, World Bank; ADB estimates.

telecommunications and transport. One possible reason is that capital markets and the institutional environment are more stable and accommodative in economies at higher development levels.

For several DMCs, budgets show the contribution of domestic and foreign sources to public funds. Foreign resources include official development finance (ODF)[37] channeled through multilateral development banks (MDBs) and bilateral partners, loans from other foreign financial institutions or through the flotation of government securities in the international market. For example, MDBs, national development banks and development agencies accounted for around 90% of the foreign loans in

the Maldives' 2015 budget, while bilateral lending accounted for the rest.[38] Under the assumption that most public sector foreign financing is provided through ODF, we can infer that the contribution of ODF to DMCs is typically small in large economies and large in small DMCs (Figure 3.4).

How do other measures compare?

How do the BUDGET + PPI estimates compare with other measures? The BUDGET + PPI measure is generally on the low side, as expected, based on data for 2011.

The differences can be large between the various measures (Figure 3.5). In particular, the divergence between BUDGET + PPI and other measures exceeds 5% of GDP for the PRC, Mongolia, and Bhutan. These

---

37 ODF consists of official development assistance (ODA) and other official flows (OOF). ODA is concessional finance (or has a grant element of at least 25% of the total), whereas other official flows are official transactions not meeting ODA criteria and are nonconcessional. ODF can be channeled bilaterally or through multilateral institutions, including MDBs (Organisation for Economic Co-operation and Development 2015).

38 Donors to Maldives in 2015 include Saudi Arabia, Kuwait Fund, Abu Dhabi Fund, OPEC Fund, ADB, IDB, IFAD, Exim Bank of China, Exim Bank of India, and French Development Agency.

Figure 3.4: Sources of Budget Financing for Infrastructure: Domestic vs. Foreign, various years*

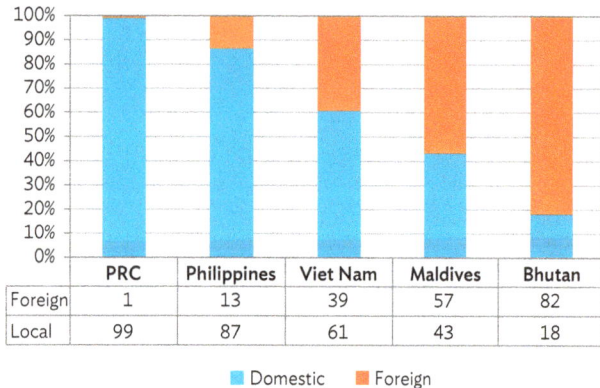

	PRC	Philippines	Viet Nam	Maldives	Bhutan
Foreign	1	13	39	57	82
Local	99	87	61	43	18

■ Domestic ■ Foreign

PRC = People's Republic of China.
Note: Time coverage is as follows: The average of 2010–2014 for the PRC and the Philippines, the average of 2010–2012 for Bhutan, the average of 2011–2013 for Maldives and 2012 for Viet Nam.
Source: Country sources; World Development Indicators, World Bank; ADB estimates.

differences are partly from the different scope of the three alternatives as discussed earlier. For example, the wide gap between the BUDGET + PPI measure and the other two measures of the PRC can be largely explained by their differences in sector coverage.[39]

Moreover, it is possible that the lumpy nature of infrastructure investments could accentuate differences in the three measures if a particularly large investment is made in one year and included/ excluded in one of the other measures. This is more likely in small economies. Another possible source of the divergence between the measures is the quality variation of different statistics. Hence, improving the quality of statistics on infrastructure investments should be a priority for national and international agencies.

At the same time, correlations between the three measures (as share of GDP) are positive. The rank correlation between BUDGET + PPI and GFCF(CE) is 0.57; the rank correlation between BUDGET + PPI

and GFCF(GG) + PPI is 0.63 (the rank correlation between BUDGET and GFCF(GG) is 0.63); while the rank correlation between GFCF(GG) + PPI and GFCF(CE) is 0.45.[40]

There is also a fair degree of consistency between the physical measures of infrastructure stock described in Section 2 and GFCF(GG) + PPI— for which a long time-series is available (Box 3.5).

Comparing the three alternative measures—and considering the global distribution of the GFCF(CE) measure (Box 3.6)—suggests the following groups of economies in developing Asia by the extent of their infrastructure investment:

i.   **The PRC is in a league of its own** (if nothing else because of its sheer size). The PRC invests significantly more than other DMCs in all three measures (all above 5% of GDP). The annual average of 2010–2014 infrastructure investment was almost $700 billion (in 2015 prices), or over three times the total of the other 19 DMCs with budget data available.

ii.   **Bhutan and Viet Nam also invest substantially in infrastructure**, with government budget based infrastructure investment rates above 5% and GFCF(CE) and GFCF(GG) + PPI investment placing them among the top 10 and top 30th percentiles of their respective global distributions.

iii.   **Economies with high to medium infrastructure investment to GDP ratios** (with at least two measures above 5%): India and Mongolia.

iv.   **Economies with medium to low infrastructure investment to GDP ratios**

---

39   Expanding the coverage of Budget + PPI (four major infrastructure sectors) to include more broadly defined infrastructure, such as management of public facilities, water conservancy, and storage, would raise the infrastructure-GDP ratio from around 6% to around 14% in 2011.

40   For GFCF(GG), real general government GFCF as share of GDP from the Investment and Capital Stock Dataset, 1960–2015, IMF was used.

Figure 3.5: Alternative Measures of Infrastructure Investment, Selected Economies, 2011
(% of GDP)

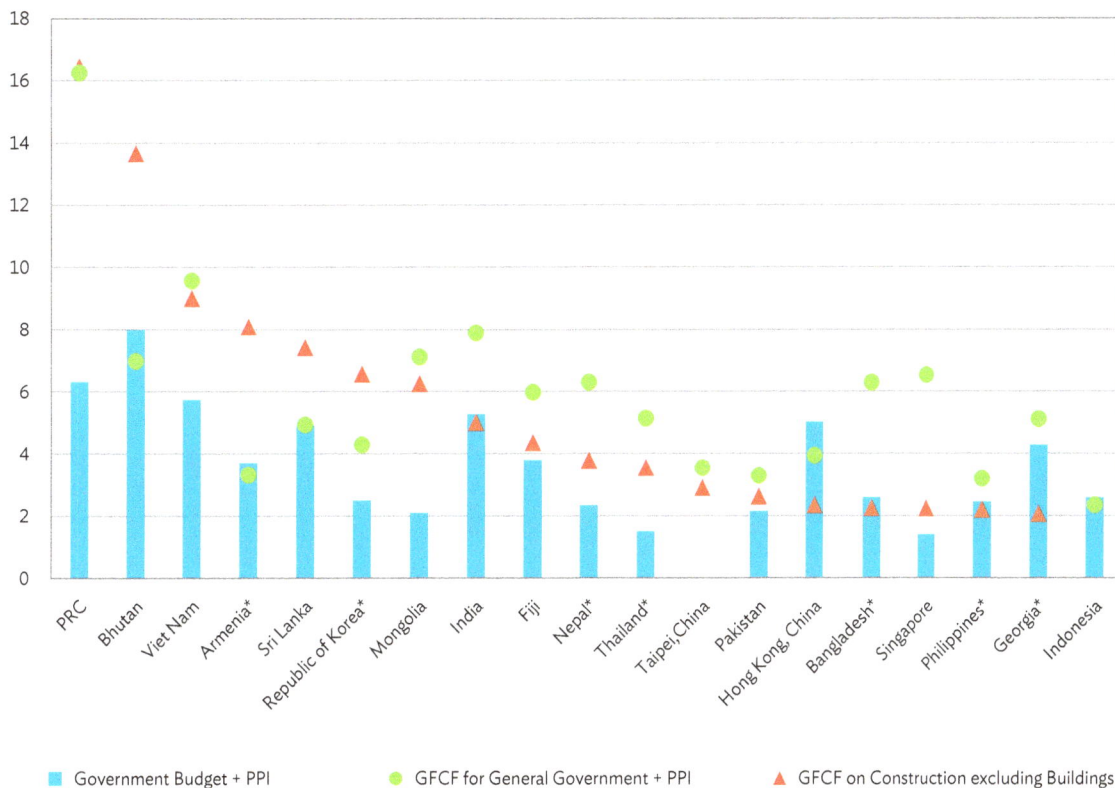

■ Government Budget + PPI   ● GFCF for General Government + PPI   ▲ GFCF on Construction excluding Buildings

GDP = gross domestic product; GFCF = gross fixed capital formation; PPI = private participation in infrastructure; PRC = People's Republic of China.
*Central government budget only.
Note: Countries are arranged by GFCF on Construction excluding Buildings or GFCF(CE). The Republic of Korea government budget + PPI figure includes both capital and operational expenditures and excludes PPI. Indonesia's estimates of GFCF(CE) are not shown because they were exceptionally high in 2011 and 2005, exceeding 10% of GDP. India's government budget + PPI data is for 2012.
Source: Country sources; International Comparison Program of ADB and the World Bank; Investment and Capital Stock Dataset, 1960–2015, IMF; Private Participation in Infrastructure Database, World Bank; World Bank (2015a and 2015b); World Development Indicators, World Bank; ADB estimates.

(with at least two infrastructure investment-GDP ratios below 5%): Armenia; Bangladesh; Fiji; Georgia; Indonesia;[41] Nepal; Pakistan; Philippines; the Republic of Korea; Taipei,China; and Thailand. Several economies in this group do not report subnational government investments. Including these could raise them into the high investment group.

___

41 Infrastructure investment based on GFCF(CE) suggest unusually high investment rates for Indonesia in 2011 and 2005, exceeding 10% of GDP, while government budget information suggests the country has been a relatively low investor in infrastructure in recent years. Disaggregated data is required to better explain this. However, it is possible that civil engineering investment related to mining and natural resource processing may be behind the divergence between the GFCF(CE) and budget-based measures.

3.3. Infrastructure investment and growth revisited

The considerable variations in infrastructure investment across DMCs are understandable given differences in economic characteristics—such as stage of development, geography, population density, and urban concentration, among others. For example, there is a tendency for higher income economies to spend less on public capital as a share of GDP than lower income economies—in part driven by the possibility that building new infrastructure often consumes considerably more resources than

Box 3.5: How Well Do Infrastructure Investment Measures Track Physical Infrastructure Stock

Measuring infrastructure investment is complicated by the limited availability of high-quality data. Thus, analyses of infrastructure investment often use imperfect measures. It would be reassuring if these measures effectively track infrastructure stock—as captured by physical measures such as the length of a road network or power generation capacity.

Among the various measures of infrastructure investment, general government gross fixed capital formation or GFCF(GG) is often used to analyze public infrastructure investment due to its relatively wide availability across countries and over time. A critical question is what GFCF(GG) can tell us about stocks of physical infrastructure. One of the simplest ways to check is to evaluate the extent to which the two measures are correlated. A simple regression is used here to describe the relationship between GFCF(GG) and the physical infrastructure measure (International Monetary Fund 2014).

Based on 2000–2011 annual flows of real GFCF(GG) per capita, cumulative GFCFs are constructed (no depreciation or initial stocks assumed) as proxies for public capital stocks for 18 of the Asian Development Bank's (ADB) developing member countries. A single index (the first principal component) is constructed to summarize eight types of per unit infrastructure stock measures averaged during the period. Then, the index of aggregate infrastructure stock is regressed on the log of accumulated GFCF per capita.

The regression result in Box figure 3.5.1 shows a statistically significant high correlation between the per unit physical infrastructure measure and accumulated per capita general government GFCF. The estimated results show that a 1% increase in per capita accumulated general government GFCF corresponds to an increase in physical infrastructure by 0.78%. This finding is quite consistent with International Monetary Fund results covering its member countries from 2005 to 2011.

Box figure 3.5.1: Relationship Between Infrastructure and Accumulated Real GFCF(GG) per capita
(average, 2000–2011)

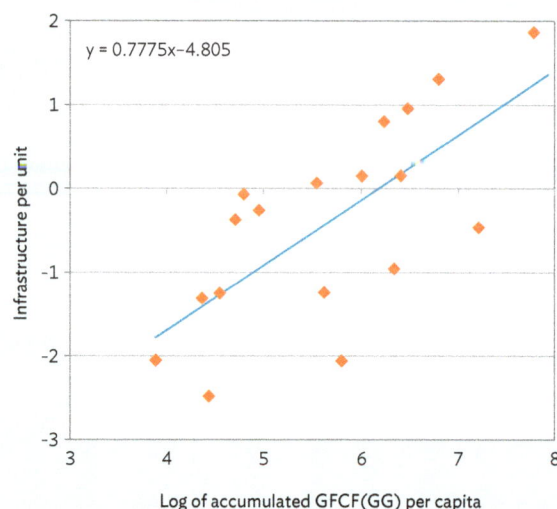

$y = 0.7775x - 4.805$

GFCF = Gross Fixed Capital Formation; GFCF(GG) = general government GFCF.

Note: The infrastructure measure is the first principal component of road, air passenger, electricity, telephone, mobile, broadband, water, and sanitation. Each dot represents an ADB developing member country—Armenia, Azerbaijan, Bangladesh, Bhutan, Cambodia, People's Republic of China, Fiji, Georgia, India, Kazakhstan, Kyrgyz Republic, Lao People's Democratic Republic, Malaysia, Mongolia, Nepal, Pakistan, Philippines, Sri Lanka, and Uzbekistan. Infrastructure stocks are measured based on the following indicators: road = kilometers (km) per 1,000 square km land area; air passenger = number of passengers per 100 population; electricity = kilowatts of installed electricity generation capacity per capita; telephone = number of subscriptions per 100 population; mobile = number of subscriptions per 100 population; broadband = number of subscriptions per 100 population; water = % of population with access; sanitation = % of population with access.

Source: ADB estimates.

maintaining or even upgrading existing infrastructure (Figure 3.6); selected outliers are identified.[42] This would partly explain why public investment as captured by GFCF(GG) of a high income economy like Singapore is considerably below a low middle income country like Viet Nam.

From a policy perspective, the important question is whether infrastructure investments are optimal or not. This is exceedingly difficult to answer with any precision, especially using macro-level aggregate data, regardless of whether based on physical indicators or investments (Straub 2008). One reason is that infrastructure has a spatial nature—that it is located in a particular place (region or city, among others). This spatial nature means a given amount of infrastructure investment may be "optimal or grossly inadequate" depending on how the investment is distributed within the economy and relative to the distribution of other production inputs.

Nevertheless, the aggregate data used here show some interesting and suggestive patterns—for example, when comparing the average share of

---

42 It is possible that excluding private sector investments might account for the negative relationship between per capita income and infrastructure investment. This could happen, for example, if higher income economies have a greater private sector component in infrastructure investment. Though correct, this would need to be balanced by the possibility that a larger fraction of GFCF(GG) is for noninfrastructure related expenditures in higher income economies.

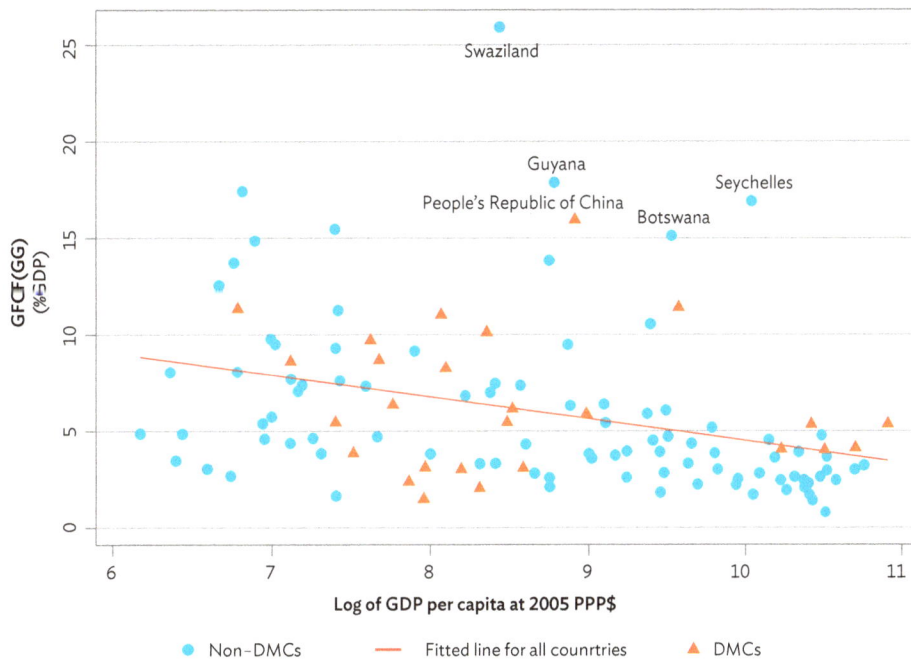

Figure 3.6: Gross Domestic Product per Capita and Public Investment, 2011

DMC = developing member country; GDP = gross domestic product; PPP = purchasing power parity; PRC = People's Republic of China.
Note: Countries with population less than one million and oil exporters are excluded for the samples.
Source: Investment and Capital Stock Dataset, 1960-2015, IMF.

public investment in GDP (an admittedly imperfect measure of infrastructure investment) and growth of real GDP per capita over 1960–1989 and 1990–2013 (Figure 3.7).[43] Breaking down data into these two time periods allows a look at today's higher income DMCs during an earlier phase of development. It also shows us how infrastructure investment growth changed across two time-periods, where many economies had generally more liberal economic policies during the later period.

The results suggest that those economies that have grown faster have also tended to have larger infrastructure investments relative to GDP. Of course, one cannot ascribe causation. In fact, it is likely the positive relationship reflects both the effect of greater infrastructure on economic growth and the higher economic growth that allows for greater infrastructure investment.

There are several other interesting patterns worth highlighting. First, as is widely known, the PRC has been quite an outlier in its public investment strategy, even with its high growth. However, it has become less so more recently as seen when comparing its data points across the 1960–1989 and 1990–2013 periods relative to the respective regression lines.

Second, high rates of economic growth over long periods (say 4.5%–5.0% annual growth in GDP per capita for 15 years or longer) very rarely go alongside relatively low infrastructure investment rates. This is consistent with the idea that developing economies with limited infrastructure investment are unlikely to see sustained high rates of economic growth. The notable exception to this is the Republic of Korea in the 1960s–1980s (see Figure 3.7).

Third, public investment rates in East Asia's high performing economies of the 1960s–1980s declined as these economies matured and reached upper middle and high income status—the idea that infrastructure investment is typically high during an economy's high-growth phase—as seen for

<hr/>

43 We omitted information on private infrastructure investments from the PPI Project database for this analysis. Given the very minor role played by private sector investment in infrastructure prior to 2000, the exclusion of information on private sector investment in the analysis carried out here is unlikely to change the analysis significantly.

Box 3.6: Global Distributions of Gross Fixed Capital Formation on Construction Excluding Buildings or GFCF(CE)

Global data on GFCF(CE) from the International Comparisons Program provide a useful basis for understanding the amount of infrastructure investment in Asian Development Bank (ADB) developing member countries (DMCs), especially from a global perspective. As noted earlier, a key feature of GFCF(CE) data is that it involves investments in civil engineering works—a major component of infrastructure investment—by all institutions—government (national and subnational), state-owned enterprises, and the private sector. However, GFCF(CE) leaves out machinery and equipment essential for generating infrastructure services.

Box table 3.6.1 shows that, in comparison with other regions, Asia's DMCs had the highest investment rates in GFCF(CE) globally in 2011. There is, however, considerable variation in infrastructure investment rates at the country/territory level as seen from the mean and median values of GFCF(CE) investment rates for various economic groupings.

There is considerable persistence in GFCF(CE) investment rates over time. The correlation coefficient between GFCF(CE) investment rates over 2005 and 2011 is 0.70 for the sample of 128 economies.

The 25 DMCs covered can be categorized in terms of whether their GFCF(CE) investment rates were in the top, middle, or lower third of global distributions in 2011 (greater than 4.9%; from 2.4%–4.9%; and less than 2.4%, respectively) and 2005 (greater than 4.3%; from 2.2%–4.3%; and less than 2.2% respectively) (Box table 3.6.2).

This categorization is fairly consistent with what the budget and Private Participation in Infrastructure (PPI) Project database measures say about infrastructure investment. There are some surprises, however. For example, Indonesia, for which GFCF(CE) investment rates were relatively high in 2011 (and 2005), government budget information suggests the country has been a relatively low investor in infrastructure in recent years. Disaggregated data is required to better explain this. However, it is possible that civil engineering investment related to mining and natural resource processing may be behind the divergence between the GFCF(CE) and Budget + PPI data show.

Box table 3.6.1: Investment Rates in GFCF(CE)
(% of GDP)

	Number of economies	2005 Mean	2005 Median	2011 Mean	2011 Median
ADB DMCs	25	9.6	4.2	11.5	4.3
DMCs excl. People's Republic of China	24	6.0	4.0	6.0	4.3
Central Asia	5	3.3	3.0	5.4	6.0
Central Asia including Pakistan	6	3.4	3.2	4.2	4.3
East Asia	5	11.4	4.5	14.2	6.2
South Asia	5	7.4	5.7	7.4	5.7
South Asia including Pakistan	6	6.9	4.9	4.7	4.4
Southeast Asia	8	5.9	3.3	8.3	3.9
The Pacific	1	5.7	5.7	4.3	4.3
Developed Regional Member Countries	3	5.4	3.1	4.7	4.3
Sub-Saharan Africa	41	3.3	3.3	4.3	3.3
Middle East and North Africa	14	2.6	2.5	3.8	3.3
Latin America and Caribbean	10	2.4	3.3	4.1	3.5
North America	2	2.0	3.2	2.8	4.2
Europe and Central Asia	33	1.9	2.6	2.4	2.4

ADB = Asian Development Bank; DMCs = developing member countries; GDP = gross domestic product; GFCF(CE) = gross fixed capital formation in construction excluding buildings.
Note: GDP at current US dollars is used as weights for aggregation; Developed Regional Member Countries include Japan, Austrailia, and New Zealand.
Source: The International Comparison Program of ADB and the World Bank.

Box table 3.6.2: GFCF(CE), 2011 and 2005
(% of GDP)

2005 GFCF(CE) / 2011 GFCF(CE)	High >4.9%	Mid =2.4%–4.9%	Low <2.4%
High >4.3%	India Lao People's Democratic Republic Republic of Korea Sri Lanka Viet Nam Bhutan Indonesia People's Republic of China	Azerbaijan Taipei,China Fiji	Georgia
Mid =2.2%–4.3%	Tajikistan Mongolia Kazakhstan	Pakistan Thailand Nepal Malaysia	
Low <2.2%	Armenia		Cambodia Philippines Singapore Bangladesh Hong Kong, China

GFCF(CE) = gross fixed capital formation in construction excluding buildings.
Source: The International Comparison Program of ADB and the World Bank.

Figure 3.7: Economic Growth and General Government Gross Fixed Capital Formation or GFCF(GG)

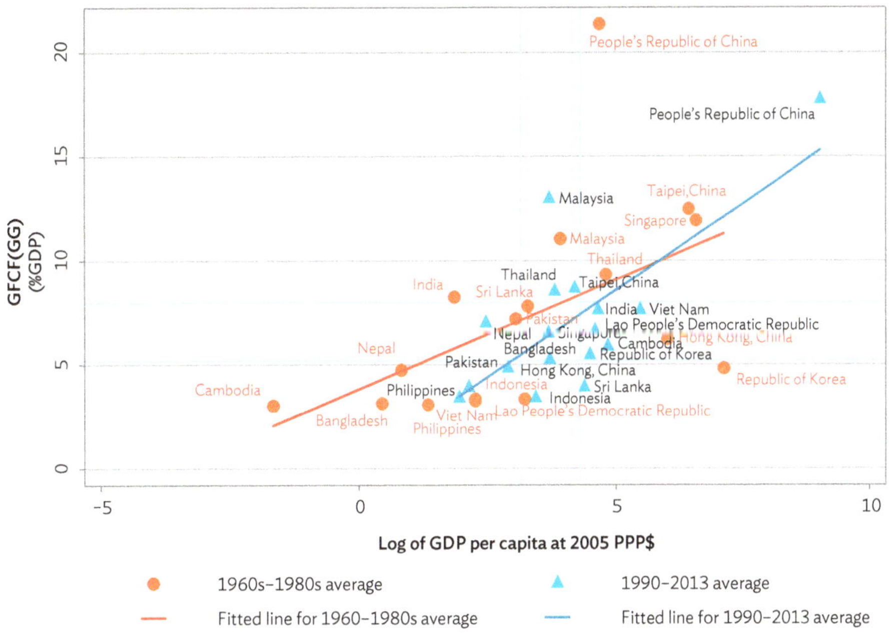

GDP = gross domestic product.

Note: The reference lines represent the lowest and highest terciles of public investment rates and GDP
per capita growth rates during 1960–2013.

Source: Investment and Capital Stock Dataset, 1960–2015, IMF.

Hong Kong, China; Singapore; and Taipei,China. Again, the Republic of Korea does not fit the mold— while its economic growth slowed during the second period, its investment rate remained relatively moderate (and, in fact, increased slightly from just below 5% to slightly above 5%).

Fourth, relatively large infrastructure investments do not guarantee high growth. Prior to the 1990s, India's average public investment was around 8.1% while GDP per capita grew only around 2.4% annually. It is possible that growth was low due to several exogenous shocks during the earlier period (involving both drought and conflict). However, it is also possible that public investment after 1990 was more effective in raising growth once the economy had significantly deregulated. In other words, infrastructure alone is not sufficient for growth; factors such as a conducive business climate are also important.

Finally, the Republic of Korea is an economy that appears to have generated high economic growth without very high rates of infrastructure

investment.[44] Yet it rapidly increased its infrastructure stock—as seen from evidence examined in Section 2. In particular, while public investments were not extraordinarily high, they were remarkably stable over time. Part of the Republic of Korea's success in achieving high growth without very high levels of infrastructure investment was its focused approach to development during its post-war reconstruction and period of export-oriented economic policy (Box 3.7).

Infrastructure investment may be difficult to measure, both conceptually and with current data limitations. The approach has varied significantly across economies, as has the likely contributions to investment growth. Given the wide range of conditions across and within developing Asian

---

44   It is possible that the omission of SOE investments in GFCF(GG) is serious in the case of the Republic of Korea. This data is difficult to gather. However, in transport—where data are available from 1980 to 2011—data suggest a large majority of investment (typically between 80%–90%) came from central and local governments (Shon 2016). SOE investments ranged from 6.8% (1985) to 15% (1995). Also, private sector investment was around 5% or less most years (though in some it accounted for a fair amount; in 2005 for example, private sector investment was as high as 15.3%).

economies, this is not surprising. There are many possible definitions and potential measures of infrastructure assets and services, with differing emphases on the relevant temporal and spatial aspects, investor/ownership structures, externalities, and subsidy elements. But considering the importance of infrastructure investment to economic and social development—and its importance in government planning and budgeting—efforts must continue and improvements must be made.

Box 3.7: Infrastructure Investment in the Republic of Korea

By the end of the Korean War in 1953, there was little infrastructure left on the peninsula. Electricity that had mostly been generated above the 38th parallel was no longer available. Only 2.4% of roads in the Republic of Korea remained paved. Limited financing prevented large-scale power plants from being built or roads to be constructed or rehabilitated.

It was the 1962–1966 First Five-Year Plan that prioritized infrastructure investment in support of the government's planned economic development. With the top priority to create an export-oriented economy, many new power plants were built in the 1960s and 1970s to supply electricity for manufacturing. Several new expressways and expanded ports provided good, low-cost logistics. Road rehabilitation—both national and local—took a back seat. New, modern infrastructure was the priority, along with the creation of new industrial complexes.

This targeted, continuous rapid economic development in the 1970s and 1980s brought more infrastructure investment. But as a percent of gross domestic product (GDP), it remained relatively low—transport and electricity were 1.38% and 2.67% of GDP respectively in 1980 (Box table 3.7).

Power plant investment continued into the 1980s and beyond to meet rising demand. And continued rapid economic growth led to an explosion in vehicle ownership from the mid-1980s, causing serious congestion across all types of roads. The urban congestion led to considerable new metrorail construction since the 1980s in Seoul and other cities. Extensive road transport investments began in earnest from the 1990s into the mid-2000s. New expressways, expanding national roads, and rehabilitating other types of roads became priorities.

In the late 1990s a new high-speed railway was built to ease congestion on the Seoul-Busan corridor. And the significant increase in international freight and passenger demand led to continuous seaport and airport investment.

Yet, while infrastructure investment since 1980 has continuously increased, its ratio to GDP has remained relatively steady. While a high 2% in the 1980s, it decreased in the 1990s and has averaged around 1.0% to 1.5% since. For transport it grew from 1.38% in 1980 to 1.75% in 1990, 2.30% in 1995 and 3.51% in 2000, before decreasing to 2.74% in 2005 and 2.42% in 2010. The ratio of telecommunication was also reduced from 1.08% in 1990 to less than 1% in the 2000s.

Box table 3.7: Infrastructure Investment in the Republic of Korea
(W billion)

	1980	1985	1990	1995	2000	2005	2010
Transport	538	1,293	3,350	9,426	21,176	23,714	28,370
(GDP ratio)	1.38%	1.51%	1.75%	2.30%	3.51%	2.74%	2.42%
Electricity	1,044	1,745	1,677	5,993	7,107	7,333	13,515
(GDP ratio)	2.67%	2.04%	0.88%	1.46%	1.18%	0.85%	1.15%
Telecommunication	N.A.	N.A.	2,060	4,291	5,069	6,011	6,018
(GDP ratio)			1.08%	1.05%	0.84%	0.69%	0.51%
GDP (W trillion)	39.1	85.7	191.4	409.7	603.2	865.2	1,173.3

GDP = gross domestic product; W = Korean won.
Source: Shon (2016).

Section 4. Estimating Infrastructure Needs for 2016–2030

Estimating future infrastructure investment needs—even if the result is a generic "birds-eye view"—can aid policy makers determine where future infrastructure development and priorities should lie. Planning, design, finance, and construction for any large-scale project can be daunting. For infrastructure projects—where investments stretch over lengthy periods—it can be even more difficult. Financing requirements must be balanced between public budget allocations and other funding arrangements. At the national level, coordinating infrastructure investments with economic development policies and spatial planning are all part of the equation.

This section presents our estimates (or projections) of infrastructure investment needs for all of ADB's 45 developing member countries (DMCs) for 2016–2030. The estimates are generated in two major steps. First, we apply a "top-down" methodology used to estimate infrastructure needs (as in Fay and Yepes 2003, Bhattacharyay 2010, and Ruiz-Nunez and Wei 2015) to obtain a set of baseline estimates. These represent updates to the estimates of the region's infrastructure needs provided in the study, *Infrastructure for a Seamless Asia* (ADB and ADBI 2009).

Second, we adjust our baseline estimates of infrastructure investment needs so that they factor in the costs of climate mitigation and adaptation. The baseline estimates are closely tied to the average historical relationship between the infrastructure an economy has built and key economic and demographic factors that have influenced demand and/or supply of infrastructure services. This approach could lead to pronounced biases in estimates of infrastructure needs if the historical relationship fails to hold into the future. One new factor that is likely to influence the demand and supply of infrastructure services is climate change. Therefore, we factor in its impact on infrastructure investment to construct climate change-adjusted estimates. This is done by considering the implications of climate change adaptation—ensuring infrastructure is resilient to projected climate change effects—through "climate proofing" of existing or new infrastructure. The projections also consider climate change mitigation—by investments in infrastructure and technologies that reduce or prevent greenhouse gas emissions. Given the complexity of estimating climate change related infrastructure needs, we mainly rely on existing estimates from recent studies to derive our climate change-adjusted estimates.

It is important to note that the infrastructure estimates here are not meant as forecasts for optimal infrastructure investments in the future for the region or individual countries. They are instead simply a guide on how infrastructure needs will likely evolve based on a broad set of assumptions on shifts in economic activity, structure, and demographics. The estimates here cannot substitute for the detailed, often bottom-up, analysis of an economy's infrastructure needs, which requires a granularity impossible at a cross-country level.

4.1. Estimates without climate change adjustment

Generating the baseline estimates first requires estimating the relationship between physical infrastructure stocks (for example, kilometers of roads or megawatts of electricity generated) and key economic and demographic factors that influence demand and/or supply of infrastructure services, including lagged infrastructure stock, per capita gross domestic product (GDP), population density, share of urban population, and the shares of agriculture and industry in GDP. These are estimated using data for developing Asia from 1970 to 2011. The regression estimates generally suggest that, *ceteris paribus*, a country's infrastructure stock increases with GDP per capita, but the incremental needs decrease with existing stock. Other economic and demographic factors such as population density, urbanization, and shares of agriculture and manufacturing in GDP are associated with some types of infrastructure but not with others. For example, increased population density and urbanization is significantly associated with greater road and sanitation infrastructure, and a higher share of manufacturing in GDP is significantly associated with greater seaport and mobile phone infrastructure.

Future physical infrastructure stocks are then estimated using projections of those same economic and demographic factors, and annual needs for additional infrastructure are calculated as a year-by-year difference in infrastructure stocks. Empirically-estimated unit costs are then applied to the annual increments in infrastructure stock to derive the monetary values of new investment needs. Unit costs capture the cost of building one unit of a given type of infrastructure (for example, how much it costs in US dollars to generate one megawatt of electricity). Also maintenance and rehabilitation costs are estimated as the depreciated part of the stock—a percentage of the previous year's stock multiplied by the unit cost. The total infrastructure investment need for a country over the 2016–2030 forecasting period is thus the sum of new investment needs plus maintenance and rehabilitation costs across different sectors and years. Appendix 4.1 contains detailed descriptions of projection methodology and data; Appendix 4.2, projections of GDP; and Appendix 4.3, estimates of unit costs for each sector.

Table 4.1 presents infrastructure investment needs without factoring in climate change (baseline estimates) as well as forecasted GDP per capita and population by region. Over the next 15 years, developing Asia's investment needs will reach $22,551 billion or $1,503 billion a year. This is equivalent to 5.1% of the region's forecasted GDP. The projections show that East Asia—mainly the PRC—will account for more than 60% of the required investments given its high levels of GDP and population, as well as its enormous existing infrastructure stock, which requires significant maintenance and rehabilitation.

South Asia follows, with infrastructure investment needs projected at $5,477 billion, or 24% of developing Asia's total. The investment needs amount to 7.6% of the subregion's projected GDP, significantly higher than East Asia's 4.5% and the developing Asia average. This is mainly due to South Asia's current lower GDP and expected faster GDP growth. Southeast Asia, Central Asia, and the Pacific will account for 12%, 2%, and 0.2% of the total investment needs, respectively. Investments are expected to account for relatively larger shares of GDP in Central Asia and the Pacific than in Southeast Asia.

It may be noted that these estimates also do not explicitly account for cross-border infrastructure that facilitates regional integration (Box 4.1).

Table 4.1: Projected Population and GDP and Infrastructure Investment Needs (Baseline Estimates) by Region, 2016–2030

Region	2015 UN Population Estimates (million)	2030 UN Population Projection (million)	2015 GDP per Capita ($ in 2015 prices)	Projected Average GDP Growth (%)	2030 Projected GDP per Capita ($ in 2015 prices)	Investment Needs	Annual Average	Investment Needs as % of Projected GDP
Central Asia	84	96	4,495	3.1	6,202	492	33	6.8
East Asia	1,460	1,503	9,022	5.1	18,602	13,781	919	4.5
South Asia*	1,744	2,059	1,594	6.5	3,446	5,477	365	7.6
Southeast Asia	632	723	3,838	5.1	7,040	2,759	184	5.0
The Pacific	11	14	2,329	3.1	2,889	42	2.8	8.2
Asia and the Pacific	3,931	4,396	4,778	5.3	9,277	22,551	1,503	5.1

GDP = gross domestic product.
*Pakistan and Afghanistan are included in South Asia.
Source: 2015 Revision of World Population Prospects, United Nations; World Development Indicators, World Bank; ADB estimates.

Box 4.1: Estimating Regional Infrastructure Investment Needs Beyond 2020

Most estimates for infrastructure investment in Asia are based on national infrastructure needs—which normally include border infrastructure, whether land, sea, or air. There are no comprehensive studies assessing the infrastructure investment needs for regional infrastructure across Asia and the Pacific. In Bhattacharyay, Kawai, and Nag (2012), it is estimated that an additional $320 billion would be needed for 1,202 regional connectivity projects—covering energy, transport (air, rail and road), trade facilitation and logistics—with a $29 billion average annual infrastructure investment required between 2010–2020 (about 4% of total national infrastructure investment needs).

When looking beyond 2020, the Asian Development Bank (ADB) identified infrastructure investment needs in its recently approved Operational Plan for Regional Cooperation and Integration (ADB 2016c) and other strategy documents for several subregional cross-border programs. These include the Central Asia Regional Economic Cooperation (CAREC) Program, the Greater Mekong Subregion (GMS) Program, and South Asia Subregional Economic Cooperation (SASEC) Program—all supported by ADB. Regional infrastructure financing estimates for the Pacific come from ADB staff projections. The estimations only touch on those sectors where a strategy has been in place or future project needs are projected. Box table 4.1 presents a summary of the estimates by program and sector. While not comprehensive, they can give an idea of the demand and financing challenge ahead.

Box table 4.1: Indicative Investment Needs for Regional Infrastructure by Regional/subregional Program and Sector
($ billion)

Sector \ Program	CAREC	GMS	SASEC	The Pacific	Total*
Transport	37.5	44.1	56.8	2.1	140.5
Road	24.6	13.3	24.4	-	62.3
Rail	10.2	30.1	22.5	-	62.8
Air	1.4	-	4.4	0.7	6.5
Maritime	1.1	0.3a	5.4d	1.4	8.2
Logistics	0.2	-	-	-	0.2
Others	-	0.5b	-	-	0.5
Trade facilitation	1.3	0.03	0.5	-	1.83
Energy	40.9	3.2	58.0	-	102.1
ICT	-	0.6	-	0.4	1.0
Other sectors	-	3.1c	-	1.5e	4.6
Total*	79.7	51.03	115.3	4.0	250.03

CAREC = Central Asia Regional Economic Cooperation; GMS = Greater Mekong Subregion; SASEC = South Asia Subregional Economic Cooperation; ICT = information and communication technology.

Note: CAREC covers Afghanistan, Azerbaijan, the People's Republic of China (PRC), Kazakhstan, the Kyrgyz Republic, Mongolia, Pakistan, Tajikistan, Turkmenistan, and Uzbekistan. GMS covers Cambodia, the PRC (Yunnan Province and Guangxi Zhuang Autonomous Region), the Lao People's Democratic Republic, Myanmar, Thailand, and Viet Nam. SASEC includes Bangladesh, Bhutan, India, Maldives, Nepal, and Sri Lanka.

a GMS maritime transport infrastructure includes sea ports, river ports, and inland waterways.
b GMS other transport infrastructure includes bridges, cross-border facilities, inland container terminals, etc.
c GMS other infrastructure sectors include agriculture, urban, tourism, environment, and multisector/cross-border economic zones.
d SASEC maritime transport infrastructure includes ports and inland waterways.
e The Pacific other infrastructure sectors include investments for climate change adaptation of regional infrastructure.
* Some figures may not add up to total due to rounding.
Source: ADB (2013, 2014a, 2015b, 2016c); ADB estimates.

4.2. Comparison with *Infrastructure for a Seamless Asia*

In 2009, ADB and ADBI estimated infrastructure needs for developing Asia for the 11-year period from 2010 to 2020 in *Infrastructure for a Seamless Asia* (Seamless Asia). The oft-cited Seamless Asia estimates showed infrastructure investment needs would total $8 trillion (in 2008 prices) for the 32 ADB DMCs covered—or an annual average $750 billion (in 2008 prices). This report uses more up-to-date and complete data to estimate investment needs for all 45 DMCs (including the 32 economies covered in Seamless Asia) for a 15-year period from 2016 to 2030. To make the estimates of the two studies more comparable, we limit the annual investment needs to the 32 economies covered in Seamless Asia and convert our updated baseline infrastructure needs estimates into 2008 prices (Table 4.2).[45]

---

45 We compare the Seamless Asia estimates with our baseline estimates as the former did not consider climate change-related infrastructure needs.

Table 4.2: Baseline Scenario in Comparison with *Infrastructure for a Seamless Asia+*

Region/Subregion	Total for the Period ($ billion in 2008 prices)		Annual ($ billion in 2008 prices)	
	Seamless Asia+	This report	Seamless Asia+	This report
Time period	2010–2020	2016–2030	2010–2020	2016–2030
DMCs covered	32	32	32	32
Central Asia	374	396	34	26
East Asia	4,378	9,728	398	649
South Asia*	2,370	5,095	215	340
Southeast Asia	1,095	2,171	100	145
The Pacific	6	36	1	2
Asia and the Pacific	8,223	17,426	748	1,162

DMC= developing member country.
+Seamless Asia refers to the *Infrastructure for a Seamless Asia* (ADB and ADBI 2009) publication.
*Pakistan and Afghanistan are included in South Asia.
Source: ADB and ADBI (2009); ADB estimates.

This report projects $1,162 billion (in 2008 prices) per year for the same set of 32 economies, 55% higher than the Seamless Asia estimate. The difference is mainly because this report covers a more distant future period (2016–2030 versus 2010–2020 in Seamless Asia) in which the region's economies will have higher GDP levels and thus require more infrastructure investments. If we held GDP constant since 2016, our estimate would be very close to that from the Seamless Asia estimates.

4.3. Infrastructure investments with climate change adjustment

We now examine our climate change-adjusted estimates that account for additional infrastructure investment needs to mitigate carbon emissions and to increase resilience to climate change.

On climate change mitigation, a recent ADB (2016d) report indicates that fossil fuels contribute over two-thirds of carbon emissions in developing Asia. For the region to progressively transit to low-carbon growth it must reduce carbon intensity in the energy sector.[46] To limit the average rise in global mean surface temperature to 2 degrees Celsius (2°C) above preindustrial levels,[47] carbon emissions from developing Asia will need to be reduced by three-quarters from our baseline scenario through investments in renewable power, smart grids, energy storage, and energy efficiency and, where applicable and feasible, carbon capture and storage, among others. We adopted the report's estimates of the additional investments required for the power sector of various economies and subregions to achieve the 2°C goal, and add these to our baseline estimates (see Appendix 4.1).

---

46 The transport sector also has a major role to play in mitigating greenhouse gas (GHG) emissions. The implications of sustainable transport on infrastructure mainly arise from shifts from more carbon-intensive modes of travel (like private cars) to less carbon-intensive modes (public transit and railways). Some recent studies suggest that these shifts will likely be less costly than a "business as usual" approach over the longer term (Cooper, Lefevre, and Li 2016; International Energy Agency 2013; Replogle and Fulton 2014). The main underlying reason is that the shifts will require less roads and more rails to be built; although the latter will not offset the former.

47 A 2°C rise above preindustrial levels is the critical threshold before more intense and severe coastal inundation and erosion, wildfires, heavy precipitation, and drought are expected (and may become unmanageable).

It should be noted that these additional costs are only one component of the macroeconomic costs of mitigation policies, which also include the costs of a larger set of changes in economic activity needed to reduce emissions. However, the additional costs of limiting warming to 2°C are vastly outweighed by their longer term benefits (ADB 2016b).[48]

Regarding climate adaptation, our estimates focus on "climate proofing" investments in the sectors covered in this report. Countries must ensure their infrastructure is resilient to the projected impact of climate change, as phenomena such as sea level rise and intensified extreme weather events can damage infrastructure, thus reducing its lifecycle and performance. While the precise costs of climate proofing infrastructure remain uncertain—costs related to, for example, elevating road embankments,

relocating upstream water intake and treatment works, and enhancing design and maintenance standards—we sourced our estimates of additional investment as a percentage of baseline investment from ADB project experience in water and sanitation (not including irrigation and flood control) and recent studies that estimate these costs (ADB 2014b; United Nations Framework Convention on Climate Change 2007; World Bank 2010).

Besides climate proofing in the sectors covered in this report, climate adaptation requires shifts in portfolio and significant investments in sectors not covered here, such as irrigation and food security, disaster risk management (flood control in particular), and coastal protection to maintain and build climate change resilience.

Table 4.3: Infrastructure Investments by Region, 2016–2030
($ billion in 2015 prices)

Region/Subregion	Baseline Estimates			Climate-adjusted Estimates		
	Investment Needs	Annual Average	Investment Needs as % of GDP	Investment Needs	Annual Average	Investment Needs as % of GDP
Central Asia	492	33	6.8	565	38	7.8
East Asia	13,781	919	4.5	16,062	1,071	5.2
PRC	13,120	875	5.0	15,267	1,018	5.8
South Asia*	5,477	365	7.6	6,347	423	8.8
India	4,363	291	7.4	5,152	343	8.8
Southeast Asia	2,759	184	5.0	3,147	210	5.7
Indonesia	1,108	74	5.5	1,229	82	6.0
The Pacific	42	2.8	8.2	46	3.1	9.1
Asia and the Pacific	22,551	1,503	5.1	26,166	1,744	5.9

DMC= developing member country; GDP = gross domestic product; PRC = People's Republic of China.
*Pakistan and Afghanistan are included in South Asia.
Source: ADB estimates.

48 Estimates in the *Asian Development Outlook Update* 2016 show that the economic benefits (avoided damages due to less climate change and co-benefits from mitigation) will exceed mitigation costs by 2025 in an "optimal" scenario of early action. In gross terms, the optimal 2°C scenario leads to policy costs for developing Asia that reach nearly 2% of GDP by 2030, peak in 2035 and then decline to 1.7% of GDP by 2050. At the same time, mitigation leads to substantial co-benefits from improved air quality, even when measured against improving air pollution control through end-of-pipe measures. By 2050 an additional 560,000 deaths from particulate matter and ozone pollution are averted annually, and nearly 7 million tons of crops are not destroyed under the 2°C scenario. Over the longer term, avoided economic losses from climate change—such as avoided losses in agriculture and labor productivity, avoided increases in storm damage, and losses from lower tourism—become the dominant source of benefits. Benefits and co-benefits collectively exceed policy costs of the 2°C scenario by the early 2020s, and policy costs involved generate a 15% internal rate of return for 2016–2050, which is far above most public investments.

Compared with the baseline estimates, our climate change-adjusted estimates are 16% higher—rising from $22.6 trillion to $26.2 trillion, or from $1.5 trillion to $1.7 trillion annually (Table 4.3). As a percentage of GDP, infrastructure investment needs will increase from 5.1% to 5.9% on average for the next 15 years. This is a considerable increase to baseline infrastructure investment needs, with most incremental costs going to power sector mitigation, as large decarbonization is needed to remain below the 2°C threshold.

Box 4.2: Factoring Climate Change and Disaster Risk into Infrastructure Design

Asian Development Bank (ADB) developing member countries face significant disaster and climate risk. Between 2006 and 2015 alone, direct physical losses as a consequence of extreme weather events and geophysical hazards averaged $46 billion per annum—equivalent to $126 million per day. Losses included damage to infrastructure, homes, and businesses, with indirect economic and social consequences for jobs, productivity and the provision of services. The failure of insufficiently resilient infrastructure also contributed to over 337,000 disaster-related fatalities over the same period.

High levels of disaster risk reflect the region's multiple river basins, the location of many countries within the tropical cyclone belt, and high, increasing population densities—particularly in coastal areas, on flood plains, and in seismically active areas. Climate change brings further challenges, with increased frequency and intensity of extreme hazards and rising sea levels, saline water intrusion and higher temperatures. Moreover, expanding economic connectivity accentuates indirect consequences of disasters, creating expanding layers of systemic risk. Damage to industry and transportation networks in one country can affect production and the delivery of services elsewhere, as amply demonstrated in 2011 when the Tōhoku earthquake and tsunami in Japan and floods in Thailand caused regional and global supply chain disruptions.

However, rising disaster losses are not inevitable. Disaster and climate resilience measures can be incorporated into infrastructure investments, sometimes with relatively little incremental expense.

The cost of incorporating investments against natural hazards can be as low as a few additional percentage points on the baseline construction cost. For instance, much of the cost in earthquake design is in more robust structural frames using additional materials like extra reinforced steel and concrete. Affordable advanced technologies can be applied as well. In ADB's East Asia and the Pacific subregions, these additions are estimated to add just 2%–4% to overall construction costs (Yanev 2010). Longer-term climate proofing may cost somewhat more but should not be prohibitive. ADB reported that climate adaptation financing over 2011–2015 was 4.5% of total project financing, and has ranged between 2% and 6% on an annual basis.[a]

Disaster and climate risk should be factored into the design and location of all infrastructure—during initial screening of investment proposals, site selection, detailed feasibility and design phases, economic analysis, and subsequent monitoring and evaluation. Forward-looking, flexible design features are required, reflecting the dynamic nature of disaster risk and potential climate change, and to ensure continued resilience throughout the intended life of an investment. For example, increasing flooding risk was identified as a major concern in designing a $35 million ADB rural roads improvement project in Cambodia's Tonle Sap basin. To address both current and future flood risk, the project includes elevated road segments, the use of highly absorptive subgrade materials, tree and grass planting on embankments, the development of an early warning flood system, and government capacity development (ADB 2010).

a   ADB, along with the other multilateral development banks, reports both mitigation and adaptation finance from internal resources through the Joint MDB Reports on Climate Finance issued annually since 2011.

East Asia, and the PRC in particular, is expected to account for the majority share of investments for climate change mitigation and adaptation. In fact, $152 billion out of the $241 billion in additional investments annually will be for East Asia, mainly to create more climate friendly power generation, transmission, and distribution. South Asia and Southeast Asia will also need to considerably increase climate change-related investments. Including climate change-related needs, the required infrastructure investments in percent of GDP will be highest for the Pacific (9.1%), followed by South Asia (8.8%) and Central Asia (7.8%).

4.4. Estimates by sector, income level, and geography

Estimates with and without climate-related investments are also calculated by sector (Table 4.4). Power and transport are the two largest sectors under both scenarios—accounting for 52% and 35%, respectively, of total infrastructure investments for the baseline estimates; and 56% and 32%, respectively, of total climate change-adjusted investments. The power sector share in total investments increases because most greenhouse gas mitigation investments go to the power sector. Among the incremental

Table 4.4: Infrastructure Investment Needs by Sector, 2016–2030
($ billion in 2015 prices)

Sector	Baseline Estimates			Climate-adjusted Estimates			Climate-related Investments (Annual)	
	Investment Needs	Annual Average	Share of Total	Investment Needs	Annual Average	Share of Total	Adaptation	Mitigation
Power	11,689	779	51.8	14,731	982	56.3	3	200
Transport	7,796	520	34.6	8,353	557	31.9	37	–
Telecommunications	2,279	152	10.1	2,279	152	8.7	–	–
Water and Sanitation	787	52	3.5	802	53	3.1	1	–
Total	22,551	1,503	100.0	26,166	1,744	100.0	41	200

Note: – denotes not applicable.
Source: ADB estimates.

investment needs ($241 billion per year) to deal with climate change, investments in the power sector to reduce carbon emissions are about $200 billion. Investments in transport will increase 7%, or $37 billion per year accounting for the majority of climate proofing costs ($41 billion per year). Telecommunications and water and sanitation are relatively smaller, accounting for 9% and 3%, respectively. However, the figures by no means suggest the sectors hold less importance for the economy or individual welfare.

Our estimates suggest much future infrastructure investment will go to maintenance and rehabilitation costs. The ratio of new investment to maintenance and rehabilitation is

4:3 for our baseline estimates and 3:2 with climate change factored in. In fact, the maintenance and rehabilitation account for a larger share than new investment in transport, telecommunications, and water and sanitation—given the high depreciation ratios assumed for those sectors.[49] Moreover, year-specific projections show that maintenance and rehabilitation play an increasingly important role when infrastructure stock increases.

The lack of comparable data limits our estimates from covering, for example, urban transit systems (in particular subways), which have developed rapidly in Asia since the 2000s. A simple estimate suggests that subway investment will continue to develop rapidly in several Asian economies (Box 4.3).

Table 4.5: Infrastructure Investment Needs by Income and Geography, 2016–2030
($ billion in 2015 prices)

Category	Baseline Estimates			Climate-adjusted Estimates		
	Investment Needs	% of GDP	Share of Total	Investment Needs	% of GDP	Share of Total
Income group						
Low income	82	9.9	0.4	87	10.5	0.3
Lower middle income	7,729	7.1	34.3	8,894	8.2	34.0
Upper middle income	13,845	4.9	61.4	16,099	5.7	61.5
High income	895	1.9	4.0	1,086	2.3	4.2
Geography						
Landlocked	626	7.4	2.8	708	8.4	2.7
Coastal	21,046	5.1	93.3	24,428	5.9	93.4
Island	879	4.2	3.9	1,030	5.0	3.9
Total	22,551	5.1	100.0	26,166	5.9	100.0

GDP = gross domestic product.
Note: See Appendix 4.4 for country/territory classification.
Source: ADB estimates.

49 In the projections, water and sanitation infrastructure is proxied by the percentage of households with access, so new investment is not required once access reaches 100%.

Box 4.3: Asia's Explosive Growth in Subway Development

In recent decades, rapid urban migration and expanding metropolitan areas has driven demand for more efficient mass transit. In many countries, subway development has provided an answer.[a] By 2010, 138 cities worldwide had 627 subway lines covering 10,672 kilometers of track, stopping at 7,886 stations (Box table 4.3). Asia accounted for some 30%–40% of the total, the highest share of any continent. And the majority of new subway systems between 2001 and 2010 were built in Asia. Of the 25 subway systems inaugurated worldwide in 2001–2010, 14 (56%) were in Asia. Half of these new systems and more than half of new tracks, stations and subway lines were in the People's Republic of China (PRC).

Looking forward, these trends will likely continue. There are many Asian cities where growing populations and economic capacity will make building subway attractive—Mumbai, Dhaka, Karachi, Jakarta, Chennai, Bangalore, and Hyderabad, among others.[b] Simple projections using recent trends in subway construction by country suggests that there could be about 2,300 kilometers of new

subway tracks and an additional 1,100 stations constructed in Asia between 2016 and 2030. Not surprisingly, the PRC is projected to dominate new construction with about 1,600 kilometers of track. India is second with 240 kilometers of track spread over 128 subway stations. The Republic of Korea is third with some 100 stations and 180 kilometers of track. Other countries with moderate subway construction expected over the next 15 years include Azerbaijan, Japan, Malaysia, Philippines, Singapore, and Thailand.

Construction costs for a subway system vary greatly—from $50 million per kilometer to more than $500 million (Levy 2013). The unit cost of subway construction in the PRC is around $100 million per kilometer, falling on the low end of the international range. Since 70% of the projected subway routes are to be built in the PRC, we apply the PRC's unit cost to the projected mileage of new subways. Thus, the total investments in subway construction are projected to reach $230 billion in Asia over the next 15 years (2016–2030).

Box table 4.3: World Subway Systems in 2010 and Growth During 2001–2010

	Subways in 2010				Subway growth (2001–2010)			
	Total Cities Covered	Total Subway Stations	Total Kilometers	Total Subway Lines	New Cities Covered	New Subway Stations	New Kilometers	New Subway Lines
World	138	7,886	10,672	627	25	1,150	2,722	130
Africa	1	51	56	2	0	0	0	0
Europe	40	2,782	3,558	233	3	190	477	23
North America	30	1,598	2,219	140	4	76	267	13
South America	14	478	627	36	4	67	220	12
Asia	53	2,977	4,210	216	14	817	1,757	82
PRC	13	883	1,427	69	7	521	1,063	45

PRC = People's Republic of China.
Source: Gonzalez-Navarro and Turner (2016).

a   "Subway" is defined as an electric-powered urban rail system completely separate from vehicular traffic and pedestrians. This excludes most streetcar systems which affect traffic at stoplights and crossings—although it includes underground streetcar segments. It is intracity and thus excludes heavy rail commuter lines. Data do not distinguish between surface, underground or above ground subways so long they have exclusive right of way.

b   Of course, while some of these cities are large, the local context may make subway construction a low priority item.

Table 4.5 shows how the total infrastructure investment needs will be distributed across countries by income group and geographic characteristic.[50] Most infrastructure investment (96%) will be concentrated in lower and upper middle income economies. Yet infrastructure needs as a share of GDP will be substantial in low income countries,

decreasing as income levels rise. Infrastructure investment as a percentage of future GDP in landlocked countries will be above the regional average. Considering climate change, the distribution of investment needs shifts slightly to the upper middle and high income countries mainly because they have more mitigation needs.

---

50 Appendix 4.4 classifies countries/economies in different categories.

Table 4.6: Climate-adjusted Infrastructure Investment Needs under Low and High GDP Growth Scenarios, 2016–2030
($billion in 2015 prices)

Region	Low Growth Scenario				High Growth Scenario			
	Projected Average GDP Growth	Infrastructure Needs	Average	% of GDP	Projected Average GDP Growth	Infrastructure Needs	Average	% of GDP
Central Asia	2.1	526	35	7.9	4.1	605	40	7.6
East Asia	4.1	14,807	987	5.3	6.1	17,389	1,159	5.2
PRC	4.6	14,097	940	5.9	6.6	16,504	1,100	5.7
South Asia*	5.5	5,930	395	9.0	7.5	6,777	452	8.5
India	5.8	4,811	321	9.0	7.8	5,504	367	8.5
Southeast Asia	4.1	2,951	197	5.9	6.1	3,355	224	5.5
Indonesia	4.5	1,158	77	6.3	6.5	1,304	87	5.8
The Pacific	2.1	43	2.9	9.3	4.1	49	3.3	8.8
Asia and the Pacific	4.3	24,257	1,617	6.0	6.3	28,175	1,878	5.8

GDP = gross domestic product; PRC = People's Republic of China.
*Pakistan and Afghanistan are included in South Asia.
Source: ADB estimates.

4.5. Infrastructure investment estimates under different growth scenarios

Accurately forecasting long-term economic growth is extremely difficult, if not impossible. So the estimates with climate change adjustments here are checked for sensitivity to low and high growth scenarios (Table 4.6). The low (high) growth scenario used is one percentage point lower (higher) than the baseline case for each economy and each year. One percentage point difference in GDP growth can be substantial as most forecasted growth rates range from 2% to 7%.

Under the low growth scenario, total climate change-adjusted infrastructure investment needs decline 7.3% from $26,166 billion to $24,257 billion for developing Asia during 2016–2030. The high growth scenario shows total investment needs rising 7.7% to $28,175 billion. The percent changes of investment needs in each subregion all are about +/- 7%, and investment needs as a percent of GDP remain essentially unchanged. This analysis suggests that the sensitivity of infrastructure investment needs to GDP growth is moderate. This may be due to other factors such as economic structure, urbanization and a country's time-invariant characteristics that will also independently affect future infrastructure needs—and a significant investment share goes to maintenance and rehabilitation.

Box 4.4: Comparison with Other Infrastructure Needs Estimates

Several recent studies estimate future infrastructure investments/spending. However, they differ in several aspects such as methodology, geographical and sector coverage, and forecast periods. Two studies—Ruiz-Nunez and Wei (2015) and McKinsey Global Institute (2016)—provide sufficient details that allow us to make a cross-study comparison (Box table 4.4).[a]

Ruiz-Nunez and Wei (2015) cover 145 emerging markets and developing countries from 2014 to 2020. McKinsey Global Institute (2016) covers 75 countries, including the People's Republic of China (PRC), India and other emerging Asian economies from 2016 to 2030. The projections in both deal with investments in energy, transportation, telecommunications, and water and sanitation. Neither takes climate change formally into account.

On methodology, this report and Ruiz-Nunez and Wei (2015) use a common approach of econometric estimation with historical infrastructure data. Both predict future infrastructure stock using forecasted gross domestic product (GDP) per capita, population density, industrial composition and urbanization rate. In contrast, McKinsey Global Institute (2016) assumes a fixed ratio of infrastructure investments to forecasted GDP for each country.[b]

While differences in countries, time periods, and sectors covered across the studies make precise comparison difficult, in general, the Ruiz-Nunez and Wei (2015) projections in terms of investment needs as a percent of future GDP are on the low side for East Asia and the Pacific relative to our baseline estimates and those of McKinsey Global Institute (which may be inferred from the numbers for the PRC). Their estimates for South Asia are higher, perhaps due to differences in estimates of GDP growth.

Box table 4.4: Comparison of Estimated Annual Infrastructure Investments Across Selected Studies

	This report ($ billion in 2015 prices)				Ruiz-Nunez and Wei (2015) ($ billion in 2011 prices)		McKinsey Global Institute (2016) ($ billion in 2015 prices)	
	Baseline Estimates		Climate-adjusted Estimates					
Number of economies	45		45		145		75	
Period covered	2016–2030		2016–2030		2014–2020		2016–2030	
Total annual	1,503	(5.1%)	1,744	(5.9%)	1,104	(2.2%)	3,300	(3.8%)
East Asia and the Pacific	922	(4.5%)	1,074	(5.2%)	212	(3.7%)	-	
South Asia	365	(7.6%)	423	(8.8%)	304	(14.9%)	-	
People's Republic of China	875	(5.0%)	1,018	(5.8%)	-		949	(5.5%)
India	291	(7.4%)	343	(8.8%)	-		196	(5.7%)
Indonesia	74	(5.5%)	82	(6.0%)	-		N/A	(4.4%)

Note: Investment as share of gross domestic product in parentheses.

a   Besides these studies, World Economic Forum (2013) consolidates estimates from various sources on different sectors and predicts that global infrastructure investments amount to $5.0 trillion per year globally and $3.3 trillion for the sectors covered in this report. A study published by Boston Consulting Group (2013) estimates $4.0 trillion globally for social, water and waste, oil and gas transmission and storage, electricity, port, airport, railway, and road. PricewaterhouseCoopers LLP (2014) forecasts capital project and infrastructure spending would total more than $9 trillion by 2025 for five industries—extraction, utilities, manufacturing, transport and social—for 49 countries accounting for 90% of global economic output and 95% of fixed investment.
b   An earlier report (McKinsey Global Institute 2013) compares results and finds similarities between the approach here and one assuming infrastructure stock is valued at 70% of GDP, and with a consolidated projection based on various third party estimates.

Section 5. Meeting the Challenge of Infrastructure Development

The analysis thus far shows Asia and the Pacific will need to invest around 6% of gross domestic product (GDP) in infrastructure from 2016 to 2030 to continue its recent history of generally high economic growth, while ensuring new investments address the increasing urgency of infrastructure-related climate change mitigation and adaptation.[51] With a majority of developing member countries (DMCs) currently investing considerably less than 5% of GDP in infrastructure, meeting projected infrastructure needs will be quite challenging.[52] In this section we delve into these challenges by examining issues related to funding and financing infrastructure—both public and private—and the institutional issues related to planning and implementing infrastructure projects; and maintaining the assets thereafter.

A few points must be made up front. First, to build a foundation based on available data, we restrict our analysis to 25 DMCs—which still cover 96% of the population and 85% of the GDP of the 45 DMCs.[53,54] Second, we limit our time-frame for assessing infrastructure investment finance to 5 years (from 2016–2020). Detailed information on public expenditures is needed for a meaningful comparison of actual infrastructure investments against investment needs. This is particularly important given the dominant role the public sector will continue to play as a source of infrastructure

planning and finance. It is also necessary for making a meaningful assessment of infrastructure investment "gaps"—the difference between the estimated level of infrastructure investment needs and countries' actual infrastructure investment over recent years.

Third, projected investment needs—and thus investment gaps presented here—are based on projections of a set of economic and demographic variables that influence demand and/or supply of infrastructure services and the historical, cross-country relationship between physical infrastructure stocks and these variables (notwithstanding the projected adjustments made due to climate change).

Given these caveats, we estimate infrastructure needs and gaps—with and without factoring in climate change-related effects—by region and income category over the 5-year period from 2016 to 2020 (Table 5.1). We also provide estimates of current infrastructure investment.[55] Infrastructure investment gaps are expressed in terms of annual investment levels and as a share of projected GDP.

The 25 DMCs invested almost $881 billion in infrastructure in 2015—well below the estimated $1.34 trillion annual investment needed over the 5-year period from 2016 to 2020 if climate change-related expenditures are included. This infrastructure investment gap amounts to 2.4% of annual average projected GDP over the same period.

---

51 As discussed, the analysis covers the estimated investment needs of ADB's 45 DMCs in transport, power (energy), telecommunications, and water and sanitation from 2016–2030.

52 Only 5 of the 22 DMCs covered have invested 5% or more in infrastructure in recent years (see Figure 3.2).

53 The 25 DMCs include Afghanistan, Armenia, Bangladesh, Bhutan, Cambodia, PRC, Fiji, India, Indonesia, Kazakhstan, Kiribati, Kyrgyz Republic, Malaysia, Maldives, Marshall Islands, Federated States of Micronesia, Mongolia, Myanmar, Nepal, Pakistan, Papua New Guinea, Philippines, Sri Lanka, Thailand, and Viet Nam.

54 In this section, the coverage of the PRC's current investment estimate is made consistent with the sector coverage of future needs estimates as discussed in Section 4. The PRC data is sufficiently disaggregated to allow for a close match of sector coverage with future needs estimates.

55 Current investment in infrastructure is computed by multiplying 2015 GDP with the average of available infrastructure investment to GDP ratios from 2010–2014. The latter are measured by BUDGET+PPI to GDP ratios for 19 DMCs. There are two points to be noted. First, infrastructure investment to GDP ratio may have changed by 2015, which would bias the estimated infrastructure investment in 2015. Another caveat is that for six DMCs, BUDGET+PPI is unavailable. Their investment to GDP ratios are approximated based on their GFCF(GG)+PPI values, or by using their respective subregion's average investment to GDP ratio.

Table 5.1: Infrastructure Investments and Gaps, Selected Economies and Subregions, 2016–2020 ($ billion in 2015 prices)	Estimated Current Investment (2015)	Baseline estimates			Climate-adjusted Estimates		
		Annual Needs	Gap	Gap (% of GDP)	Annual Needs	Gap	Gap (% of GDP)
Total (25)	881 [5.5]	1,211	330	1.7	1,340	459	2.4
Total without PRC (24)	195 [3.8]	457	262	4.3	503	308	5.0
Selected Low to Lower Middle Income Countries (18)	178 [4.2]	422	244	4.7	465	287	5.6
without India (17)	60 [2.9]	192	132	5.4	203	143	5.9
Selected Upper Middle Income Countries (7)	703 [6.0]	789	86	0.6	876	172	1.2
without PRC (6)	17 [2.0]	35	18	1.8	39	21	2.2
Selected Central Asia Countries (3)	6 [2.9]	11	5	2.3	12	7	3.1
Selected South Asia Countries (8)	134 [4.8]	294	160	4.7	329	195	5.7
Selected Southeast Asia Countries (7)	55 [2.6]	147	92	3.8	157	102	4.1
Selected Pacific Countries (5)	1 [2.7]	2	1	6.2	2	2	6.9
India	118 [5.4]	230	112	4.1	261	144	5.3
Indonesia	23 [2.6]	70	47	4.7	74	51	5.1
PRC	686 [6.3]	753	68	0.5	837	151	1.2

GDP = gross domestic product; PRC = People's Republic of China.

Numbers in parentheses refer to number of selected countries. Numbers in brackets refer to investment as percentage of GDP.

Note: The gap as a % of GDP is based on the annual average of projected GDP from 2016 to 2020. The 25 ADB developing member countries included are listed in Appendix 3.1. Income grouping is based on current World Bank classification (see Appendix 4.4).

Source: ADB (2016a); Country sources; Investment and Capital Stock Dataset, 1960–2015, IMF; Private Participation in Infrastructure Database, World Bank; World Bank (2015a and 2015b); World Development Indicators, World Bank; ADB estimates.

These aggregate figures mask wide diversity and unevenness in infrastructure spending across the region. Given the large size of the PRC economy—and its considerable investment in infrastructure—the aggregate numbers are driven in large part by the PRC. Excluding the PRC, the infrastructure gap as a share of projected GDP rises considerably, to around 5%, as many economies in the region with large infrastructure needs currently invest well below the levels required to support economic growth and meet climate change-related needs.

This is especially true for low to lower middle income economies. For these economies, the gap between future needs over the 5–year period from 2016 to 2020 and current investment levels is around $287 billion annually when accounting for climate change—or around 5.6% of projected GDP. Excluding India raises the gap to 5.9% of annual average projected GDP, reflecting in part India's fairly robust infrastructure investment in recent years.

There are certainly other ways of determining infrastructure needs. For example, they could be defined in terms of investment required to ensure a country's citizens have access to infrastructure services of the type and quality of those in a developed economy. Box 5.1 estimates infrastructure needs using this method for the People's Republic of China (PRC)—an economy that has led the developing world in infrastructure development. A large gap remains when comparing current infrastructure stock in the PRC with that of the OECD. It will take more than several decades to fill even with the PRC's current investment intensity.

Also, while we factor in the effects of climate change in our estimates of needs and gaps, some specific economies will likely be much more affected than others. This is especially true for the island economies in the Pacific where vulnerability to rising intensity of natural hazards may well require significantly more investment than our approach suggests (Box 5.2).

Box 5.1: How Much Infrastructure is Needed? Comparing the People's Republic of China with Developed Economies

The People's Republic of China (PRC) is often cited for its widespread, substantial infrastructure investment—it has been one of the largest infrastructure investors in the world. Nevertheless, it still has some ways to go in providing infrastructure services at the level and quality that developed economies do. Getting a sense of how much investment this would take offers an alternative gauge of future infrastructure investment compared with our projections made in Section 4.[a]

Our calculation suggests there remains a significant gap. In terms of highways, for example, a sizable gap remains between the PRC and Organisation for Economic Co-operation and Development (OECD) members despite the high investment over the past decades (Box figure 5.1 and Box table 5.1.1). To obtain the total stock value of "quality" PRC roads, the total lengths of express ways, national highways, and regional roads are multiplied by their respective unit costs and then added.[b] Similar OECD calculations are done based on its physical "quality" road stock (though the PRC unit costs are used for OECD road stock value to find out how much the PRC would have to spend to close the gap).[c] The stock value of these "quality" roads in the PRC is estimated at $283 million (in 2015 prices) per square kilometer—a mere 22% of the OECD average in 2011[d]—mainly due to the gap in regional roads. This implies $9.3 trillion in investment is needed to make the PRC highway network equal to the OECD average. This is equivalent to 86% of the PRC's gross domestic product (GDP) in 2015, and almost three times our projected 2016–2030 investment estimated in section 4. It would appear huge demand remains for quality roads in the PRC.[e]

Box figure 5.1: The PRC's Infrastructure Investment Needed to Catch up to Developed Economies
(% of GDP)

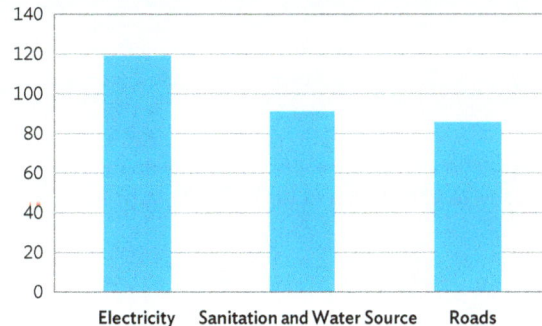

PRC = People's Republic of China.
Note: Roads data are for 2011. Electricity and water storage capacity data are for 2014. Flood and storm water control, irrigation, and water environment data are from various years. Water data refers to water storage capacity, flood and storm water control, irrigation, and water environment.
Source: International Development Statistics Online Databases, OECD; International Energy Statistics, US Energy Information Administration; International Road Federation (2012); New Energy Finance, Bloomberg; World Development Indicators, World Bank; ADB estimates.

Investment needs for power is comparable to that of highways. The electricity generation capacity of the PRC is 1.03 kilowatts per capita, 46% lower than the OECD in 2014. Multiplying this gap by the PRC population and the average unit cost, the total gap between the PRC and OECD reaches $12.9 trillion (in 2015 prices), or 1.19 times the PRC's 2015 GDP.

Box table 5.1.1: Comparison of Infrastructure Stock Between the PRC and OECD

Subsector	PRC Current Stock Value Density ($ million in 2015 prices)	OECD-Benchmark Stock Value Density ($ million in 2015 prices)	Investment Needed to Fill OECD-PRC Gap ($ billion in 2015 prices)	Ratio of OECD-PRC Gap to PRC GDP
Roads	282.76*	1,275.61*	9,321.13	0.86
Electricity	79.55+	174.33+	12,929.61	1.19

GDP = gross domestic product; OECD = Organisation for Economic Co-operation and Development; PRC = People's Republic of China.
Note: * per 1,000 square kilometer.; + per 10,000 population; Infrastructure data on roads is for 2011, data on electricity is for 2014.
Source: International Development Statistics Online Databases, OECD; International Energy Statistics, US Energy Information Administration; International Road Federation (2012); New Energy Finance, Bloomberg; World Development Indicators, World Bank; ADB estimates.

a   Projections are built on the past relationship between physical infrastructure stock and how an economy is structured, then adjusted according to evolving economic trends.
b   Assuming that unit cost for expressways is twice that of national highways and that regional roads have the same unit cost as national highways.
c   OECD average density of each type of road is calculated by first summing up the total road length, and then dividing it by the total land area of OECD. Similarly, for electricity generation capacity per capita of OECD, the total generation capacity was divided by the total population of OECD.
d   Data on OECD road length with breakdown by different grades are obtained from International Road Federation (2012) and the latest year available is 2011. The calculated road density gap of OECD over the PRC was 1.4, 18.2 and 174.0 kilometer (km) per 1,000 km^2 for motorway, national roads and regional roads, respectively.
e   Two caveats need to be noted in this exercise. First, the quality of the same type of roads may be higher in OECD than in the PRC. This may cause a downward bias in our estimate of road investment needs in the PRC. Second, the optimal spatial distribution of road network may differ in the PRC and OECD due to different geographic or economic conditions, while our current comparison does not take into account this difference.

continued on next page

Box 5.1: How Much Infrastructure is Needed? Comparing the People's Republic of China with Developed Economies *(continued)*

Infrastructure for water resources development, flood control, irrigation, wastewater management, and water environmental improvement in the PRC remain much lower than developed countries, and will need huge investments. For example, in 2014 water storage capacity was 612.2 cubic meters per person in the PRC, approximately one-third that in the United States.[f] To fill this gap, the PRC would need to invest $6.5 trillion, or 74% of the PRC's 2015 GDP. In addition, based on national plans,[g] $1.5 trillion would be needed to improve flood and storm water control, irrigation, and water environment. These add up to $8 trillion, or 91% of PRC's 2015 GDP.

Other critical infrastructure investment in the PRC is needed as well. There is about $1.1 trillion of needed investment on "intangible" infrastructure, such as ecological/environmental protection infrastructure (Zhu et al. 2015). In addition, the country's rapid urbanization requires expanded or improved urban public transit, metro networks, and solid waste treatment systems in the next 5 to 10 years (Box table 5.1.2). For example, in 2013 PRC's urban sewer pipe length per 10,000 urban population was just 17% of Japan's 2006 level, whereas in 2012 only 18.2% of anthropogenic wastewater was treated (ADB 2016e). Thus, total investment needs for general urban infrastructure could reach $6 trillion over the next 15 years. Box table 5.1.2 estimates investment needs by urban infrastructure subsector.

Box table 5.1.2: Investment Needs for Urban Infrastructure in the PRC (2016–2030)	
Infrastructure Subsector	Investment Needs+ ($ trillion in 2015 prices)
Urban Water Supply	0.3
Urban Wastewater Management	0.3
Municipal solid waste management	0.3
Urban Roads	2.2
Subways	1.9
District Heating	0.3
Urban Climate Change Mitigation*	1.0

PRC = People's Republic of China.
Note: *Urban Climate Change Mitigation needs are from 2016–2020.
+Investment needs (total for 2016–2030) by infrastructure subsector were derived as follows: annual investment needs (2018–2030) as percent of gross domestic product (GDP) is multiplied to the arithmetic mean of GDP for 2018–2030 from International Development Statistics Online Databases, OECD. The product is then multiplied by 15 (years).
Source: Paulson Institute, Energy Foundation China, and Chinese Renewable Energy Industries Association (2016); World Bank and Development Research Center of the State Council, the People's Republic of China (2014).

---

[f]   ADB estimates are based on Total Water Storage Capacity data from Japan Dam Association for US and Statistical Yearbook of Water Resources 2014 for the PRC. Population data is from World Development Indicators, World Bank.

[g]   The estimate is based on the sum of necessary investments in irrigation, drainage, reservoirs, flood control (2011 Number 1 Decree on Water released by the State Council), storm water control (2014 National Plan for Enhancing Urban Storm Water and Drainage Capacities) and water environment (2013 Clean Water Action Plan).

Meeting developing Asia's infrastructure needs will require simultaneous action on two levels: first, undertaking steps to ensure that sufficient finance is available for infrastructure development; and second, tackling institutional issues of how infrastructure projects are planned, implemented, and maintained. The latter involves conducting comprehensive feasibility studies, cost-benefit analysis, and assessing carefully all available technology options before undertaking infrastructure projects, among others. These issues are discussed in greater detail below.

5.1.   Infrastructure finance

Figure 5.1 presents an indicative snapshot of the major ways in which infrastructure is funded across public and private sectors. Public sector infrastructure financing is primarily derived from public transfers of tax revenues (current and future), though other sources can make important contributions. These include user charges against publically provided infrastructure services, tools such as land value capture (see Figure 5.1), and international transfers such as grant funding of infrastructure through official development assistance (ODA) for low income countries. Crucially, future tax revenues provide the basis for government borrowing domestically and from international sources, such as multilateral development banks (MDBs), foreign governments, and the foreign private sector. Sources of public infrastructure finance include national and subnational governments, development financial institutions—which   include   MDBs,   national

Box 5.2: Infrastructure Investment Needs in the Pacific

With the exception of Papua New Guinea (PNG) and Timor-Leste, the Pacific developing member countries (DMCs) are small, highly dispersed islands or island groups spread over vast ocean territories. The islands are far from other DMCs in the region, and most of the population lives within an average 1.5 kilometers of the coast. Their small geographic size and isolation make it costlier to organize trade and logistics (ADB 2016f).

While the estimates in Table 5.1 account for additional infrastructure needs for island economies, they may understate the needs in some Pacific DMCs. For example, constructing a road on a remote island can be four times more costly than in densely populated large economies.[a] Moreover, high exposure to the effects of climate change and natural hazards make them extremely vulnerable to shocks. Even though estimates attempt to factor in costs associated with tackling climate change mitigation and adaptation, the needs for restoring infrastructure damaged by natural disasters are not estimated. For example, in Fiji, which has the highest gross domestic product (GDP) per capita among the Pacific DMCs, tropical cyclone Winston in 2016 alone caused $118 million (3% of 2015 GDP) worth of damages and losses in four major infrastructure sectors, and total recovery and reconstruction needs reached some $136 million (Box table 5.2) (Government of Fiji 2016).

The estimates in Table 5.1 would also be well below what it would take an economy to provide infrastructure at the level of a typical Organisation for Economic Co-operation and Development (OECD) economy. For example, more than half the roads in the Pacific DMCs remain unpaved (Box figure 5.2.1). Many of these countries are also characterized by low road density, especially in PNG. There are few alternative routes, so access is subject to disruptions from heavy rainfall, flooding, landslides, and bridge failure. Frequent natural hazards and inadequate maintenance leave the road network in disrepair. The issue is further exacerbated by overloaded vehicles in many countries such as Fiji, Solomon Islands, and PNG, where forestry, sugarcane, construction, and other heavy industries operate with either poor regulation or enforceable weight limits.

Utilities coverage in the Pacific DMCs is also well below OECD levels (Box figure 5.2.2). Only 29.4% of the Pacific population has access to electricity. In countries like PNG and Vanuatu, where access to modern energy is very low, investments must be more inclusive. In other countries, assets are either approaching or surpassed their useful lives, thus requiring significant investment for replacement. People living in rural areas have far less access to drinking water and basic sanitation than those in urban areas. And the sanitation level in urban centers remains well below OECD countries. Future infrastructure investment must bridge these gaps.

Box table 5.2: Recovery and Reconstruction Needs after Tropical Cyclone Winston
($ million)

	Recovery	Reconstruction	Resilience	Total	Percentage of 2015 GDP
Total	7.29	119.38	8.95	135.62	3.12
Transport	1.52	83.19	–	84.71	1.95
Water	1.71	9.86	–	11.57	0.27
Electricity	1.00	12.33	2.76	16.10	0.37
Communication	3.05	14.00	6.19	23.24	0.53

GDP = gross domestic product.
Note: Numbers are converted based on Government of Fiji (2016). Foreign exchange rate used: F$2.10 = $1.00.
Source: Government of Fiji (2016); World Development Indicators, World Bank.

---

a   Based on a four-lane road rehabilitation in Fiji, where the cost was estimated at $2 million per kilometer; compared to an estimate of $500,000 per kilometer in rural Australia.

continued on next page

development banks, and other financial institutions (for example, the India Infrastructure Finance Company in India and the China Development Bank in the PRC, among others)—and ODA. Private sector infrastructure finance primarily rests on user fees—the revenue stream that supports financing through either equity (for example, public or private equity)

or debt (for example, borrowing from commercial banks or by issuing bonds). Private financing can be domestic or foreign. Moreover, public and private finance can be combined to deliver infrastructure services—such as public-private partnership (PPP) infrastructure projects.

Box 5.2: Infrastructure Investment Needs in the Pacific *(continued)*

Box figure 5.2.1: Road Density and Pavement Conditions in the Pacific

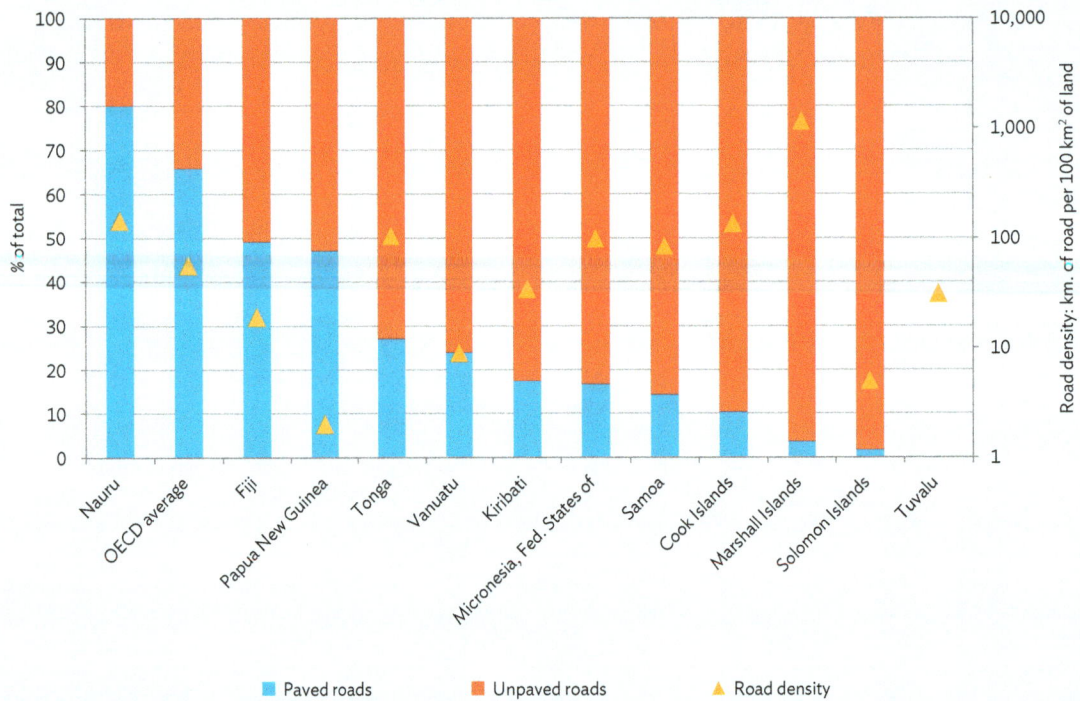

■ Paved roads   ■ Unpaved roads   ▲ Road density

km = kilometer; OECD = Organisation for Economic Co-operation and Development; km² = square kilometer.
Note: OECD average for percentage of paved and unpaved roads excludes Czech Republic, Germany, Greece, Japan, Latvia, Netherlands, Norway, Portugal, Spain, Turkey, and United States.
Source: Pacific Region Infrastructure Facility (2016 and 2017); World Development Indicators, World Bank.

Box figure 5.2.2: Utilities in the Pacific versus OECD

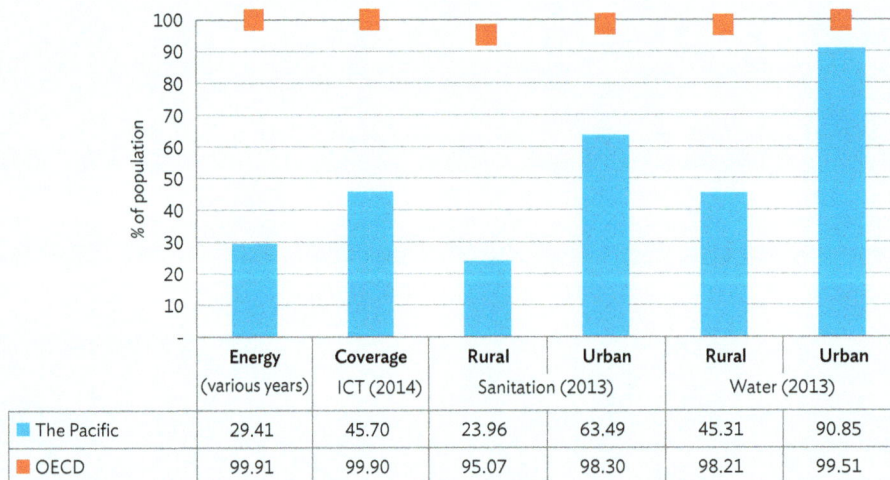

	Energy (various years)	Coverage ICT (2014)	Rural Sanitation (2013)	Urban Sanitation (2013)	Rural Water (2013)	Urban Water (2013)
■ The Pacific	29.41	45.70	23.96	63.49	45.31	90.85
■ OECD	99.91	99.90	95.07	98.30	98.21	99.51

ICT = information and communication technology; OECD = Organisation for Economic Co-operation and Development.
Note: ICT refers to percent of population with access to 3G Mobile Network; OECD data for ICT is Japan only; ICT, sanitation and water do not include Cook Islands as data unavailable; year coverage for energy: 2009: Fiji, Solomon Islands, Vanuatu; 2010: Federated States of Micronesia (FSM), Kiribati, Papua New Guinea (PNG); 2011: Nauru, Marshall Islands, Samoa, Solomon Islands, Tonga; 2012: Palau, Tuvalu; the Pacific island countries included in energy: Fiji, Solomon Islands, Vanuatu, FSM, Kiribati, PNG, Cook Islands, Nauru, Marshall Islands, Samoa, Solomon Islands, Tonga, Palau and Tuvalu; the Pacific island countries included in ICT: Fiji, FSM, Kiribati, PNG, Samoa, Solomon Islands, Tonga and Vanuatu; the Pacific island countries included in sanitation: Fiji, FSM, Kiribati, Nauru, Palau, PNG, Marshall Islands, Samoa, Solomon Islands, Tonga, Tuvalu and Vanuatu; the Pacific island countries included in water: Fiji, FSM, Kiribati, Nauru, Palau, PNG, Marshall Islands, Samoa, Solomon Islands, Tonga, Tuvalu and Vanuatu.
Source: Pacific Region Infrastructure Facility (2016 and 2017); World Development Indicators, World Bank; Global SDG Indicators Database, United Nations.

Figure 5.1: Key Sources of Infrastructure Finance

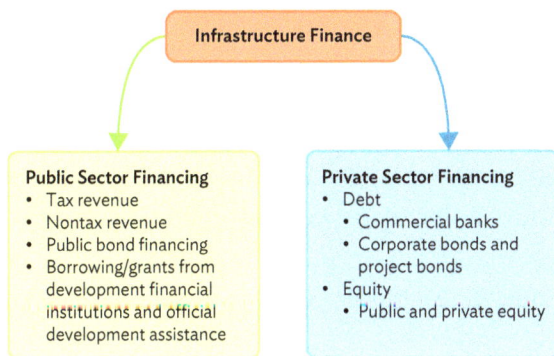

Infrastructure Finance

Public Sector Financing
- Tax revenue
- Nontax revenue
- Public bond financing
- Borrowing/grants from development financial institutions and official development assistance

Private Sector Financing
- Debt
  - Commercial banks
  - Corporate bonds and project bonds
- Equity
  - Public and private equity

Source: ADB staff conceptualization.

Figure 5.2: Public and Private Infrastructure Investment, Selected Economies, 2010–2014
(% of GDP)

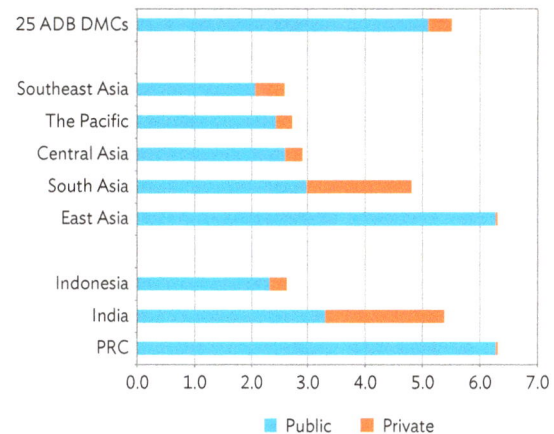

DMC = developing member country; GDP = gross domestic product; GFCF = gross fixed capital formation; PRC = People's Republic of China.
Note: Numbers are based on 25 selected DMCs listed in Appendix 3.1.
Source: ADB (2016a); Country sources; Investment and Capital Stock Dataset, 1960–2015, IMF; Private Participation in Infrastructure Database, World Bank; World Bank (2015a and 2015b); World Development Indicators, World Bank; ADB estimates.

5.2. Scaling up public infrastructure investment in developing Asia: How much room is there?

The public sector provides over 90% of the region's overall infrastructure investment.[56] This amounts to 5.1% of GDP annually, far above the 0.4% of GDP coming from the private sector. Moreover, public infrastructure investment rates vary widely across subregions and economies (Figure 5.2; also see Figure 3.3). On one hand, infrastructure investment in East Asia is dominated by the public sector. On the other, public sector infrastructure investment is not as dominant in South Asia, with the private sector accounting for a considerable portion of investments. In between are Southeast Asia, the Pacific, and Central Asia, where public sector shares in infrastructure investment are smaller than in East Asia but larger than in South Asia.

Given the region's large infrastructure needs and the public sector dominance in providing infrastructure, it is critical that policy makers evaluate

how much room they have to increase infrastructure investment. A three-pronged approach can be used to assess fiscal space for infrastructure.[57] First, policy makers need to find out how much they can reasonably increase government revenues through taxation and other reforms. Second, depending on spending priorities, there may be room to reorient public spending toward infrastructure—for example by reducing certain types of current expenditures or poorly targeted subsidies. Third, policy makers must determine how much they can borrow while keeping public debt sustainable. The assessments cited here draw on the most recent country staff reports from the International Monetary Fund (IMF), which provide both IMF and government views on fiscal

---

56 Public infrastructure investment here is defined as infrastructure investment undertaken by the general government (consolidated national and subnational government) and state-owned enterprises (SOEs). Due to data restrictions, in several DMCs only the component of SOE investment financed by government transfers can be covered, except in India, Indonesia and the PRC, where data cover all SOE infrastructure investment.

57 Heller (2005) defines fiscal space as "room in a government's budget that allows it to provide resources for a desired purpose without jeopardizing the sustainability of its financial position or the stability of the economy." He notes that fiscal space can be generated by reprioritizing expenditures, raising revenues, increasing borrowing (with an eye to ensuring sustainability), and boosting efficiency. Here we focus only on the first three, as these are more amenable to quantification. Improvements in public investment efficiency are discussed in greater detail in Section 5.5.

policy and debt sustainability.[58] The analysis here is restricted to the 25 ADB DMCs for which the necessary information is available—these countries account for 96% of the region's total population.[59]

Most economies in the region can sustainably increase revenues through changes in tax policy, improving tax administration, or a combination of the two. In most economies, specific policies have already been identified and their impact on revenues quantified. In the Philippines, for example, the IMF and World Bank have estimated that tax reform (including rationalization of tax incentives and reducing value-added tax or VAT exemptions) along with improving tax administration can yield an estimated 2%–3% of GDP in additional revenue. This is in line with the government's own estimates. In Sri Lanka, simplifying the tax system and broadening the tax base can generate 2.9% of GDP in additional revenue. Overall, IMF estimates suggest that 22 of the 25 developing Asian economies analyzed could sustainably increase revenues via policy reform (Appendix 5.1).

Reorienting other budget expenditures toward public investment can also increase resources for infrastructure. Energy subsidies are one major source. They remain large in some countries, particularly in Central Asia. Studies show subsidies are often poorly targeted, with most benefits accruing to the wealthiest households. They also lead to energy overconsumption which harms the environment. Reforms of loss-making SOEs are another possibility. In addition, some budgets in the region have excessively large public sector wage bills. IMF estimates suggest at least 14 developing Asian economies could reorient expenditures toward public investment (see Appendix 5.1).

Finally, any discussion of fiscal space must deal with public borrowing capacity and debt sustainability. High debt makes public finance and the broader economy vulnerable to growth and interest rate shocks. Debt servicing costs would consume a large share of government expenditures, restricting other priority spending. High public debt can also hurt the private sector, as the prospect of tax hikes or cutbacks in government spending to service debt can dampen investor sentiment and economic activity. Increased government borrowing can also crowd out private investment.

Debt sustainability analysis helps assess how much spending can increase while keeping debt levels manageable. For a given set of macroeconomic assumptions, one can compute the primary balance— fiscal balance excluding interest payments—that will stabilize or raise public debt. Stabilizing public debt may not make sense in all cases—where those with low debt burdens could allow an increase to provide more room for priority spending. In the following analysis, for economies with public debt greater than 50% the target is to stabilize public debt at current levels.[60] On the other hand, "low" debt economies— with public debt below 50% of GDP—can raise public debt toward the 50% of GDP threshold over a decade.

The fundamental point for developing Asia is that—considering revenue and expenditure measures along with debt sustainability—regional economies have some fiscal space to increase infrastructure investment (Figure 5.3).[61] Looking at individual

---

58 The IMF regularly monitors member economies, including all ADB DMCs, and holds consultations with authorities to assess developments and discuss economic and financial policies with government and central bank officials—as required under Article IV of the IMF Articles of Agreement. Most resulting Article IV country reports are posted on the IMF website, and provide the views of IMF staff as well as of the authorities.

59 For most economies, raising public infrastructure investment is explicitly mentioned as a fiscal priority (see Appendix 5.1, Appendix table 5.1).

60 The 50% threshold is the lower bound of the range IMF estimates as the long run debt level for developing economies, i.e. the level where the public debt to GDP ratio converges over the long run.

61 19 of the 25 DMCs in this analysis have at least 2% of GDP in fiscal space. Abiad, Ablaza, and Feliciano (forthcoming) provides a detailed discussion of fiscal space on individual economies.

Figure 5.3: Fiscal Space in Developing Asia
(% of GDP)

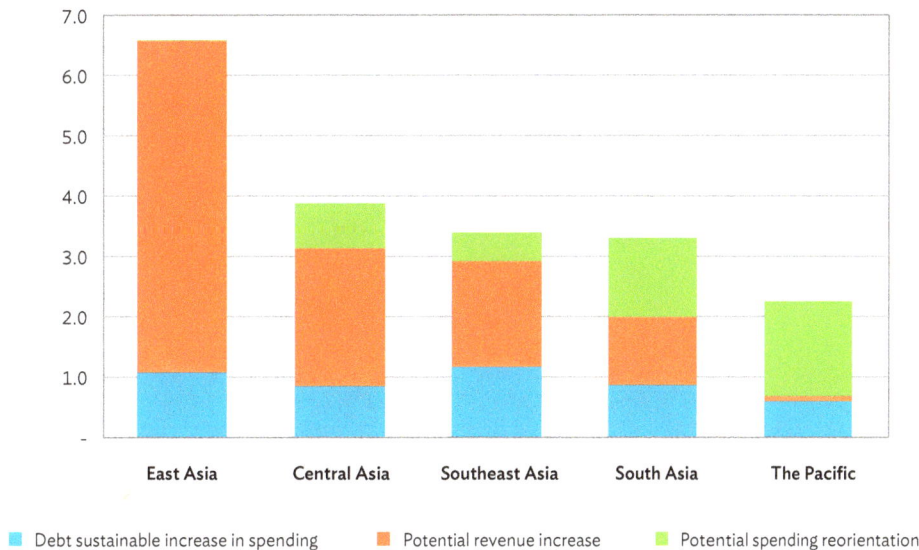

Source: ADB estimates; International Monetary Fund (2017).

countries, some economies have more potential fiscal space than others. In Afghanistan, for example, this arises from its potential to raise revenues from its current low base, and low post-debt relief levels.[62] In the Marshall Islands, fiscal space comes mainly from reorienting spending (reducing government current expenditures, SOE subsidies, and landowner utility transfers)—generating savings equivalent to 3.5% of GDP. At the other extreme are countries like the Maldives, where public debt and deficit levels are high and where spending would need to be reduced to keep public debt from rising rapidly.

This analysis has focused on the quantifiable aspects of fiscal space for infrastructure investment, but several other important (but less quantifiable) factors will also shape policy makers' public infrastructure investment decisions. First,

governments will often have other pressing priorities, like health and education expenditures, which will compete for available fiscal space of governments. Second, contingent liabilities—emanating from the financial sector or disaster risk, for example—are often difficult to quantify and can reduce available fiscal space. Third, governments can squeeze more out of each investment dollar by improving the efficiency of the public investment process. This issue is discussed in greater detail in Section 5.5.

Finally, there is much scope for governments in the region to increase infrastructure-related revenues. These include user fees that governments can charge for infrastructure services, which are more common for some types of infrastructure such as piped water, energy, and highways but where prices are often set below cost recovery (Box 5.3).

---

62   However, a debt-financed increase in infrastructure investment carries risks in Afghanistan, given the heavy reliance on public finance for large grants and the uncertainty regarding the magnitudes of future grants.

Box 5.3: User Charges

User fees are payments for the use of publicly provided goods and services. They influence consumers to use resources efficiently by putting a price on environmental and social externalities. User fees also play a vital role in infrastructure, in which they fund the operations and maintenance (O&M) of assets as well as the full or partial cost of capital. Nevertheless, there are several drawbacks to imposing charges on users. The biggest concern is that they limit access, particularly for those who cannot afford to pay. User fees may also be politically difficult to implement, particularly for services with large spillover benefits, such as water and sanitation. In some cases, the administrative and social costs of collecting such fees exceed the revenues that they generate.

User fees vary significantly across sectors and countries. They are generally more common for energy, piped water, and highways —sectors where access can be restricted to those who pay. Even within certain sectors, such as public utilities, the level of user fees varies per country. For instance, tariffs in most high income countries cover not just the O&M costs of infrastructure, but also part of the capital. In contrast, user fees in many low income countries do not sufficiently cover the costs of operation and maintenance (Box figure 5.3).

User fees in developing Asia are generally low particularly for public utilities. In regions such as South Asia, water tariffs are often insufficient to cover even O&M costs. Low prices have resulted in the overconsumption of scarce resources by users. At the same time, they have generated financial losses for operators and led to poor maintenance and underinvestment. Consequently, governments have had to subsidize enterprises to sustain operations and ensure that basic services are being provided.

There is substantial scope to increase user fees while protecting vulnerable groups. This can be achieved in a number of ways. One is through the use of block pricing or "lifeline tariffs", which gives poor households access to a minimum level of basic services at an affordable price. Differentiated service levels are another way of improving access while maintaining the financial viability of enterprises. In the Philippines, the *"Tubig Para Sa Barangay"* program pioneered by Manila Water offers bulk connection schemes tailored for low income groups. Another possible approach is through cross-subsidization between different types of users. In the People's Republic of China (PRC) and other developing countries for instance, the higher electricity rates imposed on industrial and/or commercial users serve as subsidies for residential consumers who benefit from lower rates.

Box figure 5.3: Level of Cost Recovery
(%)

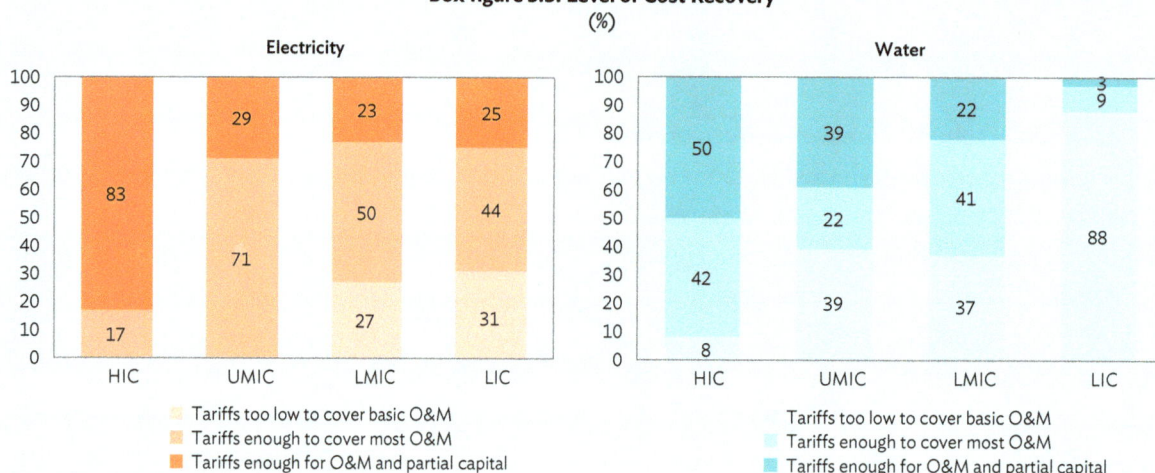

*HIC–High income countries, UMIC–Upper middle income countries, LMIC–Lower middle income countries, LIC–Low income countries
Source: World Economic Forum (2014).

Another infrastructure-related revenue stream—one underutilized by many countries as a means of financing infrastructure—is land value capture, a method by which the increase in property or land value due to public infrastructure improvements is captured through land-related taxes or other means to pay for the improvements (Batt 2001). Essentially, it enables increases in private real estate value generated by public investments to flow to the public sector.[63]

---

63 It has a number of features that complement other sources of financing. For one, most value capture instruments provide revenues upfront, thereby reducing the need for debt financing. Value capture can also aid the borrowing process, as the subsequent gains in land value can be used by subnational governments or enterprises as collateral for loans. This flexibility is particularly important for developing countries, where it is generally difficult to raise funds for infrastructure. Nevertheless, value capture has its own risks. For instance, the volatility of real estate prices could make financing unstable, especially when value capture is used as a major source of long-term funding (Peterson 2008).

Figure 5.4: Meeting the Investment Gaps: Selected ADB Developing Member Countries *, 2016–2020
(annual averages, $ billion in 2015 prices)

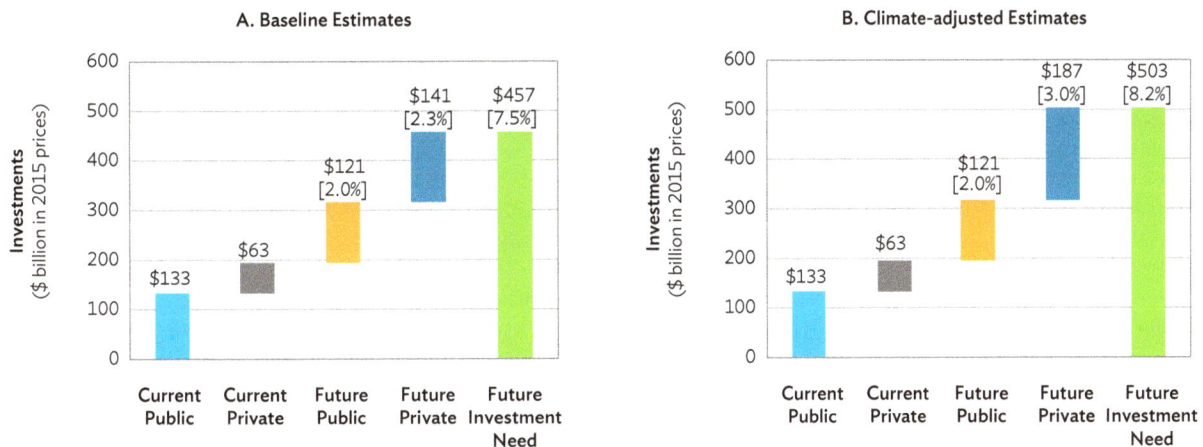

A. Baseline Estimates

B. Climate-adjusted Estimates

* Developing member countries include the 25 DMCs listed in Annex Table 2 minus the People's Republic of China; future public investments
  are based on the 50% fiscal space assumption.
  Numbers in brackets indicate percentage of GDP.
Note: Numbers may not add up due to rounding.
Source: ADB (2016a); Country sources; Investment and Capital Stock Dataset, 1960–2015, IMF; Private Participation in Infrastructure Database,
           World Bank; World Bank (2015a and 2015b); World Development Indicators, World Bank; ADB estimates.

Value capture works best for specific types of projects. In general, it produces the highest return in areas that are undergoing rapid urban growth. Development drives up land prices, creating an ideal opportunity to raise significant revenues. While value capture can be applied to a wide range of sectors, it is most appropriate for three project types: (i) new land development; (ii) major capital projects, particularly in transportation; and (iii) infrastructure that supports basic services such as water supply, wastewater treatment, and drainage. The benefits arising from these projects contribute directly to raising the value of the surrounding land, making value capture ideal (Peterson 2008).

There are many instruments through which land value can be captured.[64] The experiences of Japan, the Republic of Korea, and the PRC offer successful models of land value capture using various instruments (Box 5.4).

5.3.   How much private sector financing of infrastructure is required?

The analysis of fiscal space is a useful starting point for assessing how much private financing is needed to meet developing Asia's infrastructure needs. Significantly, the answer depends crucially on the range of actions the public sector is willing to take.

Figure 5.4 presents (i) current infrastructure financing broken down between public and private finance (captured by the two bars on the left); (ii) infrastructure needs (captured by the rightmost bar); and (iii) a breakdown of future public and private financing that together bridge the infrastructure investment gap (the remaining bars in the middle).[65]

---

64   These can be categorized into two main groups (Appendix 5.2). The first consists of instruments that generate one-time lump sum payments, such as betterment taxes, negotiated exactions, land sales, and development impact fees. The second provides ongoing sources of revenue for governments (Peterson 2008). Among the more popular instruments in this category are tax increment financing, land leases, and air rights. The choice of value capture instrument varies by country and project type. In developing countries, land sales and long-term leases are more common, given the difficulty in raising taxes, issuing debt, and increasing user fees.

65   The categorization of SOEs is a complex issue—some are commercially viable and are run like private firms, while others are loss-making and rely on government support—and data on SOE infrastructure investment is often incomplete. Infrastructure investment by the general government can often be identified using budget data, while infrastructure investment with at least 20% private participation is recorded in the World Bank's PPI Database. But the investment by firms that are largely or fully state-owned may not be captured in either budget data (except for investment funded by government transfers) or the PPI Database. In Figure 5.4, on current public investment, to the extent that infrastructure investments by SOEs are funded through the government budget and recorded there, or data on SOEs are fully available —as is the case in of the PRC, India, and Indonesia—these will be counted as public sector investments. On financing future investment needs, infrastructure investments by SOEs and funded through the government budget will be captured by the future public spending. Otherwise, future infrastructure investments by SOEs would be captured as part of future private financing.

Box 5.4: Land Value Capture

The benefits of infrastructure investment, particularly urban infrastructure, help increase land values. It aids financing new or improved infrastructure by using projected property values and the potential for developers to profit from associated commercial or residential land use. Land value capture allows governments to use some of the expected property appreciation to help pay for infrastructure—whether urban highways, public rail transport or even power and water infrastructure.

Landowning regimes differ across economies and even between cities. But governments use a variety of land-based financing techniques to support new corridor links, urban growth, or ease decongestion from overused or obsolete infrastructure.

Land acquisition models involve governments acquiring land and the associated user rights. It then sells, leases, or trades some of the land to finance projects. It can build the infrastructure itself and then impose taxes, fees or user charges on beneficiaries to cover the investment. It can also bid out projects to the private sector to build and operate the infrastructure under various schemes, or it can allow developers to lease the surrounding land for commercial or residential purposes. Here we summarize how Japan, the Republic of Korea, and the People's Republic of China (PRC) frequently use land value capture to help finance infrastructure.

Japan[a]

Financing urban infrastructure in Japan frequently benefits from increased land values on development properties. Governments and infrastructure development agencies frequently incorporate gains from these increased land values into the project cost of the new infrastructure.

Railways have typically captured the gains from rising land values. For example, Tokyu Cooperation—a major private railway operator running 105 kilometers of rail lines in the Greater Tokyo Area—is well known for combining real estate and railway development. The company carries out land readjustment projects along rail lines in collaboration with the local government. It receives the land reserved for property development, internally allocating the capital gains from real estate development as railway finance. As part of the land readjustment project, landowners willingly contribute a portion of their land because they know its value will rise once the infrastructure is in place. This type of real estate development accounted for 34% of Tokyu's net income for fiscal years 2003–2012, against about 41% generated from transport fees.

Social infrastructure—such as government buildings—can also be financed by capturing land value, particularly where cities are growing rapidly. Tokyo's Toshima Ward Government mixed-use skyscraper was financed from the 70-year upfront leasing fees received from private developers leasing the land where the old building stood. This completely offset the fiscal costs the Ward Government initially expected for the project. The government modified zoning codes and revised its maximum floor area ratio from 3.0 to 8.0, which enabled the new structure to mix revenue-generating commercial and residential floors.

Urban land-capture financing for infrastructure development can work so long as (i) the population and economy in the area are growing rapidly; (ii) project stakeholders' are clearly committed to long-term property management; and (iii) there is sufficient regulatory flexibility on issues such as zoning codes and floor area ratios. Combined with other financial resources, land capture can be an important component of large urban infrastructure financing packages.

The Republic of Korea[b]

Rapid economic development drove urban migration in the 1970s and 1980s, creating a serious housing shortage in Seoul. To reduce congestion, the government planned four new urban "districts" in Gyeonggi province in the early 1990s. The land use for the four new cities was changed from agriculture or forestry to housing or commerce. Consequently, land prices sharply rose with some of the increase captured by the developer—the Korea Land and Housing Corporation (KLHC).

KLHC financed most of the new transport infrastructure, constructing new suburban railways and expressways between Seoul and Bundang, Ilsan, and Pyeongchon. The land value captured reached nearly W3.0 trillion (Box table 5.4.1). After construction, companies bought some of the newly developed land for housing or commercial buildings. Thus, the land value capture was ultimately paid by consumers. However, as housing or building prices had by then increased substantially, users also benefited from appreciated values.

Box table 5.4.1: Land Value Capture in Four New Cities in the Early 1990s			
	Planned Area (million m²)	Planned Population ('000s)	Value Capture (W billion)
Bundang	19.7	390	1,310
Ilsan	15.7	276	927
Pyeongchon	5.2	170	415
Jungdong	5.4	170	330
Total	46.0	1,006	2,982

m² = square meter; W = Korean won.
Source: Korea Research Institute for Human Settlement (1992).

---

a   Suzuki et al. (2015).
b   Shon (2016).

continued on next page

Box 5.4: Land Value Capture *(continued)*

The model continued for new cities and housing complexes into the 2000s, particularly following a 1997 law which stipulates that appropriate land values must be captured for transport infrastructure for new developments over one million square meters or with a planned population of over 20,000. As a result, from 2001 to 2008, 38 land development projects were built in Gyeonggi with significant land capture finance (Box table 5.4.2). The average land value capture per project was around W608 billion (21.5%) of the average W2,826 billion project cost.

The People's Republic of China (PRC)

Since the 1990s, land capture has raised massive revenues for local governments as critical finance for rapid urban infrastructure development.

In most cases, land capture in the PRC involves (i) land transfer fees (LTFs)—lump-sum payments by industrial developers for leasing land (primarily through open bids for 40–70 years)—and (ii) local government borrowing using LTFs as collateral. In the PRC, urban land is owned by the state with rural land collectively owned by villages. So local governments have the power to convert rural land to urban use or redesignate urban land use. Local governments can obtain large tracts of rural land, supply infrastructure, and then lease user rights to real estate developers. Farmers are often compensated based on the land's agricultural production rather than commercial market value, allowing governments to earn premiums—given the high bids paid by developers (Liu 2015). Local governments can also acquire existing, already improved urban land to consolidate, redesignate and then strategically market the land when demand is high. The PRC's 2005–2011 property boom significantly boosted revenues from these transactions (Fung 2016).

In the past decade, over one-third of local fiscal revenue came from LTFs—growing from about 10% in the early 2000s to some 60% by 2013 (Jizao 2015). LTFs have become the predominant source of urban infrastructure finance since 2005 (Zhao 2014). In 2014, they covered some 60% of urban infrastructure operating and maintenance costs and about 14% of urban infrastructure capital outlays (Box table 5.4.3). LTFs as a share of capital outlays have fallen as the PRC urban infrastructure investment relies heavily on borrowing, through (i) allocating central government bond proceeds and (ii) innovative local government borrowing—such as *Chengtou* loans and *Chengtou* bonds (Zhao and Cao 2011).

Box table 5.4.2: Land Value Capture in Gyeonggi Projects in the 2000s,
(W billion)

	Average Land Development Project Cost	Average Transportation Infrastructure Investment Cost		
		Land Value Capture	Other Financing Sources	Total
Southern Gyeonggi	2,984	634	527	1,161
Northern Gyeonggi	2,477	550	995	1,545
Gyeonggi province	2,826	608	673	1,281

Source: Gyeonggi Province (2009).

continued on next page

Panel A pertains to the baseline estimates on infrastructure needs, while Panel B takes into account the additional infrastructure needs arising from climate change. As with the fiscal space analysis, we focus on the 5 years from 2016–2020. Figure 5.4 omits the PRC due to its very large size. Including it would drive the numbers to an inordinate degree; moreover, the PRC has done an excellent job of finding the resources to invest in infrastructure and is expected to continue to do so.

On the assumption that the public sector of the included DMCs are willing to undertake the public finance reforms outlined in Section 5.2, and that 50% of the extra fiscal space generated through those reforms is used for infrastructure,

public finance for infrastructure should expand by the amount represented by the third bar (from the left).[66] Future financing by the private sector thus emerges as a residual—the difference between future infrastructure investment needs and what the public sector will be able to provide.

Under these assumptions, $254 billion will be available from the public sector. This would leave $204 billion to $250 billion for private sector financing, depending on whether the baseline estimates is considered or climate change-related needs are included. Given that the private sector

---

66 This amount is over and above the extra expenditure on infrastructure made possible by economic growth, which is captured here by using the current ratio of public infrastructure to GDP.

Box 5.4: Land Value Capture *(continued)*

Chengtou loans and bonds are issued using land assets as collateral to boost local governments financing capacity (Liu 2015). Prior to 2014, budget law forbade local government borrowing. Most local governments, however, circumvented the restriction by creating specific financing vehicles called "Urban Development and Investment Companies" (or *Chengtou*). These could borrow commercially or issue corporate bonds on behalf of the local government. Given market flexibility and the implicit guarantee of the central government, *Chengtou* borrowing grew rapidly to finance urban infrastructure development. Annual *Chengtou* bond issuance, for example, increased some 50 times from 2005 to 2014 (Box figure 5.4). Total *Chengtou* bonds outstanding reached CNY5 trillion by December 2014—or about 8% of GDP (Ang, Bail, and Zhou 2015). These bonds were mainly used for infrastructure investment, but also for repaying *Chengtou* loans or supplementing local government operations (see China Bond Rating 2015).

This allowed the PRC to raise huge sums for urban infrastructure development. Yet the heavy reliance on LTFs and *Chengtou* borrowing has also raised concerns (Zhao 2014), where rural land conversion for urban use exceeded real demand, leaving local governments heavily indebted (Agence France-Presse 2016). To address these concerns, the PRC is experimenting with annual property tax systems as pilot programs in several cities (The Wall Street Journal 2014). It is also using asset securitization to further develop municipal bond markets (Cao 2016). And it is encouraging public-private partnerships to attract more private capital to public infrastructure and services (International Institute for Sustainable Development 2015).

Box table 5.4.3: Land Transfer Fees and Urban Infrastructure Spending in the People's Republic of China, 2014

	Capital	Operation and Maintenance	Total
Urban Infrastructure Spending (CNY billion)	1,510.0	1,289.2	2,799.2
Urban Infrastructure Spending/gross domestic product	2.4%	2.0%	4.4%
Land Transfer Fee (CNY billion)	206.8	745.2	951.9
Land Transfer Fee/gross domestic product	0.3%	1.2%	1.5%
Land Transfer Fee/Urban Infrastructure Spending	13.7%	57.8%	34.0%

Source: China Statistical Yearbook 2011–2015, National Bureau of Statistics; China Urban Construction Statistical Yearbook, Ministry of Housing and Urban-Rural Development, People's Republic of China.

Box figure 5.4: Chengtou Bond Issuance (1997–2014)

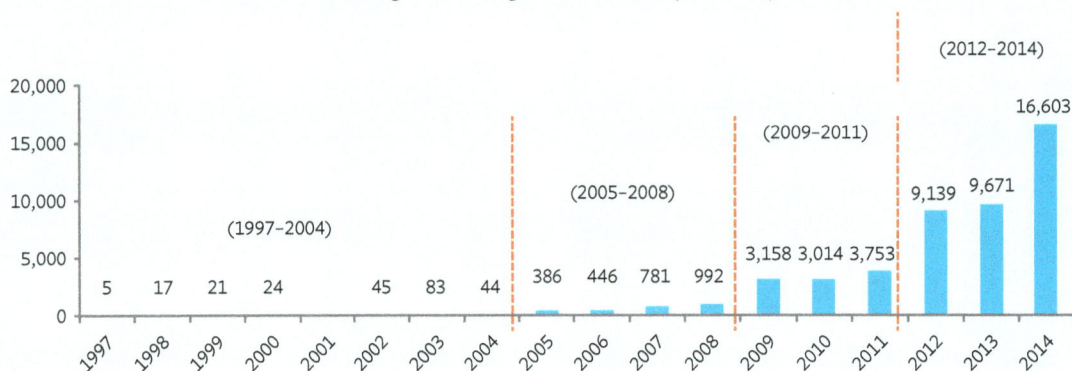

Source: Wind, Shenyin Wangguo Securities—translated from Chen 2015.

has only invested around $63 billion in recent years (the second bar on the left), the sums required are quite large. Moreover, they dwarf the finance that the MDBs have been providing or can reasonably be expected to provide (Box 5.5).

Whether or not the private sector can deliver these levels of finance depends crucially on the actions that the public sector takes to encourage greater private participation and finance in

infrastructure, something we consider next. However, there are also several actions the public sector could take to both expand funds available for financing infrastructure development and to use infrastructure expenditures more effectively. To expand funds available, increasing infrastructure-related revenues need to be considered seriously—these include more economically rational user charges, land value capture, and capital recycling (selling of brownfield assets or operating concessions and using proceeds to

Box 5.5: Multilateral Development Banks and Infrastructure Finance

Multilateral development banks (MDBs) are an important source of infrastructure financing in developing economies. Although small in scale relative to total infrastructure investment needs (Bhattacharya, Oppenheim, and Stern 2015), they provide additional value by attracting private sector investment by "improving project design and structure" and lowering transaction costs, risk and risk perception, promoting policy and institutional reforms and providing knowledge solutions (G20 2016).

MDB operations in Asia are led by ADB and the World Bank. For 2015, ADB's sovereign and nonsovereign approvals in the four major infrastructure sectors covered in this report totaled $10 billion (ADB 2015c). The World Bank Group committed about $10 billion to the same group of countries, of which $3 billion went to the private sector through the International Finance Corporation (IFC) (World Bank 2015c; IFC 2015). The Islamic Development Bank (IDB) Group approved almost $3 billion in Asian infrastructure (Country Approval, Islamic Development Bank).[a]

For 2015, these MDBs together supported about 2.5% of developing Asia's infrastructure investment.[b] However, the share rises dramatically to more than 10% if both the PRC and India are excluded.[c]

Two new MDBs with significant focus on Asia have recently been established and have just begun operations—the Asian Infrastructure Investment Bank (AIIB) and the New Development Bank (NDB). In 2016, AIIB lent a total of $1.7 billion, with around $1.2 billion going to Asian infrastructure (AIIB 2016a). AIIB and ADB cofinanced new road projects in Pakistan, each extending $100 million (AIIB 2016b; ADB 2016g); and they closed a $227 million lending package to finance natural gas production in Bangladesh—with ADB contributing $167 million (ADB 2016h). In 2016, NDB approved seven investment projects worth $1.5 billion in Brazil, the Russian Federation, India, the People's Republic of China (PRC), and South Africa (Fact Sheet, NDB). Close to $1 billion went to the PRC and India for four energy infrastructure projects (New Development Bank 2017).

As to the future, one can expect MDB support for Asian infrastructure to grow. Being newcomers, the AIIB and NDB are likely to expand their scale of operations over the next few years.[d] As for ADB, the merger of ADB's Asian Development Fund (ADF) lending operations with the Ordinary Capital Resources (OCR) balance sheet, effective 1 January 2017, will allow ADB to strengthen its financing capacity and scale up annual loan and grant approvals from $14 billion in 2014 to more than $20 billion by 2020. With this, ADB also plans to allot 70% of operations to infrastructure (ADB 2016j).[e]

A growing proportion of MDB finance is expected to be for the private sector. For ADB, nonsovereign operations—which mainly comprise private sector operations—are projected to grow from an average of 17% of nonconcessional approvals over 2012-2014 to 22% by 2019 (ADB 2016k). The World Bank Group will also likely increase private sector infrastructure lending, with IFC infrastructure lending growing by 5% to 10% annually.[f]

---

a   The figure for ADB covers its DMCs, which also account for the majority of lending by the World Bank Group. Figures for IDB include approvals to Afghanistan, Azerbaijan, Bangladesh, Brunei Darussalam, Indonesia, Kazakhstan, the Kyrgyz Republic, Maldives, Pakistan, Tajikistan, and Uzbekistan.

b   The estimated 2.5% is based on the estimates for ADB ($10 billion), World Bank ($6.6 billion), International Finance Corporation ($3.2 billion), and Islamic Development Bank ($2.7 billion) and uses total current investment for DMCs that borrow from MDBs. Except for the PRC, India, and Indonesia where BUDGET+PPI is used, current investments are estimated based on GFCF(GG)+PPI. If this information is not available, GFCF(CE), BUDGET+PPI, or subregional averages are used in its place to get a conservative share of MDB to infrastructure investment.

c   The World Bank's infrastructure lending to the PRC and India is derived by multiplying country-specific total lending by their respective subregional infrastructure share of total lending. IFC total lending to the PRC and India in 2015 is calculated by subtracting the cumulative gross commitments in 2014 from that in 2015.

d   AIIB total lending scale could rise from the current level of $1.7 billion to $3.5 billion in 2018, and NDB's total lending could increase from the current level of $1.5 billion to $5 billion by 2018 (G20 2016).

e   Since the 1960s, ADB operations have been funded by two distinct sources—Ordinary Capital Resources (OCR) and the Asian Development Fund (ADF). The main source of funding for ADF is donor contributions and transfers from OCR. Funds for OCR are raised by issuing bonds based on the subscribed capital of ADB members. Using these funds, ADB provides loans after adding a spread to cover administrative costs. OCR proceeds are then lent to borrowers at ADB's funding cost plus certain loan charges. Earnings net of administrative costs are partially retained and the rest is transferred to ADF and other special funds, which provide grants and long-term concessional loans to low income countries. Merging the OCR and ADF not only increases capital that can be used for grants and concessional loans, but also provides greater leverage for future bond issuance.

f   IFC's growth rate is based on the *MDBs Joint Declaration of Aspirations on Actions to Support Infrastructure Investment* as reported to the G20.

---

finance greenfield infrastructure investment).[67] The more effective use of infrastructure expenditures is discussed further in Section 5.5.

---

67   At the same time, it must be noted that in the analysis of fiscal space, to the extent that unquantified contingent liabilities are ultimately realized, fiscal space will be smaller, and thus private infrastructure finance needs will be higher.

Financing climate change-related needs is also a serious challenge. As noted in Section 4, factoring in climate mitigation and adaptation (through climate proofing) adds around $241 billion annually to developing Asia's infrastructure investment needs through 2030. Several issues should be considered regarding climate-related finance. There are various estimates of recent global financial flows that address climate change mitigation and adaptation from both public and private sources. The latest report from the Climate Policy Initiative, covering climate change financing in 2014, documents roughly $390 billion in climate change-related financial flows globally, covering both mitigation and adaptation. Of this, around $271 billion targeted private sector investments, the majority for renewable energy. About $25 billion came almost exclusively from public sources for climate change adaptation—emphasizing water and wastewater management, and to a lesser extent energy and other infrastructure (Buchner et al. 2015). However, these financial flows remain well below estimated adaptation funding needs. For Asia and the Pacific alone, adaptation funding needs have been estimated at approximately $40 billion per year over 2010–2050 (World Bank 2010). United Nations Environment Programme (2014) reported that adaptation funding needs (along with the funding gap) could be in fact three to four times higher than previous estimates suggest.

MDBs are important sources of targeted climate change finance. In 2012, ADB joined other MDBs to develop a joint methodology to track climate change finance more consistently and transparently. MDBs have been reporting climate finance annually since 2011. These reports indicate modest growth, with mitigation finance—mostly investments in clean and renewable energy and low-carbon transport—increasing slightly from $19 billion in 2011 to over $20 billion in 2015. Adaptation finance, largely in water and wastewater systems, energy and transport infrastructure, increased from $4.5 billion in 2011 to over $5 billion in 2015. While these trends may show some improvement, it seems clear that growth in both mitigation and adaptation finance is not keeping up with needs. How to increase public and private financing for climate change is critical.

Most climate change mitigation investment in infrastructure involves energy. Private participation in energy infrastructure generally rises as economies develop. Also, with the right policies in place and lower component prices, low-carbon energy costs in many cases are already competitive with fossil fuels. There is much potential for increasing the private sector share of resources for mitigation. But this also requires replacing perverse incentives with supportive incentives, and effectively leveraging public resources.

Fossil fuel subsidies—widespread in Asia until recently—are the principal perverse incentive for greenhouse gas emissions. Subsidies encourage inefficient public energy use, reduce investment returns in demand side efficiency, and can make renewable energy uncompetitive. At the same time, they inherently lead to deadweight welfare losses. Subsidy reform can free resources for more productive use, while encouraging emissions reduction.

Pricing carbon and other environmental effects also increases low-carbon competitiveness while raising revenues for public investment (Box 5.6). Carbon pricing can be complemented by measures that help spread low-carbon technologies—such as setting energy efficiency standards, labeling for energy consuming products, and supporting research and pilot projects. Measures to induce power utilities to increase low-carbon generation include stipulating minimum renewable shares of power generation, stable feed-in tariffs for renewable power, standardized producer purchase agreements that reduce contracts with small renewable producers, and net metering for reverse grid sales from users with renewable generation capacity.

Low-carbon energy investments can often provide attractive returns to private investors. But they carry greater risk than conventional alternatives should governments reverse policies. Thus, the public sector should ensure stable conditions and offer financial instruments that reduce investor risk, such as political risk guarantees and equity stakes.

Box 5.6: Green Taxation

Green taxation is one way developing countries can increase public revenues to support their considerable infrastructure investment needs while helping curb environmental degradation.

Broadly defined, green taxation includes all taxes levied related to the environment—including those on energy products, motor vehicles, carbon emissions, wastewater discharge, garbage, and natural resources, among others (Organisation for Economic Co-operation and Development, 2010). The original purpose of these taxes is often to raise fiscal revenues, but they effectively counter the adverse effects those products or activities have on the environment and natural resources. Another reason to adopt green taxation is to substitute environmentally-related taxes for taxes on labor as a means to boost employment, much as Europe's policy makers did in the 1990s.

Today, green taxation is playing an increasingly prominent role in advanced economies. Environmentally related tax revenues reached an average 1.5% of GDP in OECD countries in 2014, with the Republic of Korea collecting the equivalent of 2.3% of GDP and Japan 1.5% (Box figure 5.6). The ratio is relatively low in Asia's developing countries where data are available—such as India (0.95%), Malaysia (0.24%), and the Philippines (0.21%). The People's Republic of China increased rates as well as coverage of its environmentally related taxes in recent years, thus pushing its green tax revenues up to 1.3% of GDP.

An alternative to green taxes is tradable emission permits—a market-based instrument that addresses environmental issues. Permits generate public revenues when auctioned to users. But tradable emission programs with auctioned permits are rare, so they do not add much to support infrastructure investment.

In sum, environmentally related taxes such as those on fuel are important revenue sources that could be further explored by Asia's developing economies. Moving from current taxation systems to green taxation would likely involve a long optimization process as authorities decide which tax bases to tap and what rates to apply, as well as their effect on the tax structure generally. However, many governments have begun the process and its impact will grow over time.

Box figure 5.6: Revenues from Environmentally Related Taxes, 2014
(% of GDP)

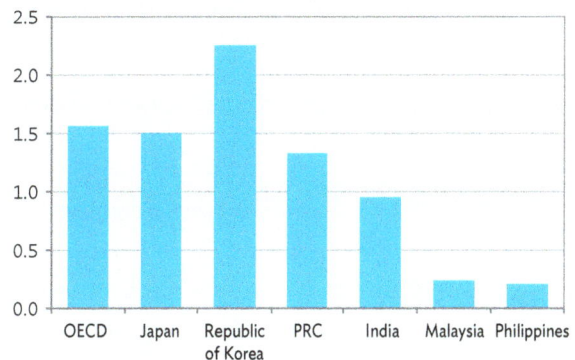

GDP = gross domestic product; OECD = Organisation for Economic Co-operation and Development; PRC = People's Republic of China.
Note: 2013 data for the Republic of Korea, Malaysia, and Philippines.
Source: International Development Statistics Online Databases, OECD.

5.4. Private participation in infrastructure: Some key issues[68]

There is large potential for attracting greater private participation in infrastructure.[69] Private investors benefit from infrastructure investment as it is a separate asset class, providing benefits through portfolio diversification. These stem from the economic characteristics of infrastructure, which often include high entry barriers, economies of scale (leading to high fixed and low variable costs), inelastic demand for services, high operating margins, and long maturities (for example, 25-year concessions or 99-year leases). The value proposition of these investments includes attractive returns, low sensitivity to swings in the broader economy (manifested through low correlation of returns with other asset classes), and stable and predictable long-term cash flows.[70]

68 This section draws on various materials, including Rao (2015).

69 Participation comes in several forms. For example, the private sector may participate by building and operating an infrastructure asset. Alternatively, private investors may finance infrastructure assets through, among others, (i) subscription to bonds issued by SOEs and/or privately owned special purpose vehicles (SPVs); and (ii) via equity investment.

70 According to Inderst (2010), time series data on performance of unlisted infrastructure funds in Australia over a 10-year period ending the second quarter of 2006 show the volatility of unlisted infrastructure (5.8%) is lower than listed asset classes but higher than bonds (4.3%) and property (1.5%). Not surprisingly, listed infrastructure shows both higher returns and risk than unlisted infrastructure assets, as financing agreements in unlisted deals allow investors to better capture key features such as lower sensitivity to economic and market swings. The Sharpe ratio for property assets is highest (3.67), while unlisted infrastructure (1.47) comes second, with stocks (0.67) and bonds (0.39) ranked lowest. This shows that, per unit of volatility, unlisted infrastructure assets provide better returns than listed stocks and bonds.

However, global experience has shown that for governments to substantially and sustainably catalyze private investment, an enabling environment that properly regulates PPPs to offer optimal value for money (VfM) solutions is a prerequisite. This in turn requires regulatory frameworks and institutions conducive to private investment—those governing procurement, design, delivery, and management of projects. It also requires financing and risk management instruments, including viability gap funds, to support project finance needs.

The importance of an enabling environment is indicated by the fact that a lack of funds per se does not seem to be the binding constraint on private investment in infrastructure. Of the estimated $50 trillion private capital managed globally by pension funds, sovereign wealth funds, insurance companies, and other institutional investors, only 0.8% has been allocated to infrastructure in recent years (The Economist 2014). Moreover, the Asia and the Pacific region is characterized by high savings. To channel available resources into infrastructure finance, an overall regulatory, legal, institutional, and financing framework that provides an effective risk allocation and risk transfer mechanism is needed to generate a pipeline of bankable projects—one that expands financial sources and instruments.

The regulatory and institutional framework for private participation

A limited pipeline of bankable projects is the proximate factor inhibiting greater private investment in infrastructure. For example, a country's development strategy may include creating a transport and economic corridor. Based on this goal, a set of projects can be identified—such as specific highways, railway corridors, and power generation and transmission lines—that require development or expansion. To become bankable, the projects should be formulated based on appropriate processes and due diligence from the prefeasibility study stage onward—including economic and financial analysis

of project costs and benefits, project structuring (for example, debt and equity requirements), specification of the procurement modality to be used (for example, build-operate-transfer [BOT] or build-own-operate-transfer), detailed project report preparation, environmental clearances, and approvals for land acquisition, among others. Developing a robust pipeline of bankable projects requires a regulatory and institutional framework that (i) specifies the types of procurement contract; (ii) ensures project identification and structuring appropriate for the specified procurement; (iii) includes a dispute resolution mechanism; (iv) contains streamlined processes for environmental and other regulatory permits for construction and operation; (v) defines costs and service levels; (vi) has defined bid parameters (for example, minimum viability gap requirements provided by the government); and (vii) has an independent tariff-setting authority.

The Philippines has been able to combine many of these elements (Box 5.7). Several other economies in the region are also undertaking reforms to encourage private participation (Economist Intelligence Unit 2014). India strengthened its policy framework by issuing a PPP toolkit, guidance papers, and enhanced selection procedures. Similarly, Indonesia, the PRC, Bangladesh, and Pakistan amended PPP policies to streamline procurement and bidding processes. Papua New Guinea, Thailand, and Viet Nam refined alternative dispute mechanisms by including mediation and arbitration procedures. Kazakhstan has established independent PPP units dedicated to providing project guidance and technical support—its Private-Public Partnership Center, established in 2008, has approved more than 30 projects worth $3 billion since its inception. Political support for PPPs has also increased, such as in the PRC, where the government has launched a policy agenda aimed at increasing the private sector's role in infrastructure.

While PPPs hold much promise, governments and policy makers should also be aware of the risks and potential liabilities. By nature, infrastructure

Box 5.7: Successfully Promoting Public-Private Partnerships in the Philippines

Conducive regulatory frameworks and effective institutions are essential for attracting private investment in infrastructure. While this is no easy task, they can develop with appropriate commitment and support—and in a relatively short period of time. A good example is the promotion of public-private partnerships (PPPs) in the Philippines. In the 2014 edition of the PPP Readiness Index for Asia and the Pacific, the Philippines was ranked among the developed group of countries in the study—it had been previously classified as an emerging country in 2011. The Philippines was among those improving the most and had the most-improved score on regulatory and institutional frameworks. It also scored among the leading countries 'for improved investment climate and financial facilities. The Philippines has one of the oldest build operate and transfer (BOT) policies in Asia and the Pacific, and introduced a new subnational regulatory framework. And it has used its increased capacity and transactional experience in recent years to promote capacity-building in emerging PPP markets within the region' (Ordinario 2015).

The Public-Private Partnership Center (PPPC) of the Philippines is the main driver of the PPP program. This central government agency was reorganized in 2010, mandated to help implement the national PPP program and designated projects. It is the central coordinating and monitoring agency for all PPP projects in the Philippines. PPPC assists and supports implementing agencies and departments on all aspects of project preparation: by (i) managing the country's project preparation facility; (ii) providing project advisory and facilitation services; and (iii) monitoring and empowering agencies through various capacity building activities. The government supports the PPPC's central institutional role

through policy circulars that (i) articulate the government's position and process for assessing value for money in PPP projects; (ii) appoint probity advisors for the procurement of PPP projects; (iii) appraise and select projects for PPP schemes; and (iv) use public funding to fill viability gaps in project proposals.

The government's commitment to introduce well-prepared projects is a key pillar to creating an enabling environment— as demonstrated through the establishment of the Project Development and Monitoring Facility (PDMF) in 2010. Managed by the PPPC, the PDMF is a revolving facility funded by the Philippine government, donor countries, and the Asian Development Bank (ADB) to provide high-quality resources and advisors to project preparation. The PDMF has a robust pipeline of viable and well-prepared PPP infrastructure projects. By end of September 2016, PDMF has supported 36 of the 53 projects in the PPP program, committing a total of nearly $56 million to help preparation costs. From PDMF-supported pipeline, more than $4.3 billion of private investment has been secured, through 11 PPP projects either operating or under construction across several sectors.

In addition to successfully attracting private investment, the PPPC was recently recognized globally, receiving "Best Central/Regional Government PPP Promoter", "Agency of the Year", and "Asia Pacific Grantor of the Year". These accolades to the PPPC also reflect the Philippines' commitment to develop and implement clear policies and the priority it gives PPPs in the government's national infrastructure agenda. This is important for any government that seriously seeks to engage and sustainably attract private investment for infrastructure.

---

projects carry a wide variety of risks—including project performance and completion risks, fuel and input risks, market risk, payment risk, financial risk, and environment risk, among others (Reside 1999). While the private sector can best handle some, others should be passed on to government, particularly when outside private sector control. A well-designed regulatory and institutional framework allocates risk to where it can be managed best.

Optimal risk sharing: An important part of PPPs is creating an explicit risk sharing arrangement between parties through regulatory and institutional mechanisms. A risk matrix is developed after assessing risks in quantitative and/or qualitative terms. An example of a detailed risk matrix provides a framework for risk identification, assessment and mitigation (Table 5.2). Although risk allocation can

vary from project to project, governments should shoulder risks associated with land acquisition, environmental clearances, changes in the legal and regulatory environment, and foreign exchange in the absence of market hedging mechanisms (Reside 1999).

The allocation of risk across public and private sectors varies by PPP modality—for example, whether it is a service or management contract, a lease arrangement, or a BOT arrangement. This determines the private party's role in assuming associated risks and earning appropriate returns on investment, with implications for the financing mode used.

Typically, in service or management contracts and some lease arrangements, where the government assumes the largest share of capital investment and risk, the private party raises commercial bank loans—serviced through government fees and grants (lower left segment of Figure 5.5). In these cases, government support usually comes from taxes, and government domestic and international borrowing (including loans from MDBs).

Figure 5.5: Risks by PPP Type

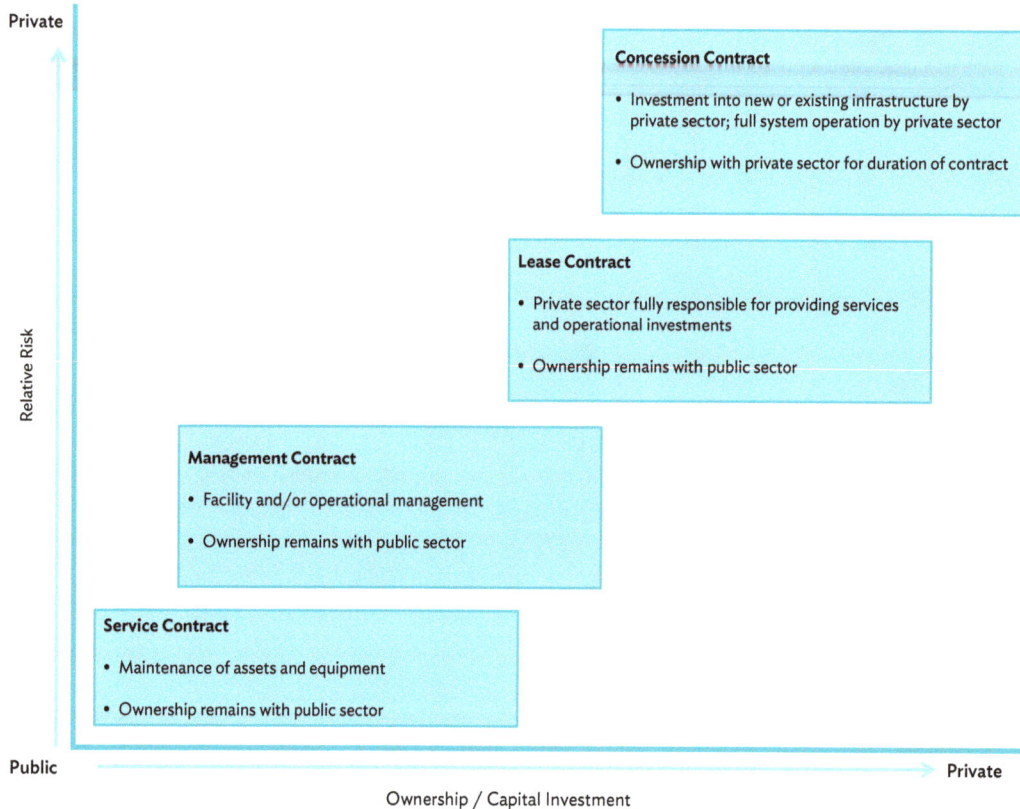

Source: ADB (2012); ADB staff conceptualization.

Table 5.2: Risk Allocation Table

Risk	Contractor	Operator	Equity	Lenders	Government	Insurance	Unallocated
Construction overruns/ delays	✓						
Change in legal regime					✓		
Land Acquisition					✓		
Approvals licenses/ permits	✓				✓		
Variations	✓				✓		
Taxation	✓		✓	✓	✓		
Tariffs and charges		✓	✓		✓		
Revenue / Traffic/ Demand			✓	✓	✓		
Operation		✓					
Maintenance		✓					
Defects liability		✓					
Natural disaster						✓	
Industrial action		✓	✓		✓		
Environmental			✓		✓		
Civil disobedience		✓			✓		
Insurance						✓	
Force majeure							✓
Confiscation					✓		
Interest rate			✓	✓			

Source: United Nations Economic and Social Commission for Asia and the Pacific (2008).

Box 5.8: Public-Private Partnerships and Contingent Liabilities in Power Sector Development

Governments need to develop a comprehensive framework for managing contingent liabilities related to infrastructure investments. For starters, the public sector needs to develop a system for allocating risks. As much as possible, risks that can be controlled or managed by the private sector should not be guaranteed by the government. Given scarce resources, guarantees must be allocated efficiently—by pricing them according to market conditions and relative risks. It is also essential for the public sector to determine how much guarantee it can sustainably provide given its fiscal position. In addition to having a framework in place, the proper accounting and monitoring of contingent liabilities is also critical. In many countries, contingent liabilities are unaccounted for in government budgets given their noncash nature. Beyond these measures, policies that reduce risks and promote competition and macroeconomic stability can help minimize contingent liabilities.

As an example, consider the case of a small open economy trying to raise electrification rates using power sector public-private partnerships (PPPs). The government, through the state power company (SPC), enters into power purchase agreements (PPAs) with independent power producers (IPPs).[a] The SPC agrees to buy all power produced by the IPP at a price specified in the PPA. With a signed PPA contract in hand, an IPP can borrow from banks to build a power station.

If the economy holds a modest credit standing, the purchase commitment alone may not sufficient to address developers' and lenders' concerns about the creditworthiness of the SPC, especially where the end-user tariff is less that the tariff payable to the developer. Force majeure and termination sale clauses in PPAs also create contingent liabilities. Under a PPA, the government typically has a call option—a right to terminate and buy the IPP's assets triggered by events such as material default by the IPP or a court order for liquidation (nonremedial events). Conversely, the IPP has a put option—or a right to terminate the PPA and require the SPC to buy the project, which can be triggered by a payment

default by the SPC or a political or natural force majeure event. While a termination sale requires a large payment by the SPC (or government), it is more a liquidity than solvency problem as the SPC (or government) takes over high-value project assets. The recovery rate could be high especially if it happens near the end of the project life with substantial or full depreciation of the assets. However, given the large contingent liabilities associated with the project, lenders and developers often want explicit government guarantees for the SPC payment obligations even if it is already implicitly supported by the government. In fact, even an explicit sovereign guarantee might not convince lenders/developers to invest in a project if a country's sovereign credit rating is below investment grade. As such, deals are often supported by concessional credit or credit enhancement.

The SPC uses "cost-plus" pricing in selling power to businesses and households. Given the low electrification rate in the country, the SPC can almost certainly sell all the power it buys, thus ensuring profitability. However, it charges end-users in local currency while obligated to pay the IPPs in US dollars. Moreover, the cost-plus pricing system does not account for possible changes in oil and gas prices in international markets. With some PPA payments indexed to fuel prices, SPC profitability thus rests critically on exchange rate and fuel price stability.

With an underdeveloped foreign exchange market, the SPC must get the dollars it needs to buy IPP power from the central bank, which in turn, buys them from local banks or sources them from government bonds or other borrowings.[b] Given a sufficiently large dollar purchase, the SPC could singlehandedly create downward pressure on the local currency. This creates a dilemma for the SPC and central bank. The more power the SPC buys from IPPs, the more pressure to depreciate, increasing its payment obligations. Should the SPC default, the government would have to cover its obligations under the PPAs.

a   These can be accompanied by power transmission agreements (PTAs).
b   If it cannot, the central bank would need to use international reserves.

Private financing and innovative instruments are important where the private sector carries the majority of the risk and undertakes the bulk of investment. These are mostly concession-type PPP arrangements (upper right segment of Figure 5.5). In these cases, more complex financing instruments such as corporate and project bonds, mezzanine instruments, securitized and asset-backed instruments are required. Servicing these instruments comes from user fees, which require appropriate regulatory arrangements for setting tariffs and government viability grant support, when required.

Importantly, risks assumed by government could result in large, unexpected public sector liabilities. The government must therefore also consider the size of each contingent liability based on type of risk. For instance, liabilities associated with market demand risk may require the government to pay a minimum amount of revenue to the infrastructure provider. This is most common in the power sector, where state-owned power companies act as off-takers or buyers of electricity from independent power producers (Box 5.8). On the other hand, contingent liabilities arising from legal, regulatory, and other country risks are usually

Figure 5.6: Historical Composition of PPI, Debt Versus Equity, various years

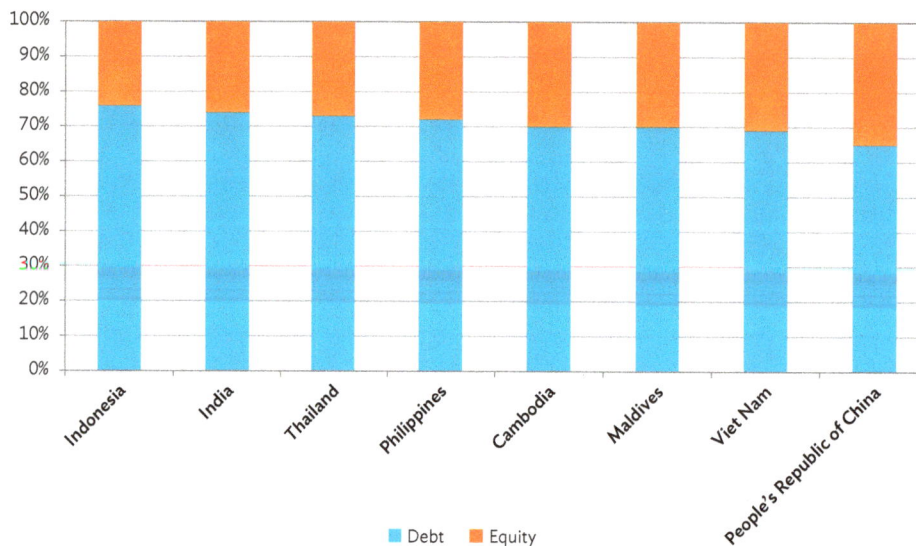

PPI = Private Participation in Infrastructure; PRC = People's Republic of China.
Note: PPI values are spread over 5 years. Time coverage is as follows: the average of 2006–2015 for Indonesia, 2011–2015 for India, 2008–2015 for Thailand, 2010–2015 for the Philippines, 2010–2015 for Cambodia, 2010–2014 for Maldives, 2006–2015 for Viet Nam, 2006–2015 for the PRC, and 2011–2015 for Bangladesh.
Source: Private Participation in Infrastructure Database, World Bank.

based on buyout or termination prices. When these risks materialize, the private sector has the option to invoke the buyout or termination clause in its PPP contract, thus creating a government liability.

Private infrastructure finance

Private infrastructure finance can be broadly divided into project and corporate finance. Project finance—otherwise known as limited recourse financing—utilizes an SPV to raise funds for acquiring or constructing an infrastructure asset.[71] Once operational, the cash flows generated by the project SPV are used to pay for its costs. In corporate finance, projects are undertaken by companies themselves and funded through their own balance sheets. While corporate finance is more flexible and less complicated than project finance, companies can only take on as much debt as their equity allows.

Moreover, large projects may cause excessive balance sheet exposure. Thus corporate finance is commonly used in relatively smaller infrastructure projects (PPP in Infrastructure Resource Center 2016).

Both corporate and project finance rely on a combination of debt and equity. Equity investors need a high level of expertise to assess the bankability of a project, and typically include construction companies or governments. In some cases, equity may be directly provided by insurance companies or private equity funds (Ehlers 2014). In general, however, infrastructure projects tend to be highly leveraged, with equity accounting for only 25% of total capital on average. The World Bank's PPI database shows that among countries reporting required data, Indonesia has the highest share of debt financing at approximately 75%, while the PRC has the lowest at roughly 65% (Figure 5.6).

Public equity markets: Listed infrastructure companies represent about 6% of the global equity market, or 4% of global GDP, with Asia having a 10%–20% weight in global infrastructure indexes. Asian

71 Project financing is 'limited' or 'nonrecourse' to shareholders. In nonrecourse financing, the project company awarded the concession for building and operating the asset is generally a limited liability SPV. In case the SPV defaults, the lenders' recourse will be limited primarily or entirely to project assets (including completion and performance guarantees and bonds).

infrastructure indexes have a market capitalization of up to $500 billion, or about 2.5% of GDP. Asian infrastructure funds are reportedly generating a deal volume of $20 billion–$30 billion a year—0.1%–0.2% of GDP—or less than half the global average. Since the mid-2000s, interest in unlisted vehicles, especially infrastructure funds, has risen. Yet the overall allocation remains small (globally about 1%–2% of assets, and even lower in Asia). Consequently, there is clearly a need to expand infrastructure equity finance in the region (Inderst 2016).

Asian equity markets have grown substantially over the past two decades with their share in global stock-market capitalization increasing from 21% in 2003 to 31% by the end of 2011. This increase was mainly driven by growing investment from international investors seeking diversification, coupled with deepening regional financial integration, a growing domestic institutional investor base, and structural improvements to market infrastructure. However, Asian equity markets still hold tremendous potential. Market capitalization as a percentage of GDP is just 66% in Asia compared with 104% for the United States (Essrich 2013). Taken as a whole, this suggests investors could expand their investments in Asian infrastructure funds to benefit from both growth potential and portfolio diversification (Inderst 2010).

Private equity markets: Private equity investments in Asia and the Pacific has centered on GDP growth factors.[72] Powered by a rising middle class, these emerging economies have grown significantly faster than the rest of the world. A surge of investment in Asian infrastructure assets drove global deal activity in the private equity market in 2016 with around $36 billion in financing, or 51% of total global deal value, despite accounting for just 27% of global transactions. While managers are

concerned about the trend of increasing capital being concentrated in fewer, higher-priced infrastructure assets, the sustained investment shows there remains a healthy investor appetite for this asset class (Preqin 2016).

Bank debt: While debt can be sourced through bank loans or bonds, banks hold several advantages over bonds—such as their ability to closely monitor project status through the loan agreement. They are also more flexible in disbursing funds and negotiating any restructuring due to unforeseen events (Bank for International Settlements 2014).

With the large amounts of financing required for a typical infrastructure project, bank loans are often syndicated due to regulatory limits on single-party exposure. Table 5.3 presents data on syndicated loans for key infrastructure sectors over 1993–2015 showing $649 billion in loans to 12 major Asian economies, with the PRC accounting for 31% by volume, followed by India (24%). Hong Kong, China; Singapore; the Republic of Korea; and Taipei,China accounted for 27%, while Indonesia, Malaysia, Philippines, Thailand, and Viet Nam took up 18%. During 2010–2015, syndicated infrastructure loans averaged around $58 billion, significantly higher than before the global financial crisis.

With larger infrastructure financing needs and the prominent role that banks play, how can the region ramp up infrastructure lending? For economies with less developed banking systems, financial systems will likely deepen as economies grow. However, the inherently short-term nature of deposits constrains banks from offering loans with the significantly longer maturities required. In addition, Basel III regulations introduced in the wake of the global financial crisis will increase the capital buffers banks must hold and require banks to better

72 Most unlisted infrastructure funds have traditional closed-end private equity-type fund structures with General Partners as fund managers and Limited Partners committing fund capital. The partnership generally has a 10–12 year life span.

manage asset-liability mismatch risk.[73] Along with other prudential regulations, this has significantly reduced banks' ability to provide long-term project finance.

Thus economies need to develop bond markets to raise additional capital. Banks and bonds play a complementary role, as they use different methodologies when monitoring borrowers (Berlin 2012). While bank financing is crucial in the initial greenfield stage of a project, bonds can be important once projects are constructed and cash flows start (when project completion risks no longer exist). Thus, post completion, fixed-rate bond finance can 'take-out' bank finance, allowing banks to recycle capital for new greenfield projects. Accordingly, there is much synergy between local capital market development and an efficient local banking industry (Bank for International Settlements 2014).

Many Asian countries have nascent bond markets with limited liquidity in lower-rated assets and longer tenors. Distinguishing between project

Table 5.3: Syndicated Loans to Infrastructure—Selected Economies, 1993–2015

Economy	Aggregate ($ billion)
People's Republic of China	200
India	157
Taipei,China	45
Hong Kong, China	44
Republic of Korea	41
Indonesia	28
Thailand	27
Philippines	24.5
Malaysia	21
Viet Nam	16
Sri Lanka	0.4

Source: Hansaku and Levinger (2016).

Table 5.4: Size of Local Currency Bond Markets
(% of gross domestic product)

	2000			2015		
	Government	Corporate	Total	Government	Corporate	Total
People's Republic of China	16.41	0.29	16.70	38.52	20.54	59.06
Hong Kong, China	8.12	27.16	35.28	38.68	28.73	67.41
India*	28.57	6.16	34.74	40.70	14.09	54.79
Indonesia	35.39	1.36	36.75	13.00	2.16	15.16
Republic of Korea	24.37	46.32	70.69	52.74	76.90	129.64
Malaysia	38.04	35.21	73.25	52.86	43.84	96.70
Philippines	29.09	0.21	29.30	29.65	6.12	35.77
Singapore	26.17	20.58	46.75	45.52	32.22	77.74
Thailand	22.16	4.42	26.58	55.38	18.60	73.98
Viet Nam	0.30	–	0.30	21.53	0.79	22.32
Total	56.03	19.34	75.36	71.26	21.98	93.25

*India figures are computed by dividing Bloomberg LP and SEBI outstanding LCY bonds with GDP data from World Development Indicators, World Bank.
Source: AsianBondsOnline, ADB; Bloomberg LP; Statistics on Issues and Redemptions and Total Outstanding Corporate Debt 2000–2016, Securities and Exchange Board of India; World Development Indicators, World Bank.

---

73 Under Basel III, banks are required to maintain a minimum capital to risk-weighted assets ratio to absorb losses during stress. Basel III will require a bank capital ratio of 8%, made up as follows: (i) at least 6% in Tier 1 capital, of which at least 4.5% must be in the form of common equity—the remaining 1.5% may be "additional going concern capital," which is subject to strict conditions to ensure it is equity-like in its ability to absorb losses; (ii) 2% in Tier 2 capital which must be subordinate and meet strict loss absorption criteria. In addition, Basel III imposes a "capital conservation buffer," which requires banks to maintain another 2.5% of common equity. One expected result of Basel III is that the quantity of common equity, which is an expensive form of capital, could quadruple, having a significant economic impact.

and corporate bonds, bond market weakness is acutely evident by the low volumes of project bonds—estimated at just $1 billion–$3 billion in recent years (Inderst 2016). Further, the public sector dominates, with private issuers accounting for a small portion of the market even in developed Asian markets. The exceptions are the Republic of Korea and Malaysia, where private sector bonds are sizable (Table 5.4).

Table 5.5: Credit Ratings by Local Rating Agencies for Local-currency Corporate Bonds

As a percentage of number of local-currency corporate bonds issued, 2010–Q3 2015

	AAA to AA	A	BBB	Below BBB	Unrated/Withdrawn
People's Republic of China	99.9	0.0	0.0	0.1	0.0
India	82.8	10.6	2.9	3.4	0.3
Indonesia	65.8	28.8	3.9	0.8	0.8
Republic of Korea	80.9	13.0	2.9	2.1	1.0
Malaysia	88.9	8.9	1.0	0.8	0.3
Philippines	100.0	0.0	0.0	0.0	0.0
Thailand	16.7	62.9	18.2	0.9	0.3

Source: Amstad et al. (2016).

A wider range of investment choices would provide an alternative to bank financing for less-than-high quality credits. Table 5.5 reports the credit quality for companies as measured by the rating on their foreign currency obligations from Standard and Poor's in key Asian markets. In the PRC and the Philippines, effectively all local currency corporate bond issuance is rated either AAA or AA. In Indonesia, the Republic of Korea, and Malaysia, the share in the AAA/AA category ranges between two-thirds and nine-tenths, with the lion's share of the remainder at A. Only Thailand has a ratings distribution that spans the entire spectrum of investment grade ratings. The table illustrates the need to deepen corporate bond markets, suggesting that without credit enhancement, there is limited scope for standalone infrastructure SPVs to float project bonds, given their higher risk profile.

Institutional investors, such as pension funds and insurance companies, are looking to diversify their portfolios, and are typically mandated to invest in low-risk assets. Infrastructure assets offer a viable investment alternative given their long-term, predictable income streams, low sensitivity to business cycles, and low correlation to other asset classes (Inderst 2010). However, most infrastructure bonds in developing countries—even those for completed projects—have ratings below those required by institutional investors. Thus credit enhancement mechanisms can help boost ratings, protecting senior creditors by absorbing the "first

loss" in the case of default—through credit guarantees where a third party acts as the guarantor in exchange for a fee. These can either be privately provided, by banks or specialized institutions, or governments. In recent years, MDBs like ADB have also begun to provide credit guarantees (Box 5.9).

Another factor constraining investment is the lack of credible credit ratings, particularly for project bonds, fueled by insufficient data to determine default probabilities. Credit enhancement instruments require rating agencies to provide a standalone rating to the bonds and advise on the extent of the credit enhancement (guarantee cover) required to raise the rating to the desired level. Investors will only invest in the credit enhanced bonds if the rating guidance provided by the rating agencies is credible. Stronger rating agencies will also support liquidity in instruments such as "Green Bonds"—corporate, project and sub-sovereign bonds for clean energy assets—and in enabling securitization of asset-backed securities (whereby bonds are backed by a pool of infrastructure loans and sold to investors through capital markets).

In this way, credible credit ratings can inject much needed liquidity into infrastructure bonds, especially in markets where investors cannot yet assess the bankability of infrastructure projects. Indeed, in Malaysia, the government's push to establish strong, local rating agencies was a huge factor in its bond market development.

Work is being done to increase the credibility of credit ratings and the agencies that issue them. Despite the considerable work done by the Association of Credit Rating Agencies in Asia (ACRAA), local credit rating agency (CRA) ratings are not yet fully comparable across borders—in methodology, rating criteria, definitions, benchmarks and the overall rating processes. ACCRA and its members are working to further strengthen local knowledge and understanding of their respective markets.[74] But they should also harmonize information disclosure and ratings models to members.

Box 5.9: The Asian Development Bank and Credit Guarantees

The Asian Development Bank (ADB) has launched several initiatives to help encourage the growth of bond markets in its developing member countries (DMCs). One is through the direct issuance of partial credit guarantees (PCGs), which could account for up to 75% of the bond's principal and interest. The first project backed by an ADB PCG was for the Tiwi-MakBan geothermal plants owned by AP Renewables—an indirect wholly-owned subsidiary of Aboitiz Power Corporation in the Philippines. The project company issued 10-year local currency bonds in the amount of P10.7 billion, of which 75% was covered by the PCG. On top of this, ADB also provided a P1.8 billion 5-year term loan, making it both a lender and guarantor. The transaction is a first in many ways. For one, it is a landmark use of project bonds in the region (excluding Malaysia) since the 1997/98 Asian financial crisis. It is also the first local currency project bond in the Philippine power sector and the first credit-enhanced project bond in the country.

For US dollar project bonds, ADB offers a subordinated liquidity facility in the form of a revolving irrevocable letter of credit for a fixed percentage of the value of the bonds. Although this has not yet been piloted in DMCs, this type of facility is commonly used elsewhere, especially in Europe—where it has increased project ratings by one to three notches. ADB has also played a role in spurring investments in environmentally-friendly projects through its green and climate bond certification. This allows investors to assess the bonds' environmental integrity on a common set of standards based on third party review. The Tiwi-MakBan geothermal project is the first standalone project to have secured climate bond certification among emerging markets.

---

74 Initially, ACRAA members included 15 domestic CRAs from 10 economies. Membership has nearly doubled since to 29 domestic CRAs covering 14 jurisdictions (Bahrain; Bangladesh; India; Indonesia; Japan; Kazakhstan; Republic of Korea; Malaysia; Pakistan; People's Republic of China; Philippines; Sri Lanka; Taipei,China; and Thailand).

With local CRAs such a critical component of Asian financial market infrastructure, strengthening local CRAs with technical ratings know-how—and by enforcing a Code of Ethics and Best Practices Checklist among ACRAA's members (to boost market credibility through higher performance standards, transparency, and accountability)—can help investors make responsible risk-return investment decisions.

5.5.   Institutional issues and high-technology infrastructure

Meeting developing Asia's infrastructure needs is not just about ensuring sufficient finance. It requires the capacity to plan, formulate, evaluate, and execute infrastructure projects.

These are the core institutional issues for successful, effective infrastructure investment. A recent study examines the relationship between accumulated public capital stock (a large component of which is infrastructure) and various indicators of infrastructure quality and access. It finds that on average 30% of the potential benefits of public investment could be lost due to inefficiencies in investment planning and implementation (International Monetary Fund 2015). It further notes that closing this "efficiency gap" could yield the most efficient public investors twice the output "bang" for their public investment expenditures compared with the least efficient investors. These gains require improving three key stages of decision-making: (i) planning sustainable investment across the public sector; (ii) allocating investment to the right sectors and projects; and (iii) implementing projects on time and within budget.

What is needed is a well-functioning ecosystem involving the many different stakeholders involved in different stages of infrastructure development. Figure 5.7 offers a schematic diagram of issues involved. The planning stage, for example, requires coordination across different government levels—

Figure 5.7: An Ecosystem for Planning and Implementing Infrastructure Projects

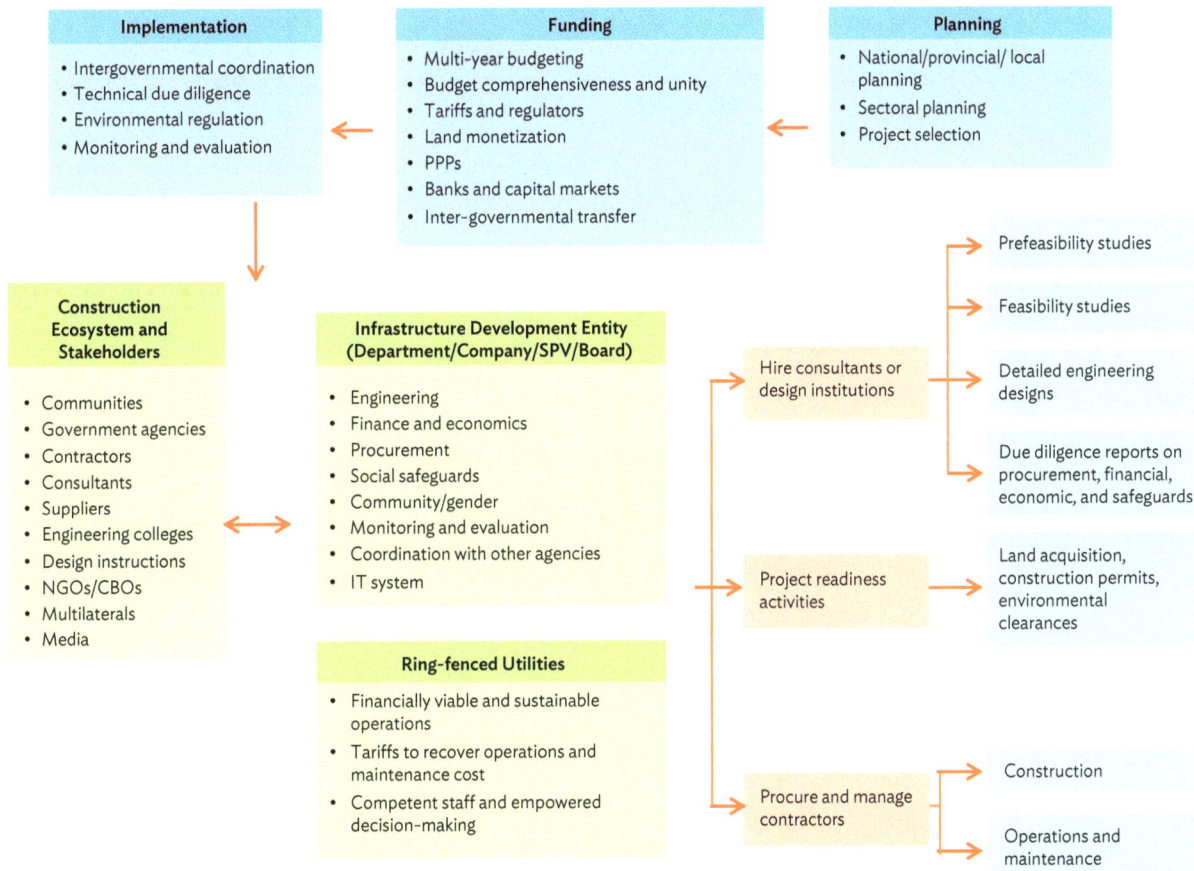

CBO = community-based organization; NGO = nongovernmental organization; PPP = public-private partnership; SPV = special purpose vehicle.
Source: ADB staff conceptualization.

spanning from national to provincial or state levels, along with critical local input. It also requires planning and coordination across sectors for infrastructure investments to be most effective. And crucially, it considers policy elements that ostensibly may have little to do with infrastructure. In planning urban public transport systems, for example, infrastructure projects need to be designed in tandem with broader economic and spatial planning, paying careful attention to regulatory issues involving land management (Box 5.10).

Similarly, funding sources must consider issues such as multiyear budgeting, tariff-setting, if and how land value capture can help fund infrastructure, which projects would work well as PPPs, and the extent of intergovernmental

transfers required, among others. Finally, efficient implementation requires considerable coordination across government agencies, the capacity to conduct technical due diligence, adhere to different (perhaps competing) regulatory standards across areas, manage contractors and the procurement process, and careful monitoring and evaluation of infrastructure projects—from construction to operations and maintenance.[75]

---

75 High-quality project preparation can play an important role not only in improving the efficiency of public investments, but also in attracting private investment. For example, if the government is seeking private investment in a particular project, a high quality feasibility study and detailed engineering design can assure potential investors the key risks associated with the project and its bankability have been considered. This ensures both greater interest in the project and its chance of overall success.

Box 5.10: Coordinating City Infrastructure[a]

Integrating and planning infrastructure projects—melding complementarities between different types of infrastructure with design specifics that fit the broader regulatory environment—is how cities such as Seoul and Singapore plan transit and other infrastructure in line with urban land use regulations.

A key element of land use regulation is the floor space index (FSI)—the ratio of the gross floor area of a building to the area of the lot. An FSI of one would require a building to have a total floor area at most equal to the total lot area. Higher FSIs thus result in taller buildings and greater population density. FSIs vary significantly across cities. For instance, Tokyo has one of the highest FSIs in the world at 20. Singapore has floor space indexes ranging from 12 to 25. By contrast, European cities such as Paris, Venice, and Amsterdam have FSIs of 3.0, 2.4, and 1.9, respectively. In reality, there is no optimal FSI. The "right" FSI will depend on several factors, such as the spatial structure of a city, street patterns and width, and the level of infrastructure in the area. When properly designed, FSIs are a powerful tool in driving the type of urbanization pursued.

Good planning involves linking floor space indexes to the actual connectivity infrastructure in place or being planned. In Seoul and Singapore, planners assign FSI levels in a granular way within the city. In particular, FSI levels vary by city location and are aligned with (i) the transit capacity of transport infrastructure, water and sanitation infrastructure, and (ii) with zoning decisions on the mix of commercial and residential activities. In fact, the city master plan, zoning and FSI regulations are adjusted based on estimates of projected population and employment growth. As Box figure 5.10 for Seoul illustrates, urban planners have allowed the largest floor space indexes along main transport hubs—for example, where Metro stations are constructed.

In this way, a city's economic density can increase without congestion crippling or eroding the benefits of gains from agglomerating economies and productivity. Put differently, good coordination of infrastructure and land use regulations in planning can enable cities to best play their role as engines of growth and job creation, generating the largest possible benefits from infrastructure provision.

Unfortunately, the urban planning approaches adopted in many Asian cities do not conform to this type of planning. Thus, FSIs are often not set with due regard to connectivity infrastructure and projections of population and employment growth. As a result, suboptimal use of scarce land leaves cities and transport networks severely congested, impacting both a city's economic strength and its livability.

Box figure 5.10: Infrastructure Zoning in Seoul, Republic of Korea

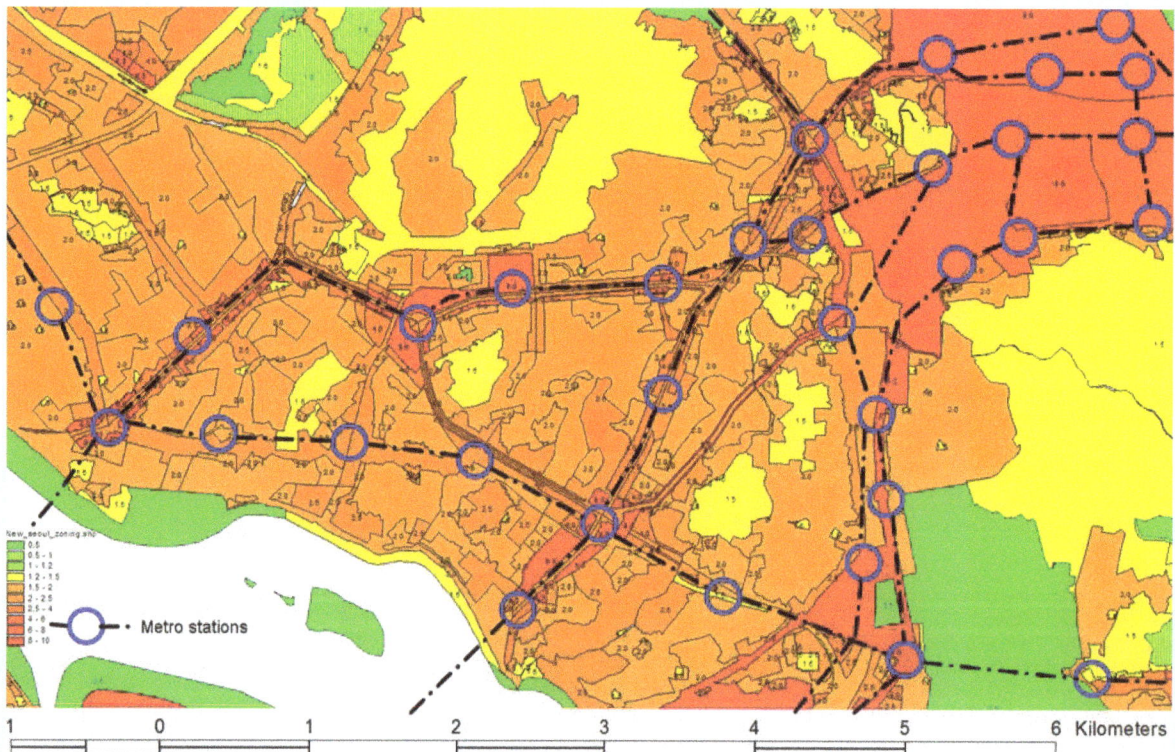

Source: Bertaud (2008).

---

a   Bertaud (2008); World Bank (2013b).

Crucially, good implementation creates demands not only from the public sector, but also from other stakeholders—such as the quality of consultants and design institutions who prepare prefeasibility and feasibility studies and detailed engineering designs. Moreover, being able to tap engineering colleges for qualified engineers is essential.

But good design is not enough. Properly sequencing activities such as land acquisition and obtaining/updating necessary permits—including environmental clearances—can avoid the considerable delays projects often face. Last, but not least, the actual construction and operations and maintenance of infrastructure projects requires capable contractors and modern procurement systems that incentivize on time, high-quality project delivery.

In the final analysis, it is no exaggeration to say that getting infrastructure right requires a fairly sophisticated ecosystem of public sector agencies across government and sector levels, a capable set of contractors, consultants, and suppliers, all backed by institutions of higher learning that promote capable engineering and management skills. Thus, improving infrastructure project planning and implementation are not the task of the public sector alone. Given the growing role private sector engineering and construction companies play in building infrastructure, any outdated practices or technologies used can take a huge toll. Adopting modern construction industry practices—in both production technology and project management—can significantly improve the effectiveness of funds earmarked for infrastructure development (McKinsey & Company 2016).

Nevertheless, the public sector has a defining role to play, especially in tackling the various institutional issues—something that is not easy and takes time. The key is to recognize there are a variety of approaches countries in the region have used to improve coordination between different agencies and build technical and managerial capacity. Box 5.11 provides some details of the institutional framework for planning and implementing infrastructure projects in the PRC that have worked quite well. Box 5.12 provides a more specific case from India—the Madhya Pradesh Road Development Corporation, wholly owned by the state government and responsible for planning and developing the state highway network and major district roads. Box 5.13 describes how better design and management of the water utility has extended coverage and improved the quality of water related services in Bangladesh. Significantly, many interventions have benefited from the experience of the Phnom Penh Water Supply Authority (PPWSA), which transformed the water utility into one of the most financially-sustainable in Asia (Box 5.14).

Choice of technology in infrastructure projects

A somewhat specific, but related issue is choosing the technology most appropriate for infrastructure projects—a choice between conventional and new or advanced technologies, including innovative practices more beneficial than conventional ones.

More specifically, advanced technologies may carry one or a combination of the following features within the country and/or regional context:

- Applications of ICT to improve efficiency and productivity in delivering services (such as smart grids and intelligent transport systems, among others)

- Climate mitigation, adaptation, and/or resilience to disaster risk (involving, for example, smart grids and renewable energy based microgrids with storage, offshore wind, concentrated solar, and early warning systems)

Box 5.11: Institutions for Planning and Executing Infrastructure Projects in the People's Republic of China[a]

The People's Republic of China (PRC) has been able to plan and implement many complex and sophisticated infrastructure projects quickly and efficiently. There are several key aspects of its institutional framework that have enabled this.

Coordination and Implementation. Inter-jurisdictional and inter-ministerial coordination is crucial in executing infrastructure projects. In the PRC, the National Development and Reform Commission (NDRC) plays the paramount role. Planning in the PRC is an iterative, detailed, bottom-up process. Plans serve as blueprints for the development of each region and are prepared by the NDRC in consultation with subnational governments. So, for example, if a port is to be built, the planning process provides for coordinated development—with appropriate involvement of all related bureaucratic entities—of ancillary infrastructure, such as rail and road access. Substantial parts of these plans are sufficiently detailed to cater to ancillary infrastructure requirements, such as hinterland development of ports. Underlying the plans are, in effect, blueprints for regions.

Beyond strategy, planning, and policy formulation, the NDRC also coordinates and monitors plan implementation. As several line ministries, institutions, and lower-level governments are involved, providing leadership in implementation is essential. The NDRC visits local areas and carries out field investigations when issues arise or as part of its implementation monitoring function (Liu 2004). To implement the plan for the power sector, for example, NDRC would coordinate with relevant central government agencies and local administrations to (i) site new plants; (ii) determine equipment manufacturers, fuel types, and suppliers; (iii) arrange for construction; (iv) facilitate all necessary approvals; and (v) determine which power-sector enterprise would operate the plant. This role, which combines top down guidance with troubleshooting, coordination, and clearinghouse functions, greatly enhances execution capacity. Arguably, it is what underlies the PRC's ability to deal with complex cross-jurisdictional infrastructure initiatives effectively (ADB, World Bank, and JBIC 2005).

This is not to say that there are no problems. The planning process for infrastructure development has not been able to prevent situations of periodic excess supply followed by acute shortages of infrastructure services. Similarly, overinvestment by enthusiastic local governments is a frequent problem and can involve building infrastructure projects without central government approval.

Furthermore, although the PRC has managed without independent regulators, as state-owned infrastructure providers become more commercial, the need for regulation will become unavoidable.

Local Ownership Creates Decision-Making Efficiency in the PRC. Project executing and implementing agencies in the PRC are almost always city-level institutions, with full decision-making powers, staff and skills for the task. Tricky decisions may reach city mayors, and rarely to provincial party officials. But routine decisions (and their responsibility) vest mainly, for example, with city-owned water supply companies. These agencies are not entirely fiscally autonomous, but they enjoy a considerable degree of functional autonomy.

It is interesting that decentralization came to PRC relatively recently. Until the early 1990's there was limited decentralization in investment decision-making, either functional or fiscal. Project related decisions were taken in Beijing at the NDRC, sometimes resulting in delays or disconnect with local decision-making levels. Since then, the PRC has extensively decentralized investment decision-making so that local authorities now oversee all matters relating to project planning, approvals and implementation.

Continuity and Accumulation of Knowledge in the PRC through Design Institutes. Executing agencies (EAs) in the PRC have relatively high levels of engineering and technical capacity relative to those in other developing countries. One reason for this is that the PRC has an institutional legacy of publicly owned regional design institutes that provide technical services for project planning, detailed engineering design and works supervision of public engineering projects in various sectors. The design institutes are engaged by the EAs to work with them at the time when projects are being prepared, and their role continues through all stages until project completion. This avoids the problem of lack of project continuity—a common problem in many developing countries—and allows feedback to incorporate good practices and lessons learned when designing the next group of projects.

Thus, the design institutes offer a vehicle through which project experience and knowledge can collectively accumulate—over time strengthening the social, environmental and institutional aspects of projects, while building on traditional strengths in project engineering. Recent efforts to partially privatize design institutes have improved access to international expertise and best practices.

---

a   ADB (2011); ADB, World Bank, and JBIC (2005); Lall, Anand, and Rastogi (2010); Liu (2004).

Box 5.12: Managing State Highways and Road Development—the Madhya Pradesh Road Development Corporation

One of India's largest states, Madhya Pradesh, has substantially reformed its road sector. A key role has been played by the Madhya Pradesh Road Development Corporation (MPRDC)— incorporated as a wholly government-owned company in 2004.[a] MPRDC develops and maintains the entire network of Madhya Pradesh state highways.

The MPRDC track record

Before MPRDC, state highways in Madhya Pradesh were of generally poor quality with inadequate coverage. The network was unable to cope with increasing demand for road transport. However, since MPRDC took over, 9,350 kilometers (km) of state highways and 2,168 km of major district roads were upgraded and extended. These were developed under a build-operate-transfer (BOT) model, using tolls for state highways and annuity for major district roads. In addition, MPRDC has been a pioneer in public-private partnership (PPP) road development. MPRDC has so far completed 29 PPP road projects with 31 projects in progress. It is also assisting other state departments on PPP projects on structuring, bid process management, monitoring and contract management. MPRDC also develops projects under a central government program for national highway development (the NHDP-IV program) and has established an innovative road accident response system designed to improve road safety and reduce the number of accidents and fatalities.

During the last few years, MPRDC has significantly improved profitability and revenues—which have grown at a compound annual rate of about 30% over the last four years. MPRDC's expenditures are budgeted mainly to (i) cover gaps between toll collections and operations (viability gap funding); (ii) payment for land acquisition and moving utility lines; and (iii) engineering, procurement and construction (EPC) contracts.

a   ADB provided a $320 million sector development program loan in 2007.

How MPRDC does it

MPRDC is thin and lean, using modern project, financial and procurement management systems. It is now regarded as a benchmark for effectively managing state highway networks. There are many factors for its success (Box figure 5.12). It is based on a well-defined organizational structure and an efficient human resource development strategy that provides hiring flexibility, transparency in career management with an emphasis on building expertise. While a large portion of its workforce is either on deputation or on contract, expertise is diversified, which allows it to do activities normally outsourced by similar organizations. For instance, MPRDC has developed in-house expertise for PPPs—such as technical, financial, and legal matter experts—so it does not require any external assistance for transaction and legal advisory services. In addition, environmental, social and management information system experts, and road data system engineers are also in-house.

MPRDC business processes are also well-defined and aligned to the needs of each stage of the project cycle—including project preparation, preconstruction activities, construction, and post construction work. For example, recognizing the importance of quality feasibility studies and detailed project reports (DPRs), MPRDC allocates sufficient time for the work to be completed (typically six months for the preparation of the feasibility study and 6–12 months for DPRs). And in an effort to minimize subsequent delays, land acquisition, and forest clearance processes are begun at the feasibility study stage.

continued on next page

- Adoption of innovative processes, methods or techniques and new or improved equipment/ materials in construction and operations, which results in lower lifecycle cost, higher durability, and better long-term performance (such as more efficient energy and material consumption; the "3Rs"—reduce, reuse, recycle)

- Reduction in environmental costs and/or social costs (including air or water pollution, resource depletion, and noise, among others)

- Creation of market opportunities for scaling up (such as innovative business models for rooftop solar installations), and

- Maximized synergies and increase in scale and impact through cross-sectoral collaboration (through solar powered desalination in island economies, for example)

Often the most important reason to adopt advanced technology in infrastructure projects

Box 5.12: Managing State Highways and Road Development—the Madhya Pradesh Road Development Corporation *(continued)*

Box figure 5.12: MPRDC's Project, Financial and Procurement Management System

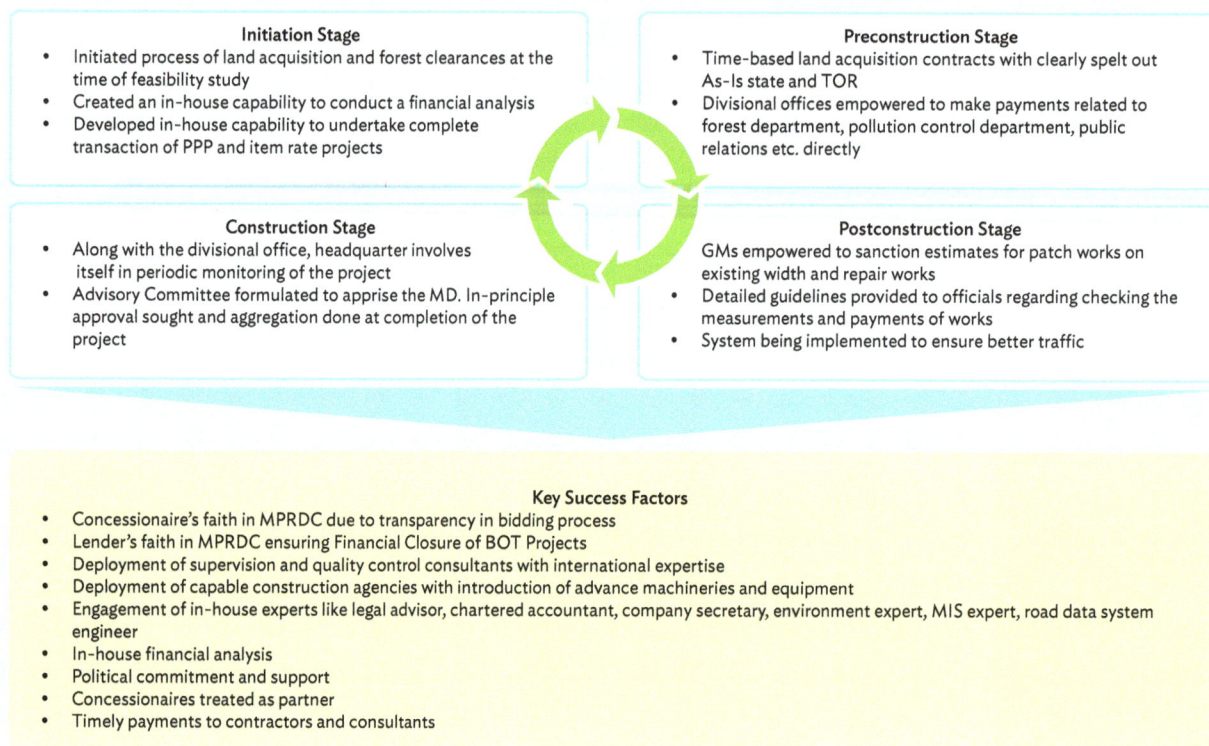

Initiation Stage
- Initiated process of land acquisition and forest clearances at the time of feasibility study
- Created an in-house capability to conduct a financial analysis
- Developed in-house capability to undertake complete transaction of PPP and item rate projects

Preconstruction Stage
- Time-based land acquisition contracts with clearly spelt out As-Is state and TOR
- Divisional offices empowered to make payments related to forest department, pollution control department, public relations etc. directly

Construction Stage
- Along with the divisional office, headquarter involves itself in periodic monitoring of the project
- Advisory Committee formulated to apprise the MD. In-principle approval sought and aggregation done at completion of the project

Postconstruction Stage
- GMs empowered to sanction estimates for patch works on existing width and repair works
- Detailed guidelines provided to officials regarding checking the measurements and payments of works
- System being implemented to ensure better traffic

Key Success Factors
- Concessionaire's faith in MPRDC due to transparency in bidding process
- Lender's faith in MPRDC ensuring Financial Closure of BOT Projects
- Deployment of supervision and quality control consultants with international expertise
- Deployment of capable construction agencies with introduction of advance machineries and equipment
- Engagement of in-house experts like legal advisor, chartered accountant, company secretary, environment expert, MIS expert, road data system engineer
- In-house financial analysis
- Political commitment and support
- Concessionaires treated as partner
- Timely payments to contractors and consultants

Source: Deloitte (2015).

are for climate change mitigation and adaptation solutions. For instance, in transportation, various climate proofing measures—such as improving the concrete mix for drainage, elevating roads and higher road embankments—help assuage the impact of increased precipitation and resulting flood risks that account for much of the climate change threat (ADB 2014b).[76]

Adopting advanced technology often requires higher initial capital investment. However, many advanced technologies actually result in lower operation, maintenance and replacement costs—

aside from better infrastructure performance—thus reducing total costs over the infrastructure lifecycle.

Renewable energy technology is a classic example that shows the relationship between advanced technology and lifecycle cost and evolution. Levelized cost of electricity (LCOE) is a standardized measure of lifecycle costs—cost of financing, capital and operating expenditures, and fuel costs—in current dollars for generating one megawatt hour (MWh) of electricity. LCOE can also be seen as the breakeven price per MWh, yielding possible comparisons across technologies.

As shown in Figure 5.8, there has been a dramatic decline in LCOE of solar photovoltaic (PV) over the last few years, and the commonly-used

---

76 This is also the case for innovative and/or modern practices. For example, ADB-funded projects have shown that "performance-based maintenance"—which incentivizes contractors to save maintenances costs—help reduce road life cycle costs.

Box 5.13: Asian Development Bank Project Helps Provide Reliable Quality Water Supply to Dhaka

The ADB-financed Dhaka Water Supply Sector Development Program (DWSSDP) helped 5.44 million people access continuous potable water directly from taps without requiring further treatment, with sufficient pressure for two-story houses. Completed in December 2016, the project was instrumental in making the Dhaka Water Supply and Sewerage Authority (DWASA) a role model for water utilities in South Asia (Box figure 5.13). DWASA effectively implemented several good practices during project implementation.

i. **Combining Infrastructure Investment and Policy Reform.** ADB support included a $150 million project loan for rehabilitating and strengthening the water supply distribution network; and a $50 million policy-based loan for implementing legal, institutional, and regulatory reforms. DWASA initiated and successfully implemented several management and operations reforms to improve efficiency and enhance service delivery.

ii. **Visionary Leaders and Turnaround Program, 2010–2016.** DWASA's Managing Director and Project Directors championed a Turnaround Program to improve operations and finance of the organization. Measures included streamlining DWASA operations for greater accountability and responsiveness; human resource development; geographic information system-based network management plans coupled with supervisory control and data acquisition; and a citizens' grievance redress system and public education campaign for greater transparency. DWASA also improved its financial performance by computerizing its customer database, billing and accounts; regular auditing; and internet payments through mobile phones and banks. DWASA recovered its operation and maintenance costs by improving coverage, billing, collection, and cost reduction. Revenue collection from water and sewerage increased from BDT3.14 billion in FY2007/08 to BDT6.52 billion in FY 2012/13. Its 2,400 million liters per day (MLD) water production exceeds current demand (2,200 MLD), while surface water sources now contribute 22% of total water production, as DWASA reduces dependence on ground water sources.

iii. **Technical innovation: District Metering Area Approach and Performance-based Contracts for Nonrevenue Water Reduction, and Trenchless Technology.** The huge amount of nonrevenue water (NRW) was substantially reduced using an innovative district metering area (DMA) approach, performance-based contracts with payments to contractors linked to NRW reduction targets, and the use of trenchless technology. The project rehabilitated 47 DMAs (2,456 km of the distribution network) benefitting 106,662 connections and 5.44 million people. This helped bring down NRW from more than 50% before the project to less than 10% in most completed DMAs. Trenchless technology enhances efficiency, reduces costs and inconvenience to residents during construction. Managing DMAs is pivotal to successful network management and sustainable service delivery.

iv. **Effective Implementation of Water Quality Monitoring System.** Effective water quality monitoring involved constructing 46 deep tube wells, 200 chlorination units, and distributed water quality test kits to pump operators. DWASA laboratory facilities were also rehabilitated and equipped with modern testing tools.

v. **Slums and Informal Settlements receive continuous water supply.** The project also served people in informal settlements and low income areas of Dhaka. Residents of Korail, the largest settlement in Dhaka, used to buy water from private vendors at exorbitant rates. Women and children fetched water daily and were exposed to water borne diseases. The project helped DWASA provide about 1,000 legal connections to user groups in Korail, benefitting 100,000 people. And Korail residents rarely miss water bills. DWASA's policy is to cover all informal settlements—about 30% (or nearly 5 million people)—with piped water.

vi. **Gender Responsive.** DWASA is the first organization in Bangladesh to adopt its own gender strategy beyond the project period. DWASA established a gender unit to promote mainstreaming gender equity through regular training on gender sensitivity, gender auditing, creating gender balance, and effective communication to raise awareness, gender disaggregated data collection, networking, gender-responsive budgeting, and monitoring and evaluation of its gender strategy.

vii. **Effective Capacity Building Programs Implemented.** DWASA refurbished and strengthened its independent, dedicated training center. Under the ADB program loan, an effective capacity building program was established, increasing the number of training courses and training center budget.

viii. **Strong Focus on Public Education Programs.** DWASA's success in reducing NRW and 24-hour water supply was also due to a strong focus on community awareness and public education programs, effectively implemented through specialized nongovernment organizations. Aside from project implementation, nonrevenue water reduction and continuous water supply, DWASA works on water conservation, demand management, sanitation, solid waste management, the "3 R's" (reduce, reuse and recycle), and health and hygiene.

Dhaka's success is closely monitored by its South Asian neighbors—who have sent several teams to study DWASA's turnaround program. In a spirit of South-South Knowledge Sharing, ADB and DWASA are actively sharing lessons and good practices with other cities in South Asia.

Box figure 5.13: Dhaka Water Supply and Sewerage Authority's Turn-Around Program

Indicator	2008	Benchmark	2015
1. Nonrevenue water %	40.38	25.00	22.00
2. Bills sent out %	93.00	99.50	99.00
3. Revenue collection %	64.50	95.00	97.50
4. Debt age / receivable (month)	14.58	3.00	5.46
5. Manpower/1,000	16.20	12.00	9.16
6. Operating ratio	0.90	0.65	0.66

Source: Dhaka Water Supply and Sewerage Authority website.

Box 5.14: From Desperate to Dependable—Turning on Phnom Penh Taps[a]

In 1993, the Phnom Penh Water Supply Authority (PPWSA) ruled a dilapidated network of disintegrating, unreliable infrastructure. The result of decades of civil war, water service was intermittent at best. Its century-old pipes were deteriorating. More than 70% of the water piped was unaccounted for. Even with low tariffs, bill collection was below 50%. Expenses topped 150% of sales (Das et al., 2010).

Within 20 years, however—with donor assistance from Asian Development Bank (ADB), Japan International Cooperation Agency (JICA), and World Bank—PPWSA transformed the water utility into one of the most financially-sustainable in Asia.

How was this possible? According to Biswas and Tortajada (2010), consultants, in close consultation with PPWSA, drew up a master plan and feasibility study of Phnom Penh's water system—using an incremental development plan that called for additional investments as milestones were reached. The blueprint guided both infrastructure development and the foreign donor finance as the plan was implemented.

Sound management and performance results were implemented and helped expand coverage. Much was attributed to the strong and unchanged leadership of PPWSA. Over the years, there were five core reform areas:

i.   Upgrading the workforce—management was strengthened, good staff identified and promoted with higher salaries and incentives; above all, teamwork was emphasized;

ii. Improving collection—water meters were installed for all connections (previously just 13% were metered), billing computerized, consumer mapping updated, nonpayers

(including several high ranking officials) were cut off if payments were delayed;

iii. rehabilitating the distribution network and treatment plants—primarily local consultants were hired; they had to manually locate existing pipes (as blueprints were destroyed during the civil war), communities were mobilized to report leaks;

iv. minimizing illegal connections and nonrevenue water— inspection teams reported illegal connections as the public were offered incentives to report illegal connections;

v.   increasing water tariffs to cover maintenance and operating costs—this was done through a three-step tariff increase spread over 7 years, although the last did not push through because by then revenues had already covered costs.

Between 1993 and 2012, PPWSA's annual water production increased from 65,000 cubic meters/day to 466,000 cubic meters/day. The area covered quadrupled. Nonrevenue water plummeted from 72% to 6%. And PPWSA became a dependable, profitable, supplier of uninterrupted water. Since 2012, PPWSA has been listed on the Cambodia Securities Exchange; its return on equity has increased yearly (PricewaterhouseCoopers (Cambodia) 2015).

The summary of lessons-learned include the following: (i) water supply should not be taken for granted—it is not free; (ii) thus, cost recovery is vital and must be publically understood; (iii) the utility operator must be autonomous; (iv) and supported by government; (v) civil society must be involved and understand water supply is a community-wide public good; (iv) investing in good staff and motivating performance significantly enhances productivity; and (vii) dynamic leadership is essential for successful reform.

---

a   Biswas and Tortajada (2010); Chan (2009); Das et al. (2010); PricewaterhouseCoopers (Cambodia) (2015); Tokyo Engineering Consultants & Nihon Suido Consultants (1993).

---

renewable technologies such as hydro, wind and solar PV are now competitive with conventional energy such as coal.[77] It is expected that the LCOEs of wind and solar PV will continue to decline as experience

accumulates rapidly (the "experience curve").[78] The lifecycle costs of these technologies may fall below those of coal and natural gas in near term. Taking into account the pronounced environmental benefits, there is substantial room to increase the share of renewable energy in total energy consumption for the region, which relies on fossil fuel by far.

---

77 With the exception of hydro, which is grid-friendly, a MWh of intermittent renewable energy only available for a portion of the day is not directly comparable to a MWh of constant power supply. Depending on time-of-day demand, other generating capacity may need to be available when intermittent renewable energy is not. This other capacity could be reduced or eliminated through storage, an integrated approach with other renewables, and/or demand side energy efficiency measures (which do have additional costs).

78 According to a literature survey (McDonald and Schrattenholzer 2001) on experience (learning) curve estimates of energy technologies, as production doubles unit costs of solar PV and wind technologies decrease by 18%–35% and 4%–32%, respectively, varying by country and time period.

Figure 5.8: Levelized Cost of Electricity (LCOE) by Technology ($/MWh)

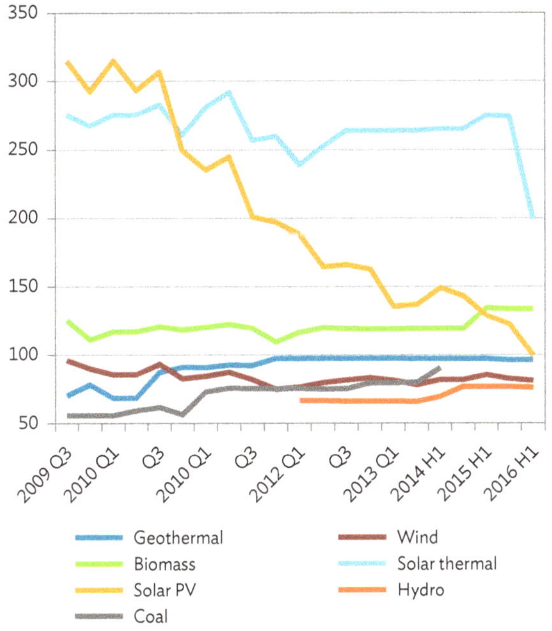

MWh = megawatt/hour; PV = photovoltaic.
Note: Wind – onshore; Solar PV – Crystalline silicon without tracking; Solar thermal – parabolic trough; Marine – tidal; Hydro – large hydro > 10MW; Biomass–incineration; Geothermal – binary.
Source: New Energy Finance, Bloomberg; World Economic Forum (2013).

Even without any specific financial advantage, using advanced technology could eliminate certain environmental and social constraints. For instance, in highly saline-prone areas, a desalination plant can treat the surface or ground water effectively before it reaches farmers, residents, and industries.

Project owners in many developing countries are often discouraged to use advanced technology due to higher upfront costs. Sometimes, they are unaware these technologies exist. Technical assistance and MDB finance could play important roles in promoting and demonstrating the advantage of using advanced technology in infrastructure. Decision makers in developing countries should assess its costs and benefits more comprehensively and consider more proactively applying advanced technology to infrastructure.

Section 6. Concluding Remarks

This report has examined in some detail the state of infrastructure across developing Asia and how much countries are investing in infrastructure. It has estimated investment needs through 2030 and examined the impact climate change will have on the costs of building and maintaining infrastructure. The report also considered the challenges the region faces in satisfying its infrastructure needs. It examined both finance as well as the institutional and capacity issues related to planning and implementing infrastructure projects.

Several findings dominate the narrative. First, a concerted effort is needed to better measure and track infrastructure investments. While data from various sources, such as government budgets and gauges of private sector investment (such as the World Bank's Private Participation in Infrastructure or PPI Project Database) allow us to get a sense of the quantum of infrastructure investments being made, we need to do better. The report proposes a way forward for measuring infrastructure investment: using more disaggregated data on gross fixed capital formation from national accounts—broken down by type of investor, type of fixed asset, and the sector making the investments.

Second, looking to the future, the report estimates total infrastructure investment needs for developing Asia will reach $22.6 trillion over the next 15 years (from 2016 to 2030) in a baseline scenario. Factoring in climate change adaptation and mitigation raises the needed investments to $26.2 trillion, or 5.9% of projected gross domestic product. A large part of the $3.6 trillion in additional investments over baseline estimates (around 83%) is for climate mitigation-related needs in producing cleaner energy, and limiting global warming to 2 degrees Celsius between now and 2100—the optimal pathway to meet the Paris Agreement goals on climate change. It entails investment in renewable power, smart grids, energy storage, energy efficiency and, where possible, that carbon capture and storage

gain traction. While the sums involved are very large, so too are the benefits. Over the longer term, economic losses from climate change—losses from agriculture and labor productivity, storm damage, even tourism—outweigh the expense (ADB 2016b).

Third, the report's discussion on infrastructure finance highlights the huge increase required in private infrastructure financing and the critical public sector role in helping make that happen. The analysis of financing issues for a selected set of DMCs over the 5-year period from 2016–2020 shows that public sector reforms on both tax revenues and expenditures—while ensuring new borrowing maintains public debt sustainability—can meet around 46% of the gap ($121 billion out of $262 billion) between current and needed investments based on baseline estimates. This leaves 54% of the gap (or $141 billion) for private sector finance (absent new avenues for generating additional public sector resources for infrastructure). Factoring in the climate change cost, public financing will be only 39% of the $308 billion gap. This means 61% of the remaining gap will have to be financed by the private sector.

With the private sector estimated to invest around $63 billion at present, expanding private finance by the required level is no doubt a major challenge. However, the numbers we present should serve as a call for action. In particular, the public sector must consider innovative means of generating income for infrastructure investment, including ramping up land value capture as an alternative means of generating finance, and charging more market-based user fees to bolster the financial condition of public utilities. Equally important, the public sector needs to establish a regulatory and institutional framework that encourages greater private participation in infrastructure—including creating bankable public–private partnerships—giving the best value to taxpayers and deepening capital markets that attract long-term private sourced infrastructure finance.

Fourth, given the public sector's dominant role in infrastructure, it must strengthen its capacity to plan and allocate investments to the right sectors and projects (including appropriate funding for maintenance), while getting projects done on time and on budget. This is vital. Indeed, high quality public sector planning and project design will also help attract private investment by expanding the pipeline of "bankable" projects.

Meeting the region's infrastructure needs is not just about raising adequate financial resources. And this is precisely why multilateral development banks have made technical assistance and policy advice on the wide range of issues above a key part of their support to members' efforts at infrastructure development (Box 6.1).

Box 6.1: ADB's Role in the Region

Multilateral development banks (MDBs) have an important role to play in public and private sector infrastructure finance. Their experience and access to multilateral expertise and the latest technology can also contribute to an economy's policy and institutional environment. Aside from helping build technical capacity in infrastructure planning and project implementation, they can help modernize procurement processes; support the development of a regulatory environment conducive to public-private partnerships (PPPs) and capital market development; and promote the use of appropriate advanced technologies, including climate-proofing design. Indeed, as the public-private mix in infrastructure finance expands and deepens, MDBs can be pivotal in providing advisory services to facilitate transactions. Finally, MDBs can play a key role as coordinator—or "honest broker"—among multiple stakeholders involved with cross-border and regional infrastructure projects that expand regional cooperation and integration.

Over the course of its 50 years, ADB has contributed to the region's development through project- and policy-based lending, technical assistance, research, knowledge dissemination, and dialogue with governments and other development partners and stakeholders. As Asia continues its steady economic advance, ADB will increase its support for the region's priorities, including infrastructure development.

As mentioned (see Box 5.5), one way is by scaling up lending capacity by merging the two sources of ADB funding (Ordinary Capital Resources and the Asian Development Fund). This allows ADB to increase annual lending to $20 billion—nearly 50% above its current capacity.

Given developing Asia's huge infrastructure demand, ADB is also working closely with the private sector to deliver more projects, including renewable energy projects like solar, geothermal, and wind. Moreover, new financial products such as credit guarantees for project bonds and subordinated loans are helping unlock the much needed private capital for infrastructure. ADB is helping unleash the potential of PPPs and offers technical expertise in helping arrange PPP projects. Currently, it provides assistance to countries such as India, Indonesia, Philippines, and Viet Nam in creating PPP laws and/or establishing PPP centers. Moreover, in 2014, the Office of Public Private Partnerships (OPPP) was created to provide transaction advisory services for PPP project preparation. Recently, the Asia-Pacific Project Preparation Facility was launched to support the OPPP.

ADB is also pushing the boundaries of knowledge and innovation across the region. In January 2015, seven sector groups focusing on areas such as energy, transport, and water were formed along with eight thematic groups dedicated to issues such as climate change and rural development. These groups create and promote knowledge-sharing across ADB departments and with external partners in business, academia, and the development sector. Moreover, ADB promotes the use of cleaner and more advanced technologies by revising rules on project design, bidding specifications, and bidder selection. During implementation, all projects must comply with environmental and social safeguards.

Finally, ADB's in-depth regional knowledge—coupled with its experience and technical expertise in economic integration among developing member countries—enables it to act as a coordinator facilitating cross-border and regional infrastructure projects. This includes helping negotiate regional agreements, establishing key regional institutions, and supporting connectivity "software" such as trade facilitation.

References

Abiad, A. D., C. Ablaza, and P. Feliciano. forthcoming. "Scaling-up Public Infrastructure Investment: How Much Room Does Developing Asia Have?"

ADB. 2010. *Report and Recommendation of the President to the Board of Directors: Proposed Loan, Kingdom of Cambodia: Rural Roads Improvement Project.* Manila.

_____. 2010–2015. *Annual Report 2010–2015.* Manila.

_____. 2011. *Study Report on Implementation of Urban Water Supply and Wastewater Projects in India.* Manila.

_____. 2012. *Public-Private Partnership Operational Plan.* Manila.

_____. 2013. *Overview of the GMS Regional Investment Framework (2013–2022).* Manila.

_____. 2014a. *CAREC Transport and Trade Facilitation Strategy 2020.* Manila.

_____. 2014b. *Climate Proofing ADB Investment in the Transport Sector: Initial Experience.* Manila.

_____. 2015. *Strategy and Work Plan (2016–2020) for Regional Cooperation in the Energy Sector of CAREC Countries.* Manila.

_____. 2015a. *Assessment of Power Sector Reforms in Viet Nam.* Manila.

_____. 2015b. *Key Indicators for Asia and the Pacific 2015.* Manila.

_____. 2016a. *Key Indicators for Asia and the Pacific 2016.* Manila.

_____. 2016b. *Asian Development Outlook 2016 Update: Meeting the Low-Carbon Growth Challenge.* Manila.

_____. 2016c. *Operational Plan for Regional Cooperation and Integration, 2016–2020.* Manila.

_____. 2016d. *Fossil Fuel Subsidies in Asia: Trends, Impacts, and Reforms.* Manila.

_____. 2016e. *Addressing Water Security in the People's Republic of China: The 13th Five-Year Plan (2016–2020) and Beyond.* Manila.

_____. 2016f. *Pacific Approach 2016-2020.* Manila.

_____. 2016g. *Project Agreement for Loan 3395-PAK and Grant 0482-PAK: National Motorway M-4 Gojra-Shorkot-Khanewal Section Project–Additional Financing.* Manila.

_____. 2016h. ADB Approves Second Cofinancing with AIIB to Boost Natural Gas Output, Transmission in Bangladesh. News release. 21 November.

_____. 2016i. *Asia Bond Monitor – November 2016.* Manila.

_____. 2016j. *Work Program and Budget Framework, 2017–2019.* Manila.

_____. 2016k. *Private Sector Operations, Brochure.* Manila.

_____. AsianBondsOnline. https://asianbondsonline. adb.org/ (accessed 01 December 2016).

_____. International Comparison Program. https:// www.adb.org/data/icp

ADB and ADBI. 2009. *Infrastructure for a Seamless Asia.* Manila and Tokyo.

ADB, World Bank, and JICA. 2005. *Connecting East Asia: A New Framework for Infrastructure.* Manila, Washington, DC, and Tokyo.

Agence France-Presse. 2016. China's Debt is 250% of GDP and 'Could be Fatal', Says Government Expert. *The Guardian.* 16 June.

Allcott, H., A. Collard-Wexler, and S. D. O'Connell. 2016. "How Do Electricity Shortages Affect Industry? Evidence from India." *American Economic Review* 106 (3): 587-624.

Amstad, M., S. Kong, F. Packer, and E. Remolona. 2016. A Spare Tire for Capital Markets: Fostering Corporate Bond Markets in Asia. *BIS Papers.* No. 85. Basel: Bank for International Settlements.

Ang, A., J. Bail, and H. Zhou. 2015. The Great Wall of Debt: Corruption, Real Estate, and Chinese Local Government Credit Spreads. *Georgetown McDonough School of Business Research Paper No. 2603022; Columbia Business School Research Paper No. 15-57; PBCSF-NIFR Research Paper No. 15-02*

Asher, S. and P. Novosad. 2016. "Market Access and Structural Transformation: Evidence from Rural Roads in India." Manuscript.

Asian Infrastructure Investment Bank. 2015. *Articles of Agreement*. Beijing.

———. 2016a. *2017 Business Plan and Budget*. Beijing.

———. 2016b. *Pakistan: National Motorway M-4 Project*. Beijing.

Banerjee, A., E. Duflo, and N. Qian. 2012. On the Road: Access to Transportation Infrastructure and Economic Growth in China. *Working Paper Series*. No. 17897. Cambridge, MA: National Bureau of Economic Research.

Bank for International Settlements. 2014. Long-Term Finance: Can Emerging Capital Markets Help? *BIS Papers*. No. 75. Basel.

Batt, H. W. 2001. "Value Capture as a Policy Tool in Transportation Economics: An Exploration in Public Finance in the Tradition of Henry George." *American Journal of Economics and Sociology* 60 (1): 195–228.

Berlin, M. 2012. "Banks and Markets: Substitutes, Complements, or Both?" *Business Review* Q2 1-10.

Bertaud, A. 2008. Powerpoint Presentation on Options for New Alternatives for Development Control Regulation and Justification for Increasing FSI. Mumbai. 3 April 2008.

Bhattacharya, A., J. Oppenheim, and N. Stern. 2015. Driving Sustainable Development through Better Infrastructure: Key Elements of a Transformation Program. *Global Economy and Development Working Paper*. No. 91. Washington, DC: Brookings Institution.

Bhattacharyay, B. N. 2010. Estimating Demand for Infrastructure in Energy, Transport, Telecommunications, Water and Sanitation in Asia and the Pacific: 2010-2020. *ADBI Working Paper Series*. No. 248. Tokyo: Asian Development Bank Institute.

Bhattacharyay, B. N., M. Kawai, and R. M. Nag, eds. 2012. *Infrastructure for Asian Connectivity*. Cheltenham, UK and Northampton, MA: Edward Elgar.

Biswas, A. K. and C. Tortajada. 2010. "Water Supply of Phnom Penh: An Example of Good Governance." *Water Resources Development* 26 (2): 157-172.

Bloomberg. New Energy Finance – All Clean Energy; Levelised Cost of Electricity Update: H1 2006. https://about.bnef.com/ (accessed April 2016).

Boston Consulting Group. 2013. *Bridging the Gap: Meeting the Infrastructure Challenge with Public-Private Partnership*. Boston, MA.

Briones, R. and J. Felipe. 2013. Agriculture and Structural Transformation in Developing Asia: Review and Outlook. *ADB Economics Working Paper Series*. No. 363. Manila: Asian Development Bank.

Buchner, B. K., C. Trabacchi, F. Mazza, D. Abramskiehn, and D. Wang. 2015. *Global Landscape of Climate Finance 2015*. San Francisco, CA: Climate Policy Initiative.

Busk, K. and T. Smyth. 2013. *Financial Implications of Container Terminal Automation*. Aarhus: Seaport Group.

Cao, Y. 2016. LPN Securitization from the Perspective of Supply-Side Structure Reform. *SINA Caijing*. 29 August.

Chan, A., P. Lam, D. Chan, and E. Cheung. 2008. "Risk-Sharing Mechanism for Ppp Projects – the Case Study of the Sydney Cross City Tunnel." *Surveying and Built Environment* 19 (1): 67-80.

Chan, E. K. 2009. "Bringing Safe Water to Phnom Penh's City." *International Journal of Water Resources Development* 25 (4): 597–609.

Chatterton, I. and O. S. Puerto. 2011. Estimation of Infrastructure Investment Needs in South Asia Region. *Working Paper*. No. 62608. Washington, DC: World Bank.

Chen, Y. and A. Whalley. 2012. "Green Infrastructure: The Effects of Urban Rail Transit on Air Quality." *American Economic Journal: Economic Policy* 4 (1): 58-97.

China Bond Rating. 2015. *The Analysis of Nationwide Chengtou Bond Issuance in 2014, Four-Dimension Finance*.

Coady, D., I. Parry, L. Sears, and B. Shang. 2015. How Large Are Global Energy Subsidies? *IMF Working Paper*. No. 15/105. Washington, DC: International Monetary Fund.

Cooper, E. M., B. Lefevre, and X. Li. 2016. Can Transport Deliver Ghg Reductions at Scale? An Analysis of Global Transport Initiatives. *Working Paper*. Washington, DC: World Resources Institute.

Das, B., E. S. Chan, C. Visoth, G. Pangare, and R. Simpson. 2010. *Sharing the Reforms Process, Mekong Water Dialogue Publication No. 4*. Gland: International Union for Conservation of Nature.

Datta, S. 2012. "The Impact of Improved Highways on Indian Firms." *Journal of Development Economics* 99 (1): 46–57.

Deloitte. 2015. *TA-7734 IND: Knowledge Management for Inclusive Growth, Final Report Submitted to Asian Development Bank*. Mumbai: Deloitte Touche Tohmatsu India Private Limited.

Dinkelman, T. 2011. "The Effects of Rural Electrification on Employment: New Evidence from South Africa." *American Economic Review* 101 (7): 3078-3108.

Donaldson, D. 2010. Railroads of the Raj: Estimating the Impact of Transportation Infrastructure. *NBER Working Paper Series*. No. 16487. Cambridge, MA: National Bureau of Economic Research.

Economist Intelligence Unit. 2014. *Evaluating the Environment for Public-Private Partnerships in Latin America and the Caribbean: The 2014 Infrascope*. New York, NY.

Ehlers, T. 2014. Understanding the Challenges for Infrastructure Finance. *BIS Working Papers*. No. 454. Basel: Bank for International Settlements.

Essrich, D. 2013. *Asia: Development, Financial Markets, Infrastructure and Consumption, China*. Zurich: Credit Suisse Group AG.

Faber, B. 2014. "Trade Integration, Market Size, and Industrialization: Evidence from China's National Trunk Highway System." *The Review of Economic Studies* 81 (3): 1046-1070.

Fay, M. and T. Yepes. 2003. Investing in Infrastructure: What is Needed from 2000 to 2010? *Policy Research Working Paper*. No. 3102. Washington, D.C.: World Bank

Felipe, J., U. Kumar, and A. Abdon. 2012. "Using Capabilities to Project Growth 2010-2030." *Journal of The Japanese and International Economies* 26 (1): 153–166.

Fung, E. 2016. China's 'Land Kings' Return as Housing Prices Rise. *The Wall Street Journal*. 19 June.

G20. 2016. *MDBs Joint Declaration of Aspirations on Actions to Support Infrastructure Investment*. Hangzhou: G20 Summit Preparatory Committee.

Ghani, E., A. G. Goswami, and W. R. Kerr. 2016. "Highway to Success: The Impact of the Golden Quadrilateral Project for the Location and Performance of Indian Manufacturing." *The Economic Journal* 126 (591): 317-357.

Gibson, J. and S. Rozelle. 2003. "Poverty and Access to Roads in Papua New Guinea." *Economic Development and Cultural Change* 52 (1): 159-185.

Girardin, E. and K. A. Kholodilin. 2011. "How Helpful are Spatial Effects in Forecasting the Growth of Chinese Provinces?" *Journal of Forecasting* 30 (7): 622–643.

Gonzalez Alegre, J., A. Kappeler, A. Kolev, and T. Valila. 2008. Composition of Government Investment in Europe: Some Forensic Evidence. *EIB Papers*. No. 13(1). Luxembourg: European Investment Bank.

Gonzalez-Navarro, M. and M. A. Turner. 2016. Subways and Urban Growth: Evidence from Earth. *SERC Discussion Papers*. No. 195. London: Spatial Economics Research Centre.

Government of Fiji. 2016. "Tropical Cyclone Winston, February 20, 2016." *Post-Disaster Needs Assessment*.

Government of India, National Institution for Transforming India Aayog. 2014–2015. *Annual Report*. New Delhi.

———, Planning Commission. 2013–2014. *Annual Report*. New Delhi.

———, Securities and Exchange Board of India. 2000–2016a. *Statistics on Issues and Redemptions*. Mumbai.

———, Securities and Exchange Board of India. 2000–2016b. *Statistics on Total Outstanding Corporate Debt*. Mumbai.

Gupta, K., R. Hasan, N. Kapoor, and B. Rout. 2014. "A Note on the Impact of Rural Roads on Poverty." Asian Development Bank, Mimeo.

Gyeonggi Province. 2009. *Study on Metropolitan Transport Improvement Measures, Korea (in Korean)*.

Hale, G. and J. A. C. Santos. 2008. "The Decision to First Enter the Public Bond Market: The Role of Firm Reputation, Funding Choices, and Bank Relationships." *Journal of Banking & Finance* 32 (9): 1928-1940.

Hansaku, S. and H. Levinger. 2016. *Asia Infrastructure Financing: Getting It Right Would Lift Medium-Term Growth, Current Issues: Emerging Markets*. Frankfurt am Main: Deutsche Bank Research.

Heller, P. 2005. Back to Basics – Fiscal Space: What it is and How to Get it. *Finance and Development*. June.

Inderst, G. 2010. *Infrastructure as an Asset Class*. Luxembourg: European Investment Bank.

———. 2016. Infrastructure Investment, Private Finance, and Institutional Investors: Asia from a Global Perspective. *ADBI Working Paper Series*. No. 555. Tokyo: Asian Development Bank Institute.

International Energy Agency. 2013. *World Energy Outlook 2013*. Paris.

———. 2014. *World Energy Investment Outlook: Special Report*. Paris.

International Finance Corporation. 2011–2015. *IFC Financials and Projects 2011–2015*. Washington, DC.

International Institute for Sustainable Development. 2015. *Public-Private Partnerships in China: On 2014 as a Landmark Year, with Past and Future Challenges*. Winnipeg.

International Monetary Fund. 2011. *Modernizing the Framework for Fiscal Policy and Public Debt Sustainability Analysis*. Washington, DC.

———. 2014. *Legacies, Clouds, Uncertainties, World Economic Outlook*. Washington, DC.

———. 2015. Making Public Investment More Efficient. Washington, DC.

———. Fiscal Monitor Database. http://data.imf.org/?sk=4BE0C9CB-272A-4667-8892-34B582B21BA6 (accessed 01 December 2016).

———. Investment and Capital Stock Dataset, 1960-2015. https://www.imf.org/external/np/fad/publicinvestment/ (accessed 16 January 2017).

———. 2017. "IMF Article IV Staff Reports." http://www.imf.org/external/ns/cs.aspx?id=51 (last modified 26 February).

International Road Federation. 2012. *World Road Statistics*. Geneva.

International Telecommunication Union. ICT Statistics. http://www.itu.int/en/ITU-D/Statistics/Pages/default.aspx (accessed 31 October 2016).

Islamic Development Bank. 2010–2015. *Annual Report*. Jeddah.

———. 2015. *Country Approvals*. Jeddah.

Jensen, R. 2007. "The Digital Provide: Information (Technology), Market Performance, and Welfare in the South Indian Fisheries Sector." *The Quarterly Journal of Economics* 122 (3): 879-924.

Jizao, X. 2015. End of Land Sales: Land Transfer Payments in the First. *SINA*. 25 May.

Khandker, Shahidur R., Z. Bakht, and Gayatri B. Koolwal. 2009. "The Poverty Impact of Rural Roads: Evidence from Bangladesh." *Economic Development and Cultural Change* 57 (4): 685-722.

Kharas, H. 2010. The Emerging Middle Class in Developing Countries. *Working Paper*. No. 285. Paris: OECD Development Centre.

Kholodilin, K. A., B. Siliverstovs, and S. Kooths. 2008. "A Dynamic Panel Data Approach to the Forecasting of the GDP of German Länder." *Spatial Economic Analysis* 3 (2): 195–207.

Korea Research Institute for Human Settlement. 1992. *Long-Term Road and Railway Network Development Plan in Gyeonggi Province (in Korean)*. Sejong.

Lall, R., R. Anand, and A. Rastogi. 2010. Developing Physical Infrastructure: A Comparative Perspective on the Experience of the People's Republic of China and India. In K. Gerhaeusser, Y. Iwasaki and V. B. Tulasidhar, eds. *Resurging Asian Giants: Lessons from the People's Republic of China and India*. Manila: Asian Development Bank.

Levy, A., "Comparative Subway Construction Costs, Revised." Blog. *Pedestrian Observations*, 2013. 03 June. https://pedestrianobservations. wordpress.com/2013/06/03/comparative-subway-construction-costs-revised/

Li, H. and Z. Li. 2013. "Road Investments and Inventory Reduction: Firm Level Evidence from China." *Journal of Urban Economics* 76 (1): 43-52.

Li, Z. and Y. Chen. 2013. "Estimating the Social Return to Transport Infrastructure: A Price-Difference Approach Applied to a Quasi-Experiment." *Journal of Comparative Economics* 41 (3): 669-683.

Liu, Z. 2004. Planning and Policy Coordination in China's Infrastructure Development. Background paper for the ADB–JBIC–World Bank East Asia and the Pacific Infrastructure Flagship Study. Manila.

———. 2015. Strengthening Municipal Fiscal Health in China. *Land Lines*. Cambridge, MA: The Lincoln Institute of Land Policy.

Maier, T. and M. Jordan-Tank. 2014. *Accelerating Infrastructure Delivery: New Evidence from International Financial Institutions*. Cologny: World Economic Forum.

Mayer, T. and S. Zignago. 2011. Notes on CEPII's Distances Measures: The Geodist Database *CEPII WP*. No. 2011–25. Paris: Centre d'Etudes Prospectives et d'Informations Internationales.

McDonald, A. and L. Schrattenholzer. 2001. "Learning Rates for Energy Technologies." *Energy Policy* 29 (4): 255-261.

McKinsey & Company. 2016. *Financing Change: How to Mobilize Private Sector Financing for Sustainable Infrastructure*. New York, NY.

Mckinsey Global Institute. 2013. *Infrastructure Productivity: How to Save $1 Trillion a Year*. New York, NY: McKinsey & Company.

———. 2014. *Using PPPs to Fund Critical Greenfield Infrastructure Projects*. New York, NY: McKinsey & Company.

———. 2016. *Bridging Global Infrastructure Gaps*. New York, NY: McKinsey & Company.

New Development Bank. 2017. "NDB Fact Sheet." http://ndb.int/pdf/NDB-Fact-Sheet.pdf (accessed 06 February).

Nokia. 2014. Mobile Broadband with HSPA and LTE – Capacity and Cost Aspects. *Nokia White Paper*. Espoo.

Ordinario, C. 2015. "Phl's PPP Program among World's Best." *Business Mirror*. 22 May.

Organisation for Economic Co-operation and Development. 2010a. *Taxation, Innovation and the Environment*. Paris.

———. 2010b. *Perspectives on Global Development 2010: Shifting Wealth*. Paris.

———. 2011. *Strategic Transport Infrastructure Needs to 2030*. Paris.

———. Glossary of Statistical Terms. https://stats. oecd.org/glossary/ (accessed 01 December 2016).

———. International Development Statistics Online Databases. https://www.oecd.org/development/stats/idsonline.htm (accessed 01 December 2016).

———. Official Development Finance for Infrastructure: Support by Multilateral and Bilateral Development Partners. https://stats. oecd.org/glossary/ (accessed 01 December 2016).

Pacific Region Infrastructure Facility. 2016. *2016 Pacific Infrastructure Performance Indicators 'PIPIs'*. Sydney.

_____. 2017. "Home Page." http://www.theprif.org/index.php (accessed 06 February).

Paulson Institute, Energy Foundation China and Chinese Renewable Energy Industries Association. 2016. *Green Finance for Low-Carbon Cities*. Chicago, IL; San Francisco, CA; Beijing.

Peterson, G. E. 2008. *Unlocking Land Values to Finance Urban Infrastructure, Trends and Policy Options (PPIAF)*. Washington, DC: World Bank.

Phin, "Rail Construction Costs." Blog. *Public Transport Issues in Melbourne*, 2008. https://melbpt.wordpress.com/rail-construction-costs/

PPP in Infrastructure Resource Center. 2016. "Main Financing Mechanisms for Infrastructure Projects." https://ppp.worldbank.org/public-private-partnership/financing/mechanisms (last modified 6 September).

Preqin. 2016. *Infrastructure, The Q2 2016 Preqin Quarterly Update*. New York, NY.

PricewaterhouseCoopers (Cambodia). 2015. *Phnom Penh Water Supply Authority Financial Statements for the Year Ended 31 December 2014*. Phnom Penh.

PricewaterhouseCoopers LLP. 2014. *Capital Project and Infrastructure Spending: Outlook to 2025*. New York, NY.

PricewaterhouseCoopers. 2015. *Power in Indonesia: Investment and Taxation Guide*. 3rd Edition ed. Jakarta.

Rao, V. 2015. Developing the Financial Sector and Expanding Market Instruments to Support a Post-2015 Development Agenda in Asia and the Pacific. *ADB Sustainable Development Working Paper Series*. No. 36. Manila: Asian Development Bank.

Reis, L. A., J. Emmerling, M. Tavoni, and D. Raitzer. 2016. The Economics of Greenhouse Gas Mitigation in Developing Asia. *ADB Economics Working Paper Series*. No. 504. Manila: Asian Development Bank.

Replogle, M. A. and L. M. Fulton. 2014. *A Global High Shift Scenario: Impacts and Potential for More Public Transport, Walking, and Cycling with Lower Car Use*. New York, NY and Davis, CA: Institute for Transportation and Development Policy and University of California, Davis.

Reside, R. E. 1999. Estimating the Philippine Government's Exposure to and Risk from Contingent Liabilities in Infrastructure Projects. *Discussion Paper*. No. 9914. Quezon City: University of the Philippines School of Economics.

Ruiz-Nunez, F. and Z. Wei. 2015. Infrastructure Investment Demands in Emerging Markets and Developing Economies. *Policy Research Working Paper*. No. 7414. Washington, D.C.: World Bank.

Sawada, Y. 2015. The Impacts of Infrastructure in Development: A Selective Survey. *ADBI Working Paper Series*. No. 511. Tokyo: Asian Development Bank Institute.

Shon, E. Y. 2016. Infrastructure Financing in Korea. Background paper for the Asian Development Bank's Technical Workshop on Infrastructure Finance. Manila. 18-19 August.

Straub, S. 2008. Infrastructure and Growth in Developing Countries : Recent Advances and Research Challenges. *Policy Research Working Papers*. No. 4460. Washington, DC: World Bank.

Suzuki, H., J. Murakami, Y.-H. Hong, and B. Tamayose. 2015. *Financing Transit-Oriented Development with Land Values: Adapting Land Value Capture in Developing Countries*. Washington, DC: The World Bank.

The Economist. 2014. "Investing in Infrastructure: The Trillion-Dollar Gap." 22 March.

The Wall Street Journal. 2014. "China Not Planning to Expand Pilot Property-Tax Program." 19 March.

Tokyo Engineering Consultants & Nihon Suido Consultants. 1993. *The Study on Phnom*

Penh Water Supply System in the Kingdom of Cambodia, Final Report, Vol. 1, Summary. Tokyo: Japan International Cooperation Agency.

United Nations. 2009. *System of National Accounts 2008.* New York, NY.

_____. 2015 Revision of World Population Prospects. https://esa.un.org/unpd/wpp/ (accessed 01 December 2016)

_____. 2015. *Central Product Classification Ver. 2.1.* New York, NY.

_____. Global SDG Indicators Database. http://data.worldbank.org/indicator (accessed 01 December 2016).

_____. World Urbanization Prospects, the 2014 Revision. https://esa.un.org/unpd/wpp/ (accessed 01 December 2016).

United Nations Economic and Social Commission for Asia and the Pacific. 2008. *Public-Private Partnerships in Infrastructure Development: A Primer.* Bangkok.

United Nations Environment Programme. 2014. *The Adaptation Gap Report 2014.* Nairobi.

United Nations Framework Convention on Climate Change. 2007. *Climate Change: Impacts, Vulnerabilities and Adaptation in Developing Countries.* Bonn.

US Energy Information Administration. International Energy Statistics. http://www.eia.gov/beta/international/data/browser (accessed 01 December 2016).

Wagenvoort, R., C. de Nicola, and A. Kappeler. 2010. Infrastructure Finance in Europe: Composition, Evolution and Crisis Impact. *EIB Papers.* No. 15(1). Luxembourg: European Investment Bank.

Wilson, D. and R. Purushothaman. 2006. Dreaming with Brics: The Path to 2050. In S. C. Jain, ed. *Emerging Economies and the Transformation of International Business: Brazil, Russia, India and China (Brics).* Gloucestershire, England and Northampton, MA: Edward Elgar Publishing.

World Bank. 2010. *Economics of Adaptation to Climate Change: Synthesis Report.* Washington, DC.

_____. 2013a. Pressures Mounting. *Indonesia Economic Quarterly.* March.

_____. 2013b. *Planning, Connecting, and Financing Cities—Now.* Washington, DC.

_____. 2015a. *Technical Note: Estimating Infrastructure Investment and Capital Stock in Indonesia.* Jakarta.

_____. 2015b. "High Expectation." *Indonesia Economic Quarterly,* http://www.indonesia-investments.com/upload/documents/World-Bank-Indonesia-Economic-Quarterly-March-2015-Indonesia-Investments.pdf.

_____. Enterprise Surveys Data. http://www.enterprisesurveys.org/ (accessed 01 December 2016).

_____. International Comparison Program. http://siteresources.worldbank.org/ICPEXT/Resources/ICP_2011.html

_____. PovcalNet. http://iresearch.worldbank.org/PovcalNet/home.aspx (accessed 01 December 2016).

_____. Private Participation in Infrastructure Database. http://ppi.worldbank.org/ (accessed 01 December 2016).

_____. World Development Indicators. http://data.worldbank.org/indicator (accessed 01 December 2016).

World Bank and Development Research Center of the State Council, the People's Republic of China. 2014. *Urban China: Toward Efficient, Inclusive, and Sustainable Urbanization.* Washington, DC and Beijing.

World Economic Forum. 2013. *The Green Investment Report: The Ways and Means to Unlock Private Finance for Green Growth.* Geneva.

_____. 2014. *Strategic Infrastructure Steps to Operate and Maintain Infrastructure Efficiently and Effectively.* Cologny.

_____. 2015. *The Global Competitiveness Report 2015-2016.* Edited by K. Schwab. Geneva.

Yanev, P. I. 2010. *It is Not Too Late : Preparing for Asia's Next Big Earthquake–with Emphasis on the Philippines, Indonesia, and China: Policy Note*. Washington, DC: World Bank.

Yoshino, N. and U. Abidhadjaev. 2015. An Impact Evaluation of Investment in Infrastructure: The Case of the Railway Connection in Uzbekistan. *ADBI Working Paper Series*. No. 548. Tokyo: Asian Development Bank Institute.

Yoshino, N. and V. Pontines. 2015. The "Highway Effect" on Public Finance: Case of the Star Highway in the Philippines. *ADBI Working Paper Series*. No. 549. Tokyo: Asian Development Bank Institute.

Zhang, J. and L. C. Xu. 2016. "The Long-Run Effects of Treated Water on Education: The Rural Drinking Water Program in China." *Journal of Development Economics* 122 (1): 1-15.

Zhao, Z. 2014. Making China's Urban Transportation Boom Sustainable. *Paulson Institute Policy Memorandum*. Chicago, IL: The Paulson Institute.

Zhao, Z. and C. Cao. 2011. "Funding China's Urban Infrastructure: Revenue Structure and Financing Mechanisms." *Public Finance and Management* 11 (3).

Zhu, J., Y. Yan, C. He and C. Wang. 2015. "China's Environment: Big Issues, Accelerating Effort, Ample Opportunities." *Equity Research*.

Appendix

Appendix 3.1: DMC Coverage in Selected Figures and Tables

Figure 3.1: Subregional BUDGET + PPI infrastructure investment, 2011	22 Developing Member Economies[a]
Figure 3.2: BUDGET + PPI Infrastructure Investment Rate, various years (% of GDP)	22 DMCs
Figure 3.3: Public and Private Infrastructure Investment, by income group, 2011	15 DMCs (excludes the People's Republic of China; India; Bangladesh; Hong Kong, China; Republic of Korea; Singapore; Thailand)
Figure 3.5: Alternative Measures of Infrastructure Investment, 2011 (% of GDP)	19 DMCs (includes Myanmar and Taipei,China; excludes Kiribati; Malaysia; Maldives; Myanmar; Papua New Guinea)
Table 5.1: Estimated Annual Infrastructure Investment Needs and Gaps, 25 ADB Developing Member Countries, 2016–2020 ($ billion in 2015 prices)	25 DMCs (includes Afghanistan; Cambodia; Federated States of Micronesia; Kazakhstan; Kyrgyz Republic; Myanmar; Marshall Islands; excludes Georgia; Hong Kong, China; Republic of Korea; Singapore)
Figure 5.2: Public and Private Infrastructure Investment, Selected Economies, 2010–2014 (% of GDP)	25 DMCs (includes Afghanistan; Cambodia; Federated States of Micronesia; Kazakhstan; Kyrgyz Republic; Myanmar; Marshall Islands; excludes Georgia; Hong Kong, China; Republic of Korea; Singapore)
Figure 5.3: Fiscal Space in Developing Asia (% of GDP)	25 DMCs (includes Afghanistan; Cambodia; Federated States of Micronesia; Kazakhstan; Kyrgyz Republic; Myanmar; Marshall Islands; excludes Georgia; Hong Kong, China; Republic of Korea; Singapore)
Figure 5.4: Meeting Investment Needs for 24 DMCs (PRC excluded), (2016–2020 annual average; in 2015 prices)	24 DMCs (includes Afghanistan; Cambodia; Federated States of Micronesia; Kazakhstan; Kyrgyz Republic; Myanmar; Marshall Islands; excludes the People's Republic of China; Georgia; Hong Kong, China; Republic of Korea; Singapore)

DMC = developing member country; GDP = gross domestic product; PPI = private participation in infrastructure.

a The 22 developing member economies include the People's Republic of China; Republic of Korea; Hong Kong, China; Mongolia; Bangladesh; Bhutan; India; Maldives; Nepal; Pakistan; Sri Lanka; Indonesia; Malaysia; Philippines; Singapore; Thailand; Viet Nam; Fiji; Kiribati; Papua New Guinea; Armenia; and Georgia.

Appendix 4.1: Methodology and Data for Estimating Infrastructure Investment Needs

The methodology for estimating infrastructure investment needs without climate change adjustment (baseline) is similar to that used in the literature, e.g. ADB and ADBI (2009), Fay and Yepes (2003), and Ruiz-Nunez and Wei (2015). We estimate a dynamic panel model[81] for each type of infrastructure as follows:

$$I_{it} = \alpha_0 + \alpha_1 I_{it-1} + \alpha_2 y_{it} + \alpha_3 Agr_{it} + \alpha_4 Ind_{it} + \alpha_5 Urban_{it} + \alpha_6 Popden_{it} + \delta_i + \gamma_t + \varepsilon_{it} \quad (1)$$

where I_{it} is the physical infrastructure stock (e.g. per capita electricity generating capacity) of country i in year t (the full set of dependent variables is listed in Table A4.1). I_{it} is assumed to be correlated with several variables, including lagged values of the infrastructure stock to capture persistence and partial adjustment, gross domestic product (GDP) per capita (y_{it}), shares of agriculture and industrial value-added in GDP, the urbanization rate (share of population in urban areas) and population density.

Table A4.1: Infrastructure Sectors Covered in the Study

Sector	Infrastructure stock variables
Road	Kilometer of road per 1,000 km² of land area
Rail	Kilometer of railroad per 1,000 km² of land area
Air Port	Number of Passengers per 100 population
Ports	TEU per 100 population
Electricity	Kilowatt of installed electricity generation capacity per capita
Telephone	Number of Subscriptions per 100 population
Mobile	Number of Subscriptions per 100 population
Broadband	Number of Subscriptions per 100 population
Water	Percent of population with access
Sanitation	Percent of population with access

km² = square kilometer; teu = twenty-foot equivalent unit.

81 We estimated the model with both OLS and GMM-IV estimators. In principle, GMM-IV estimates are superior as they potentially tackle the endogeneity concerns when estimating fixed effects models with lagged dependent variables. However, the results suggest that using the GMM-IV estimator has much lower explanatory power as measured by the mean squared error as compared to OLS. Moreover, the GMM-IV estimator has been found to have unsatisfactory and unstable performance in out-of-sample forecasting (Girardin and Kholodilin 2011; Kholodilin, Siliverstovs, and Kooths 2008). Considering that the main purpose of estimating equation 1 is for projecting future stocks of infrastructure, we choose to estimate the model using OLS rather than GMM.

All these variables are expressed in natural logs for the estimation of equation 1. The regression model also contains country and time fixed effects.

Second, forecasts of the right-hand side variables over 2016–2030 are substituted in the estimated equation (1) to project future infrastructure stocks for 2016–2030 (see discussion below on the source of the forecasted variables).[82]

The total investment need is assumed to depend on both investment in new infrastructure as well as maintenance cost associated with existing infrastructure stock. The investment needs for new infrastructure in a future year t is thus calculated as

$$M_{it} = c\Delta I_{it} = c(I_{it} - I_{it-1})$$

where c is the unit cost for type of infrastructure (see Appendix 4.3).

Following the literature and the views of Asian Development Bank (ADB) experts, we assume a depreciation rate of 2% for power, railway, ports and airports, 3% for roads, water supply and sanitation, and 8% for telecommunication. The maintenance cost is calculated as the product of the depreciation rate, previous year's stock and the unit cost of each type of infrastructure. The total infrastructure investment need for a country is a sum of new investment needs and maintenance costs across different sectors and over the forecasting period of 2016–2030. These are our baseline estimates.

The countries covered include 45 of the ADB's developing member countries. The data sources used to estimate equation (1) are as following: (i) GDP per capita, country land area, population and urban population, agriculture and manufacturing value-added shares to GDP, railroad length, fixed-telephone line subscriptions, mobile cellular subscriptions, container port traffic, air transport passengers, and improved water source and sanitation facilities (% of population with access) all come from the World Bank's World Development Indicators (WDI); (ii) Road length comes from WDI and is supplemented with data from International Road Federation (2012); (iii) Broadband subscriptions come from the ICT Statistics, International Telecommunication Union; and (iv) Electricity generation capacity comes from the International Energy Statistics, US Energy Information Administration.

Forecasted right-hand side variables are obtained from the following sources: (i) GDP projections (2016–2030) are based on staff estimates (see Appendix 4.2 for details); (ii) For agricultural share of GDP, using actual data for the latest year (2012) and Briones and Felipe (2013)'s projections for 16 Asian Development Fund[83] countries for 2040, values for in-between years (2013–2039) were derived by linear interpolation for these countries. The subregional average change rates were applied for countries with no projected data in Briones and Felipe (2013) from 2013 onward. The projected share is held constant when it declines to 5%; (iii) For industrial share of GDP, data for the most recent year available from WDI were used across years due to absence of any projections; (iv) Population projections (medium variant) come from 2015 Revision of World Population Prospects, United

---

82 The model estimates unreasonably high or low infrastructure needs for Southeast Asia, the Kyrgyz Republic, Tajikistan, Bhutan, and Afghanistan. Low public investment has persisted in Southeast Asia after the Asian Financial Crisis restraining infrastructure provision in these countries. Tajikistan and the Kyrgyz Republic had high levels of infrastructure provision, probably reflecting their histories as former republics of the Soviet Union. Bhutan has abnormally high infrastructure investment for several years as a result of very large hydroelectric power projects. For Afghanistan, substantial aid has been provided in its infrastructure, especially road, in recent years. The expectation however is that the pattern of infrastructure provision in these countries will not sustain in long term. Therefore, we use regional rather than country-specific fixed effects for these countries in projections.

83 The Asian Development Fund (ADF) provides grants to ADB's lower-income developing member countries (DMCs). Established in 1974, the ADF initially provided loans on concessional terms. Grants were introduced in 2005, and beginning 2017, with ADB's concessional lending financed from its ordinary capital resources (OCR), the ADF has become a grant-only operation. Activities supported by the ADF promote poverty reduction and improvements in the quality of life in the poorer countries of the Asia and the Pacific. For further details, visit https://www.adb.org/site/funds/adf.

Nations; and (v) Urban population shares are derived on the basis of linear interpolation based on 5-year projections of the World Urbanization Prospects, the 2014 Revision, United Nations.

For investment needs with climate change adjustment, we consider two additional infrastructure-related investments: mitigation and climate proofing, a key component of adaption efforts. For climate change mitigation, ADB (2016b) employs a model to estimate additional investments that are needed in the power sector for each year and subregion except Central Asia.

According to the analysis, climate change mitigation under an optimal scenario to limit warming to 2 degrees causes different relative changes to power supply infrastructure costs across Asia. These differences arise due to regional variation in the relative emissions reduction that occurs from baseline levels (countries with lower abatement costs have more mitigation), the share of mitigation that occurs through the energy sector, the share of energy sector mitigation that occurs through changes in the electricity mix, and the cost of the low-carbon electricity generation infrastructure for achieving the change in electricity mix. In general, the costs increase over time and more rapidly after 2020.[84]

The study estimates that the additional investments required for the power sector carbon mitigation from 2016–2030 amount to $2,488 billion in 2005 prices and $2,938 billion in 2015 prices for developing Asia excluding Central Asia. This is equal to 26% of our baseline projection for the power sector. We use the study's estimates for each year and subregion, adding these to our baseline power investments to capture mitigation investments. For Central Asian countries, we assume that the additional investments will be 26% of their baseline power investments.

As far as climate proofing is concerned, we sourced our estimates of additional investment as a percentage of baseline investment from ADB project experiences in water and sanitation sector and recent studies that conduct such estimation for transport and power sectors. Based on a recent ADB project database, climate proofing-related investments account for 1.9% of the total baseline investments in the water and sanitation sector. The median estimates in recent studies (i.e. ADB 2014b; United Nations Framework Convention on Climate Change 2007; World Bank 2010) suggest 7.8% for road, 0.6% for rail, seaport and airport, and 0.4% for power.

We apply these estimates to our baseline estimates to obtain investment for climate proofing. This estimate should be understood as indicative of a potentially wide and currently uncertain range of investment required to ensure a climate-resilient infrastructure base. It should also be noted that the additional cost requires for any specific project can vary by orders of magnitude, reflecting region, sector, project location, scale and complexity, and the nature and magnitude of the assessed climate risks among other factors.

Our investment projection with climate change adjustment is the sum of baseline estimates, mitigation investments, and climate proofing investments.

Appendix 4.2: GDP Growth Projections: Methodology

Section 4's estimates of infrastructure needs in Asia depend on projections of gross domestic product (GDP), population, and other variables for 2016–2030. GDP projections were derived as follows. First, 2016 and 2017 GDP growth projections for the Asian Development Bank (ADB) developing member countries (DMCs) were taken from the *Asian Development Outlook Update (ADOU) 2016* (ADB 2016b).

[84] A detailed analysis of mitigation responses, including in the power sector, across selected DMCs and subregions in the Asia and the Pacific is provided in ADB (2016b) and Reis et al. (2016) based on the World Induced Technical Change Hybrid (WITCH) model.

Second, these were combined with projections for long-term GDP growth from 2018 to 2030 based on a simple aggregate production function that relates output to contributions by two factor inputs, labor and capital—as well as a Hicks-neutral shift in the production function. To avoid sharp fluctuations in growth beyond 2017 (as ADOU short-term forecasts shift to model-based projections), a 2-year symmetric moving average (t-2, t-1, t, t+1 and t+2) of growth rates is used to provide a set of baseline estimates for GDP growth from 2016 to 2030.

Third, these baseline estimates are compared with assessments by country experts. In several cases, these assessments are based on quantitative country-specific models of long-term growth; in others, they provide qualitative information on whether the benchmark projections are on the high/low side based on economic circumstances and prospects of individual developing member countries (DMCs). The final set of "benchmark" country projections are determined by balancing these assessments with long-term growth projection ranges during 2010–2030 as proposed by Felipe, Kumar, and Abdon (2012). The long-term ranges are based on a cross-country regression model where long-term fundamentals are determined by countries' accumulated capabilities and capacity to undergo structural transformation—as captured by detailed information on export baskets, their sophistication and diversification.

Finally, GDP per capita is calculated by dividing the GDP forecasts by population estimates from 2015 Revision of World Population Prospects, United Nations. The final GDP growth projections for each subregion are listed in Table A4.2.

Turning to the details of the second step outlined above, projections were generated using the approach of Kharas (2010) and Wilson and Purushothaman (2006). In particular, a Cobb-Douglas production function is assumed with the following specification:

$$GDP_t = L_t^{\alpha} K_t^{(1-\alpha)} TFP$$

where GDP_t is gross domestic product at time t. L, K, and TFP represents labor force, capital stock, and total factor productivity, respectively. Alpha (α) is the labor share in production and is assumed to be 2/3, as in Kharas (2010). The labor force is assumed to evolve as per International Labour Organization (ILO) projections to 2030. Capital stocks are assumed to evolve as:

$$K_t = K_{t-1}(1-\delta) + I_t$$

where I is investment and captured by gross fixed capital formation and δ is the rate of depreciation, assumed at 6% per annum. Investments are projected forward by assuming these to be a function of the lagged value of the investment to GDP ratio and the GDP growth rate of the previous year; total factor productivity (TFP) growth is a function of TFP growth in the United States (US) (assumed to grow 1.3% annually), the gap in GDP per capita between the US and each DMC (to capture "convergence" effects), and past growth (to distinguish between countries converging and those that are not).

The TFP growth of DMCs is linked to TFP growth of the US, which is assumed to grow 1.3% per annum. However, this link varies by type of DMC—which are characterized in terms of past growth performance (Organisation for Economic

Table A4.2: Gross Domestic Product Growth Projections By Region

Regional Member	2000–2015	2016–2030
Developing member countries	7.6	5.3
Central Asia	7.7	3.1
East Asia	8.5	5.1
South Asia	6.6	6.5
Southeast Asia	5.2	5.1
The Pacific	3.9	3.1

Source: ADB 2015c; ADB 2016b; World Development Indicators, World Bank; ADB estimates.

Co-operation and Development 2010b); economies that have grown rapidly over the past 15 years are assumed to converge relatively faster to the US and exhibit higher TFP growth.

Appendix 4.3: Infrastructure Unit Costs

The conventional way to forecast infrastructure investment needs is to apply unit costs to projected increments of physical infrastructure stock (e.g. ADB and ADBI 2009, Fay and Yepes 2003, and Ruiz-Nunez and Wei 2015). Previous estimates were largely based on expert opinions of World Bank staff (Ruiz-Nunez and Wei 2015). To provide an additional empirical basis for the unit costs used in this chapter, the estimates are updated using information provided through ADB projects in developing Asia. The updates include road, railroad, and water supply and sanitation projects—which comprise the majority of infrastructure investments and ADB's portfolio.

The method used is relatively straightforward. We put together project-level data on total cost and quantity of the major output—such as additional kilometers of highway constructed under the project. The total cost (converted to constant United States [US] dollars) is divided by the output to calculate the unit cost for each project. To reduce the impact of outlier cases, the median of the sample is used as the sector unit cost. A few caveats are warranted. First, estimating a unit cost for any broadly defined infrastructure type—roads, for example—is quite difficult when considering the many factors that help determine its costs.[85] Even within the limited number of ADB-financed projects, the range of unit costs is sizable. So they are developed here to provide a "rough" average that can be applied to the estimated quantities of physical infrastructure demand to calculate the projected financial needs.[86] Second, for multi-output projects, only the main output is used for calculating unit costs.[87] Third, project costs include consulting services and sometimes training in addition to civil works and equipment—given its emphasis on safeguards and capacity building, ADB projects may have slightly higher shares of consulting and training costs than a typical developing country project.

Table A4.3 presents the unit costs this report uses along with estimates from some other similar studies. There are three point estimates for roads from ADB project information—$7,955,000 per kilometer (/km) for expressways, $709,000/km for highways, and $11,100/km for rural roads. Using the top-down model described in Appendix 4.1, paved roads are projected to account for about 74%, and unpaved roads for 26%, of all roads built in the region to 2030. In light of this, we assume that 1% of all roads will be expressways, 73% highways, and 26% rural roads. These percentages are then applied to the three cost estimates respectively to get a single unit cost for roads—$600,000/km.[88] This turns out very close to the Fay and Yepes (2003) estimate converted to 2010 US dollars.

The estimated unit cost for new railways is $3.855 million/km, substantially higher than the existing estimates of $0.9–$1.2 million/km. Discussions with ADB railway specialists and desk research[89] suggest the estimate is close to the lower end of unit costs (for nonelectric single track lines, for example).

---

85 For example, the costs of a road project will vary depending on (i) road specifications (such as 6-lane expressways versus 2-lane rural roads or length proportions of bridges and tunnels, (ii) geographic or natural conditions (such as terrain, soil conditions, and weather), (iii) a country or region's market and policy environment, and (iv) technological advances over time.

86 We would not recommend to use the unit costs presented here to gauge specific projects, which are to be carried out in various different contexts.

87 Some projects that produce multiple outputs with equal weights are excluded given the difficulty in assigning the cost share of each output.

88 According to ADB experts, road construction costs are significantly higher in the Pacific due to their small geographic size and isolation from the major markets. To address this concern, we assume the unit cost for road is one third higher, i.e. $800,000/km, in the Pacific.

89 See Phin (2008) for example.

Table A4.3: Estimated Unit Cost of Infrastructure ($)				
Sector	Unit	ADB (in 2010 prices)	Nuñez & Wei (in 2011 prices)	Fay & Yepes (in 2000 prices)
Road	kilometer	600,000	–	410,000
Paved	kilometer	–	500,000	–
Unpaved	kilometer	–	51,000	–
Rail	kilometer	3,855,000	1,200,000	900,000
Electricity	kilowatt	2,513	2,700	1,900
Water supply	person	161	150 (rural); 80 (urban)	400/connection
Sanitation	person	168	150	700/connection
Telephone landline	line	261[a]	200–300	400
Mobile line	line	127[a]	90–130	700 in 2000; 580, 2005 onward
Broadband	person	3.4[b]	–	–
Port	twenty-foot equivalent unit	400[c]	360	–
Airport	passenger	6.5[d]	–	–

a Chatterton and Puerto (2011); b Nokia (2014); c Busk and Smyth (2013); d Organisation for Economic Co-operation and Development (2011).

The estimate for water supply and sanitation is the unit cost per connection converted to unit cost per capita—the per connection cost is divided by the country's average household size. The median of the sample pooled across rural and urban projects is used in line with the physical projections done for the country as a whole. The estimates are close to the existing ones for both water supply and sanitation.

We derive the unit cost for electricity generation and ratio of transmission and distribution investments to generation investment for Asia based on IEA estimates (IEA 2014). These allow us to compute a unit cost for building each kilowatt generation capacity and associated transmission and distribution infrastructure, which equals $2,513 in 2010 prices. Unit costs for telephone landline and mobile line, broadband, ports and airports are obtained from Chatterton and Puerton (2011), Nokia (2014), Busk and Smyth (2013) and OECD (2011), respectively.

Appendix 4.4: Profiles of Economies

Region	Economy	Income Group	Geography
Central Asia	Armenia	Lower middle	Landlocked
Central Asia	Azerbaijan	Upper middle	Landlocked
Central Asia	Georgia	Upper middle	Coastal
Central Asia	Kazakhstan	Upper middle	Landlocked
Central Asia	Kyrgyz Republic	Lower middle	Landlocked
Central Asia	Tajikistan	Lower middle	Landlocked
Central Asia	Turkmenistan	Upper middle	Landlocked
Central Asia	Uzbekistan	Lower middle	Landlocked
East Asia	People's Republic of China	Upper middle	Coastal
East Asia	Hong Kong, China	High	Coastal
East Asia	Republic of Korea	High	Coastal
East Asia	Mongolia	Lower middle	Landlocked
East Asia	Taipei,China	High	Island
South Asia	Afghanistan	Low	Landlocked
South Asia	Bangladesh	Lower middle	Coastal
South Asia	Bhutan	Lower middle	Landlocked
South Asia	India	Lower middle	Coastal
South Asia	Pakistan	Lower middle	Coastal
South Asia	Sri Lanka	Lower middle	Island
South Asia	Maldives	Upper middle	Island
South Asia	Nepal	Low	Landlocked
Southeast Asia	Brunei Darussalam	High	Coastal
Southeast Asia	Indonesia	Lower middle	Coastal
Southeast Asia	Cambodia	Lower middle	Coastal
Southeast Asia	Lao People's Democratic Republic	Lower middle	Landlocked
Southeast Asia	Myanmar	Lower middle	Coastal
Southeast Asia	Malaysia	Upper middle	Coastal
Southeast Asia	Philippines	Lower middle	Island
Southeast Asia	Singapore	High	Coastal
Southeast Asia	Thailand	Upper middle	Coastal
Southeast Asia	Viet Nam	Lower middle	Coastal
The Pacific	Cook Islands*	Upper middle	Island
The Pacific	Fiji	Upper middle	Island
The Pacific	Federated States of Micronesia	Lower middle	Island
The Pacific	Kiribati	Lower middle	Island
The Pacific	Marshall Islands	Upper middle	Island
The Pacific	Nauru	High	Island
The Pacific	Palau	Upper middle	Island
The Pacific	Papua New Guinea	Lower middle	Island
The Pacific	Solomon Islands	Lower middle	Island
The Pacific	Timor-Leste	Lower middle	Island
The Pacific	Tonga	Lower middle	Island
The Pacific	Tuvalu	Upper middle	Island
The Pacific	Vanuatu	Lower middle	Island
The Pacific	Samoa	Lower middle	Island

* Income classification is based on OECD's DAC List of ODA Recipients.
Geography: Landlocked (definition adopted from Mayer and Zignago (2011) = Economies with no territorial access to the sea; Coastal = Economies with access to the sea while not surrounded by water bodies; Island = Economies surrounded by bodies of water.
Note: Income group is based on World Bank's income classification: Low income = $1,025 or less Gross National Income (GNI) per capita in 2015; Lower middle income = between $1,026 and $4,035 GNI per capita in 2015; Higher middle income = between $4,036 and $12,475 GNI per capita in 2015; High income = $12,476 or more GNI per capita in 2015.

Appendix 5.1: Country Information on Fiscal Space for Infrastructure Investment

Country	Is raising infra spending a priority?	Is public debt sustainability a concern?	Potential revenue increase, in % of GDP	Potential spending reorientation, in % of GDP	Source
Afghanistan	Yes; "infrastructure deficit," "pressing infrastructure needs" (Key Issues: Context, Page 6)	Public debt is low due to debt relief, but public finances are heavily dependent on large grants, whose long-term future is uncertain. (Risks, Paragraph 15, Page 9)	Measures to strengthen enforcement and compliance and improve tax policy could raise revenues by 4% of GDP (Footnote 13, Page 11 of IMF report; and page 18 of World Bank report)	Authorities aiming for a more "pro-growth recomposition of public spending," but details and impact are not quantified. Energy subsidies are 0.1% of GDP. (Paragraph 23, Page 12; MEFP, Paragraph 25)	IMF Request for ECF (2016) http://www.imf.org/external/pubs/ft/scr/2016/cr16252.pdf; and World Bank Afghanistan Development Update (2016)
Armenia	Yes; "capital and social spending remain a priority" (Paragraph 13, Page 12)	Yes; debt is high and rising and deficit is large (Paragraph 8, page 46)	Tax reforms are expected to raise revenues by 2 percent of GDP by 2021. (Box 1, Page 11)	Little room to further cut expenditures. No more energy subsidies. (Paragraph 28, Page 16)	IMF Third Review (2016) http://www.imf.org/external/pubs/ft/scr/2016/cr16246.pdf
Bangladesh	Yes; "need to ramp up public investment in critical infrastructure" (Paragraph 29, page 22)	No; debt remains stable at a moderate level (Press release, Page 1)	2% of GDP, based on new VAT (Structural Reforms, Page 46)	1% of GDP can be raised by cutting energy subsidies. (Box 4, Page 23)	IMF Article IV Staff Report (2015) http://www.imf.org/external/pubs/ft/scr/2016/cr1627.pdf
Bhutan	Yes, but a very large rise in capital spending is already in budget (Key Issues, Challenges, Page 1)	Only moderate risks, despite high debt; large hydro projects imply debt rising sharply, but these are guaranteed by Indian government and can generate significant returns (DSA, Paragraph 10, Page 5) and (DSA, Paragraph 10, Page 6, 2nd bullet)	A new GST by end-2018 will raise 0.3 percent of GDP for each PP increase in the rate; removal of tax exemptions and holidays can raise revenue by up to 2 percent of GDP. (Paragraph 16, Page 12)	Limited space; current spending has been kept limited. (Paragraph 18, Page 8; Statement by Subir Gokarn, Paragraph 6, Page 2)	IMF Article IV Staff Report (2016) http://www.imf.org/external/pubs/ft/scr/2016/cr16206.pdf
Cambodia	Yes; "growth-critical capital spending" (Paragraph 18, Page 14)	No; risk of debt distress is low (DSA, Introductory Paragraph, Page 1)	Past tax reforms generated an additional 2.2 percent of GDP in revenue; modernizing administration and tax policy will increase revenues by 0.5 percent of GDP (Fiscal Sustainability, Page 3; Footnote 12, Page13)	There was an unwelcome shift in the spending mix, raising current spending by 1.3% of GDP and cutting capital spending by 0.6% of GDP. (Paragraph 15, Page 13)	IMF Article IV Staff Report (2015) http://www.imf.org/external/pubs/ft/scr/2015/cr15307.pdf
China, People's Republic of	No; "more focus on health and social security," and infrastructure spending already "buoyant" (Article IV, Paragraph 9, Page 6)	A bit; official debt/deficit figures are low but much off-budget spending. Augmented debt and deficits are high (Article IV, Appendix III, Page 75)	Extending VAT to services, recent increases in petrol taxes, and ongoing reforms to natural resource taxation; further reforms include single VAT rate and national property tax. IMF estimates the total revenue impact to be around 4.5 to 6.5 percent of GDP. (IMF Working Paper, Paragraph 4 and 5, Page 3) and (IMF Working Paper, Table 3, Page 24)	No expenditure cuts. China plans to bring off-budget infrastructure spending on-budget, and to increase social expenditures on health and education. (IMF Working Paper, Table 3, Page 24)	IMF Article IV Staff Report (2015); https://www.imf.org/external/pubs/ft/scr/2015/cr15234.pdf China: How Can Revenue Reforms Contribute to Inclusive and Sustainable Growth, IMF Working Paper (2015) https://www.imf.org/external/pubs/ft/wp/2015/wp1566.pdf
Fiji	Yes; "need to address infrastructure gaps" (Outlook and Risks, Paragraph 13, Page 6)	No; "public debt is sustainable and forecast to decline" (Press Release, 3rd Paragraph, Page 1)	Tax reforms will largely be revenue neutral. (Paragraph 28, Page 11)	Restraint on current expenditures remains critical. (Paragraph 25, Page 10)	IMF Article IV Staff Report (2015) http://www.imf.org/external/pubs/ft/scr/2016/cr1654.pdf

continued on next page

Country	Is raising infra spending a priority?	Is public debt sustainability a concern?	Potential revenue increase, in % of GDP	Potential spending reorientation, in % of GDP	Source
India	Yes; "public investment is a key engine of growth" (Box 4, 1st Paragraph, Page 24)	Somewhat; debt is high and deficits are large, but interest costs are manageable and GDP growth is high. (Annex III, Introductory Paragraph, Page 55)	Partial implementation of GST will raise revenues by 0.8 percent of GDP. (CRISIL) Gains from tax administration are large but unquantified. (See CRISIL link)	Little space to reduce expenditures further; can pare back food and fertilizer subsidies; total food/fertilizer/petroleum subsidies about 1.5% of GDP. (Annex V, Table on Government Subsidies, Page 68)	IMF Article IV Staff Report (2016) http://www.imf.org/external/pubs/ft/scr/2016/cr1675.pdf *In fiscal correction quest, the best bet's GST*, CRISIL (2014) http://www.moneycontrol.com/news/crisil-research/in-fiscal-correction-questbest-bets-gst-crisil_1109590.html
Indonesia	Yes; "authorities will utilize fiscal space to allow for larger capital spending" (Statement by Marzunisham Omar, 1st paragraph, Page 3)	No; debt and deficits are low (Paragraph 33, page 17)	Tax reform can raise non-oil revenues by 2.5 percent of GDP by 2020 (Paragraph 15, Page 8)	No current spending cuts envisioned in reform scenario. Energy subsidies were 1 percent of GDP in 2015, with further subsidy reforms planned (Paragraph 14, Page 8; and Statement by Marzunisham Omar, 4th paragraph, Page 2)	IMF Article IV Staff Report (2016) http://www.imf.org/external/pubs/ft/scr/2016/cr1681.pdf
Kazakhstan	Yes; "addressing infrastructure bottlenecks" (Paragraph 10, Page 6)	No; public debt is low (Annex VII, Page 50)	The revenue base can be raised through measures such as strengthening the enforcement of tax collection; reducing tax exemptions; including in the Special Economic Zones; and making income tax rates more progressive. The World Bank estimated that tax reform measures could increase non-oil tax revenues by 2.3 percent of GDP. (2015 IMF Article IV, Paragraph 15, Page 12; Implementation and Status Report, Page 5)	Cuts to expenditure not specified in IMF Staff Report. Energy subsidies at 0.8% of GDP.	IMF Concluding Statement on the 2015 Article IV Mission (2015); https://www.imf.org/external/pubs/ft/scr/2015/cr15241.pdf Kazakhstan Tax Administration Reform Project - Implementation Status and Results Report (Cycle 10) http://documents.worldbank.org/curated/en/184111467285288205/pdf/ISR-Disclosable-P116696-06-30-2016-1467285272386.pdf
Kiribati	Yes; "weak infrastructure is a key obstacle to development" (Paragraph 1, Page 4)	Yes; "Kiribati is at high risk of debt distress" (Results, Page 3)	VAT already introduced in 2014. This, together with efforts to improve compliance and strengthen SOE efficiency would allow the tax ratio to increase from 14 percent to 17 percent. (Paragraph 14, Page 11)	Public sector wages and SOEs' subsidies should be contained. Impact unquantified. (Paragraph 31, Page 18)	IMF Article IV Staff Report (2015) http://www.imf.org/external/pubs/ft/scr/2015/cr15207.pdf
Kyrgyz Republic	Yes; "investments needed to close the country's infrastructure gap" (Paragraph 18, Page 11, IMF Article IV Staff Report)	Yes; "public debt has reached worrisome levels" (Paragraph 38, Page 19, IMF Second Review)	For 2016, permanent measures will yield an increase of 1.6 percent of GDP. For 2017, revenue enhancing measures will generate an additional permanent increase of 0.7 percent of GDP. (Paragraph 17 and Text Table 2, Page 12, IMF Second Review)	For 2016, permanent measures will lead to savings of 0.2% of GDP. (Paragraph 17 and Text Table 2, Page 12, IMF Second Review)	IMF Article IV Staff Report (2016); IMF Second Review of ECF (2016) http://www.imf.org/external/pubs/ft/scr/2016/cr1655.pdf http://www.imf.org/external/pubs/ft/scr/2016/cr16186.pdf
Malaysia	Yes; "continued focus on physical infrastructure" (Page 2, Press Release)	Somewhat; debt is high but projected to decline (Figure 4, Page 22)	Tax reforms (mainly implementation of GST) already done in 2015. No new measures identified or quantified. (Paragraph 3, Page 4)	Expenditure rationalization and elimination of energy subsidies already done in 2014-15. No new measures identified or quantified. (Fiscal policy, Key Issues, Page 1)	IMF Article IV Staff Report (2016) https://www.imf.org/external/pubs/ft/scr/2016/cr16110.pdf

continued on next page

Country	Is raising infra spending a priority?	Is public debt sustainability a concern?	Potential revenue increase, in % of GDP	Potential spending reorientation, in % of GDP	Source
Maldives	Yes; "public infrastructure could transform the economy;" but public investment has already been scaled up substantially (Paragraph 50, Page 20)	Yes; debt is very high and rising rapidly (Figure 4, Page 25)	Raising the GST rate, broadening the profit tax and raising the rate, and other tax measures can raise revenues by 3.6 percent of GDP. (Paragraph 25, Page 12)	Containing the wage bill, cutting electricity and food subsidies, and containing healthcare costs can reduce current expenditures by 1.9 percent of GDP. (Paragraph 25, Page 12)	IMF Article IV Staff Report (2016) http://www.imf.org/external/pubs/ft/scr/2016/cr16135.pdf
Marshall Islands	Yes; "infrastructure projects will help support growth" (Paragraph 3, Page 1, Authorities' statement)	Yes; "relatively high level of public and publicly-guaranteed debt is a constraint on future prospects" (Paragraph 3, Page 1, Authorities' statement)	Tax reforms (PIT reform, introduction of net profits tax and consumption tax, replacing import duties with excise tax) can generate 0.5 percent of GDP in revenues. (Paragraph 14, Page 9)	Cuts in the government's current expense, SOE subsidies, and landowner utility transfers can generate savings equivalent to 3.5 percent of GDP. (Paragraph 14, Page 9)	IMF Article IV Staff Report (2016) http://www.imf.org/external/pubs/ft/scr/2016/cr16260.pdf
Micronesia, Fed. States of	Yes; "plans to allocate more funds for infrastructure;" "safeguard priority spending in the social sector and infrastructure investment" (Paragraph 10, Page 5) and (Paragraph 13, Page 7)	Somewhat; "vulnerability to debt distress is mitigated by a number of factors," including concessional terms from development partners, gradual decline in Compact support, building up of trust funds (Paragraph 12, Page 5)	The tax reform package (replacement of import duties and state sales tax with a new VAT, replacing the gross revenue tax with a net profit tax, and reducing the gross wage and salary tax) will generate an additional 4 percent of GDP. (Paragraph 12, Page 6)	Fiscal consolidation should be accompanied by improvements in the quality of public spending, including through wage moderation and implementation of an updated infrastructure development plan. However, impact is unquantified. (Page 2, Press Release)	IMF Article IV Staff Report (2015) http://www.imf.org/external/pubs/ft/scr/2015/cr15128.pdf
Mongolia	Yes, "existing infra deficiencies" (Paragraph 21, Page 10)	Yes; "high risk of debt distress" (Paragraph 13, Page 7)	Scope to increase customs duties and impose taxes on social benefits; adjustment scenario shows revenue increase of 1.7 percent of GDP. (Paragraph 21, Page 10) and (Table 9, Page 29)	Scope to cut subsidies, public wage bill; adjustment scenario shows current spending can be reduced by 1.4 percent of GDP. (Paragraph 21, Page 10) and (Table 9, Page 29)	IMF Article IV Staff Report (2015) http://www.imf.org/external/pubs/ft/scr/2015/cr15109.pdf
Myanmar	Yes, "infrastructure development a priority," "lack of infrastructure services a major constraint" (Paragraph 21, Page 10)	No, "debt distress remains low;" however, fiscal deficits should be reduced not only to limit rise in debt but also to reduce inflationary pressures and anchor exchange rate (Paragraph 25, Page 11) and (Paragraph 13, Page 7)	Tax revenue can be raised by commencing the collection of the commercial tax on telecommunication services and reducing tax incentives. This will generate about 0.55 percent of GDP. (Paragraph 13, Page 8) and (Paragraph 39, Page 15)	Limiting transfers to states and regions, and eliminating recurrent but unnecessary spending will result in savings of 0.68 percent of GDP. (Paragraph 13, Page 8) and (Paragraph 39, Page 15)	IMF Article IV Staff Report (2015) http://www.imf.org/external/pubs/ft/scr/2015/cr15267.pdf
Nepal	Yes; "high public investment needed to support reconstruction and medium-term growth" (Page 2 of Press Release and Paragraph 37, Page 16; IMF 2015)	No; relatively low debt level, declining (Paragraph 6, Page 7, IMF 2015)	Various tax reforms and improved tax administration can raise revenues by 3.3 percentage points of GDP in the long term. (Box 1, Page 2, DSA, IMF 2014)	The focus is already squarely on increasing capital spending for post-earthquake reconstruction and to support long-term growth. (Paragraph 8, Page 7; Paragraph 20, Page 10, and Statement by Marzunisham Omar, Paragraph 7, Page 2)	IMF Article IV Staff Report (2015); IMF Article IV Staff Report (2014) http://www.imf.org/external/pubs/ft/scr/2015/cr15317.pdf http://www.imf.org/external/pubs/ft/scr/2014/cr14214.pdf

continued on next page

Country	Is raising infra spending a priority?	Is public debt sustainability a concern?	Potential revenue increase, in % of GDP	Potential spending reorientation, in % of GDP	Source
Pakistan	Yes; "needs substantial fiscal space for growth-enhancing priority spending on infrastructure" (Paragraph 15, Page 12, IMF 2015)	Yes; "need to firmly reduce public debt," "remains vulnerable to shocks" (Paragraph 14, Page 12, IMF 2015)	To realize full revenue potential of a further 2.2 percent of GDP increase in revenue by FY19/20, additional tax measures (Paragraph 2, Page 2, Authorities' statement, IMF 2016)	Rationalizing noncritical current expenditures, containing energy subsidies, and managing the public sector wage bill prudently (0.1 percent of GDP in FY16/17). Energy subsidies were 0.4 percent of GDP in FY15/16. (Paragraph 9, Page 7, IMF 2016; Paragraph 21, Page 15, IMF 2015)	IMF Article IV Staff Report (2015); IMF 11th Review (2016) http://www.imf.org/external/pubs/ft/scr/2016/cr1601.pdf http://www.imf.org/external/pubs/ft/scr/2016/cr16207.pdf
Papua New Guinea	Yes; "poor infrastructure is a constraint on inclusive growth" (Paragraph 2, Page 4)	Yes; "fiscal consolidation is critical for debt sustainability" (Paragraph 6, Page 3)	Limited room; the bulk of fiscal adjustment will have to come from reductions and reprioritization of expenditure. (Paragraph 14, Page 8)	There is room for spending cuts and reprioritization. These can lower deficits by about 2 percent of GDP in the medium-term. (Paragraph 13, Page 7)	IMF Article IV Staff Report (2015) http://www.imf.org/external/pubs/ft/scr/2015/cr15318.pdf
Philippines	Yes; "large infrastructure gap" (Paragraph 1, Page 4)	No; "low and declining public debt" (Paragraph 44, Page 15)	2-3 percent of GDP can be raised via tax reforms (rationalization of tax incentives, reducing VAT exemptions) (Footnote 1, Page 9)	Limited space to cut. Energy subsidies already eliminated, public wage bill is small, key public services face manpower shortages. (Paragraph 17, Page 9)	IMF Article IV Staff Report (2015) http://www.imf.org/external/pubs/ft/scr/2015/cr15246.pdf
Sri Lanka	Yes; "substantial needs for social and infrastructure spending" (Paragraph 15, Page 13; MEFP Paragraph 2)	Yes; key objective is to "reduce public debt relative to GDP and lower Sri Lanka's risk of debt distress" (Paragraph 31, Page 24)	Simplifying the tax system and broadening the tax base can generate additional revenue of 2.9% of GDP. (Paragraph 32, Page 26)	Authorities are aiming for a "revenue-based fiscal consolidation." Past consolidation already cut expenditures heavily. Energy subsidies at 0.2% of GDP will be reduced by raising prices to cost recovery levels (Fiscal Policy, Key Issues, Page 1; Paragraph 35, Page 28; MEFP Paragraph 3 and 12)	IMF Article IV Staff Report and EFF Request (2016) http://www.imf.org/external/pubs/ft/scr/2016/cr16150.pdf
Thailand	Yes; "needs to upgrade its infrastructure to keep up with regional competition, lift potential growth" (Box 1, Page 20)	No; debt is moderate and remains sustainable in the medium term (Page 1, Press Release)	Introduction of inheritance tax, review of tax system (including property taxes and PIT, raising VAT rate), but not quantified. Energy price reforms could raise up to 1 percent of GDP. (Appendix III, Page 37)	No expenditure measures are identified or quantified. Thailand does not have any energy subsidies.	IMF Article IV Staff Report (2016) http://www.imf.org/external/pubs/ft/scr/2016/cr16139.pdf
Viet Nam	Somewhat; there is a "need to narrow the infrastructure gap" but this can be done through improved public investment efficiency; public capital spending is already high (Paragraph 19, Page 12)	Yes; there is a "need to reduce the fiscal deficit and arrest the rise in public debt" (Paragraph 20, Page 12)	Revenue can raise revenue/GDP back to its long run average (i.e., by about 2 percent of GDP). (Paragraphs 18-19, Page 11)	Public wage bill is high (about 2 percent of GDP above average). Energy subsidies are about 0.5% of GDP. (Paragraph 20, Page 12)	IMF Article IV Staff Report (2016) http://www.imf.org/external/pubs/ft/scr/2016/cr16240.pdf

DSA = debt sustainability analysis; ECF = Extended Credit Facility; FY = fiscal year; GDP = gross domestic product; GST = goods and services tax; IMF = International Monetary Fund; MEFP = Memorandum of Economic and Financial Policies; PIT = personal income tax; SOE = state-owned enterprises; VAT = value added tax.

Note: Supplementary information on energy subsidies in various countries is taken from Coady et al (2015). Data available at http://www.imf.org/external/np/fad/subsidies/data/codata.xlsx. The measure relevant for fiscal space is pretax consumer subsidies, which arise when the price paid by consumers (firms and households) is below the cost of supplying energy.

Appendix 5.2: Principal Value-capture Instruments

Value capture instrument	Main features
One-time charges on land value gains	
Land value taxation	Land value tax (LVT) is a simple technique designed to recapture the value created by the provision of public services. LVT is assessment of land value rather than property value and focuses on landowners. It can discriminate against the beneficiary of the tax – that is, the tax can, for instance, be directed only toward a specific group of landowners.
Betterment tax	A betterment tax ('benefit assessment' or 'betterment levy'), is used to provide funds to cover infrastructure investment costs by means of a one-time tax or charge on the land value gain; it is targeted at the beneficiaries of increased accessibility, reduced congestion and pollution, as well as those provided with a new public amenity or lower transport costs. Betterment tax is seen as an equitable and efficient levy, and can be used for urban transport/sidewalks, parks and water/wastewater sector. It recovers the added value on private land assets accruing to property owners positively affected by the infrastructure investment.
Project-related land sales	Publicly-owned land whose value has been enhanced by zoning procedures or by infrastructure investment can be sold.
Negotiated exactions	Negotiated exactions require developers to contribute, including, if needed, by giving up part of their land or facilities in return for greater off-site benefits, such as better transport provided by the public sector. The costs to the developer are upfront, by either providing land or making a payment to be used for infrastructure serving the development. Furthermore, land can be used by the companies as collateral for construction loans. Once the investment is financed, the development company can repay its debt by selling land after its value has been enhanced.
Development impact fees	These are one-time charges applied by a local government to an applicant in connection with approval of a development project to finance a portion of the cost of public facilities related to the development project. An example of this is the requirement of a shopping mall developer to pay for the cost of road improvements to better access the new retail activity.
Joint development	Joint development, a form of public-private partnership (PPP), is a mechanism of cooperation and cost sharing between public and private operators or developers. Its advantage is that one need not identify direct and indirect impacts of the transport investment – as with betterment tax or tax increment financing (see below) – since there is cooperation between the public agency and private developers who share construction costs. Joint development promotes efficiency and equity among participants, creating a win-win situation when properly structured. Private developers benefit from better accessibility and more potential customers, and the public sector benefits through the sharing of construction costs while also securing increased demand for the transport infrastructure. It is the most easily applicable instrument – for example, within a PPP agreement – because it is technically straightforward to implement within the structure of a PPP contract.
Long term revenue sources	
Tax increment financing (TIF)	TIF schemes, used extensively in the US, operate through fiscal incentives such as tax relief, tax breaks or tax disincentives in order to encourage development in a defined urban area. Any increase in tax revenue over the "base" is determined to be attributable to the new development and escrowed into a separate account from general fund revenues. It is used to retire debt for infrastructure or other public improvements associated with the new development. TIF can be applied to income, sales or property taxes. Furthermore, this funding stream can serve as the basis for securing a bond as the new, accretive revenue stream is used to back the bond obligation by the public sector.
Special or benefit assessment districts	This approach is similar to TIF except that tax rates are increased and are typically applied only in defined districts that will benefit from the transit investment. Special assessments for urban transit are being used to channel revenues from property tax rate increases to fund transit construction, operations or related infrastructure improvements. In the US, the districts are being set up in both suburban and downtown contexts and are funding a wide variety of transit types, from metro to light rail transit (LRT) to bus rapid transit (BRT).
Land asset management	Similar to joint development and long-term leases but in contrast to land sales, land asset management has the advantage that the public sector retains ownership and control over the plots of land around the infrastructure investment over the long term, while receiving the lease revenues.
Air rights	Air rights (sale or lease) are a form of value capture that involves the establishment of development rights above the previously permitted land-use controls (e.g. increased floor area ratios of buildings), or in some cases below a new transportation facility (e.g. selling rights to build a shopping area below a rail station). These further developments are expected to lead to increases in land value, which can be captured and used to fund infrastructure investment.
Transportation utility fees	In TUF, a transportation improvement is treated as a utility (water, electricity) and is paid for by a user fee. Rather than establish a fee with respect to the value of the property, the fee is estimated on the number of trips that property would generate.

Source: Maier and Jordan-Tank (2014).